Freedom of association
and economic development

Freedom of association and economic development

Guy Caire

International Labour Office Geneva

ISBN 92-2-101455-X (limp cover)
ISBN 92-2-101466-5 (hard cover)

First published 1977

The designations employed in ILO publications, which are in conformity with United Nations practice, and the presentation of material therein do not imply the expression of any opinion whatsoever on the part of the International Labour Office concerning the legal status of any country or territory or of its authorities, or concerning the delimitation of its frontiers. The responsibility for opinions expressed in signed articles, studies and other contributions rests solely with their authors, and publication does not constitute an endorsement by the International Labour Office of the opinions expressed in them.

ILO publications can be obtained through major booksellers or ILO local offices in many countries, or direct from ILO Publications, International Labour Office, CH-1211 Geneva 22, Switzerland. A catalogue or list of new publications will be sent free of charge from the above address.

Printed by Imprimeries Réunies, Lausanne, Switzerland

FOREWORD

The title of this book and the identity of its author [1] should not call for any explanation; but it does seem necessary to show how it fits in with the aims and activities of the International Labour Organisation.

For the ILO freedom of association is more than just a field of study: since the setting up of the ILO it has been one of the Organisation's fundamental objectives, which today is more important than ever. If workers are to be able to defend their interests effectively and, more generally, to play a genuine part in economic and social life, they must have freedom of association. This freedom is proclaimed in the constitutional texts of the ILO and has been reaffirmed in some of the Organisation's most important and most widely ratified Conventions. In addition to the ILO's general supervisory system, through which the application of Conventions adopted in this field is regularly followed up, special machinery to help to protect and promote freedom of association was set up 25 years ago and is still extensively used. The importance and universal validity of the principles of freedom of association have frequently, and again only recently, been confirmed in resolutions adopted by the general conference and by regional conferences of the African, American, Asian and European States members of the ILO, as well as in appeals by those conferences to all countries to ensure full application of the principles in question.

Although no voices are raised in disagreement when these principles are being proclaimed, difficulties arise when it comes to their implementation. It is in the field of freedom of association that Conventions have been most widely ratified and supervisory procedures most fully developed; yet it would also seem to be in that field, paradoxically enough, that the application of standards

[1] Guy Caire is Professor of Economics at the University of Paris X. He has written numerous books and articles dealing mainly with various aspects of planning, industrialisation, industrial relations, trade unionism and employment.

has run up against the most serious obstacles. On reflection, however, this is not surprising. Trade union rights are so closely bound up with the organisation of society, with civil liberties and, more generally, with national life that they are inevitably influenced by national concepts and institutions, and in many cases even by the vagaries of domestic politics.

The problems that have impeded the implementation of freedom of association in many countries vary widely in nature and importance. One particular difficulty which is often cited—not only in connection with freedom of association—and which may be more or less openly referred to or may merely transpire in the course of discussions about the application of ILO Conventions, has to do with the relationship that may exist between freedom of association and economic development. Is freedom of association a possible hindrance to economic development? If so, would there be justification for restricting, or even abolishing, that freedom in order to meet the requirements of development? Or, conversely, should a slower rate of development be accepted as the price to be paid in order to preserve freedom of association?

In the view of the ILO, this is not an insoluble dilemma. In fact, it is to a large extent a false problem. For the ILO, there can be no justification for sacrificing either economic development or freedom of association. Sustained economic development has always been considered an important factor of social progress, but it is not an end in itself: rather is it a means towards achievement of social and humanitarian aims, which should not be lost from sight. This view, which the ILO has long advocated, received support from the General Assembly of the United Nations in 1970 when, in adopting the International Development Strategy for the Second United Nations Development Decade, it drew particular attention to the social objectives of development and set the economic aspect in its social context. It should therefore be possible, as qualified spokesmen have often insisted, to reconcile the requirements of development with the right of individuals to live and fulfil themselves in a climate of freedom and dignity.

People might say, however, that these are just well-meaning generalities which represent a far too idealistic view of things. What is the real relationship between freedom of association and economic development? What truth is there in the claims that they are incompatible?

A scholarly and objective study of the matter seemed to be called for. The purpose of this book is to assess whether and to what extent there is validity in an objection that is sometimes made to the principles of freedom of association, so as to be able either to show it up as false or to suggest ways of overcoming it. The intention, in other words, is to probe deeper into the problem and thus to promote a more widespread application of a standard of human freedom to which the ILO remains firmly attached.

The subject is therefore an important one, and raises fundamental issues of social policy. In more general terms, it has to do with the effectiveness of the efforts of the international community to protect human rights, at a time when the International Covenants on Human Rights of 1966 have just come into force. It is fortunate therefore that Professor Caire, a well known authority on economic and social questions, should have agreed to undertake this work. The reader will no doubt appreciate the new light he casts on this highly controversial subject, of which this is the first detailed study. The author was left entirely free to choose his methodology, and his conclusions are also his own. His findings do not represent any official doctrine, although the ILO would subscribe to many of them. Obviously, however, there may be other opinions; it may in fact be useful some day to organise a far-ranging discussion of the subject. But somebody had to clear the way, explore a field which is not without pitfalls, clarify issues on which the strongest views are sometimes heard, and do so in a responsible and independent manner. The ILO is grateful to Professor Caire for having succeeded.

Nicolas VALTICOS

Assistant-Director-General,
Adviser for International Labour Standards,
International Labour Office.

CONTENTS

Foreword v

Introduction 1

Subject 1
Points of agreement 1
Points in dispute 3
Definition of the problem 4

Approach 5
Geographical scope 5
Historical range 10
Methodology 11

Outline 11

1. Definitions 13

Freedom of association 13
Practical content 15
Individual freedom of conscience and the right to bargain collectively 18
Economic development 20
Meanings considered in this study 26

Appendix. International standards concerning freedom of association . . 28

2. The issues 31

The record 32
Institutional history 32
Statistics 38
Date of legal establishment of trade unions 38
Trade union membership figures 43

Theory . . . 47
Consumption and investment . . . 48
Labour cost and employment . . . 54
Economic role of trade unions . . . 57

Tentative conclusions . . . 60

Appendix 1. Industrial revolution, primitive accumulation and take-off . . 62

Appendix 2. Resolution concerning the independence of the trade union movement, adopted by the International Labour Conference at its 35th Session (1952) . . . 64

3. Policy implications . . . 67

Supply . . . 69
Worker protest and the trade unions . . . 69
Union weakness in the developing countries . . . 73
Restriction of the right to strike . . . 80
Effectiveness of restrictions . . . 86

Demand . . . 90
Objectives of wage policy in the developing countries . . . 90
Means of implementing a wage policy . . . 95
Effectiveness of wage policies . . . 101

The development process . . . 108
Ends . . . 108
Means . . . 119

Conclusions . . . 129

Summing up . . . 129
Concepts . . . 129
Issues . . . 130
Industrial relations policies . . . 132

Role of international standards . . . 134
Influence in the legal field . . . 135
Educational role . . . 137
Promotion of international standards through technical assistance . . . 140
The search for new international standards . . . 146

Bibliography . . . 149

INTRODUCTION

In any kind of research, the first step is to define the issues to be tackled and to decide on the method of work to be followed. This study of freedom of association and economic development is no exception. It begins, therefore, with a statement of its subject and of the approach to be followed.

SUBJECT

Even the most cursory glance reveals that, although on the surface the need for freedom of association in industrial life would appear to be broadly recognised by all concerned, the way they behave in practice does not always bear out this first impression, and their interpretation of the relationship that may exist between the principle of freedom of association and the imperatives of economic development is a subject of endless discussion and controversy.

Points of agreement

In 1973 the ILO Committee of Experts on the Application of Conventions and Recommendations conducted an over-all international survey [1] in respect of the Conventions on freedom of association and on the right to organise and collective bargaining. The survey suggests that there is widespread acceptance of the right to organise trade unions and to engage in collective

[1] In accordance with the reporting obligations laid down in articles 19, 22 and 35 of the Constitution of the Organisation. ILO: *Freedom of association and collective bargaining*, Report III (Part 4B), International Labour Conference, 58th Session, Geneva, 1973. See also ILO: *Freedom of association: An international survey* (Geneva, 1975).

bargaining.[1] Moreover, in several countries, including even some that have not ratified the relevant Conventions,[2] freedom of association is often looked upon as a basic right and, as such, has constitutional force.

In addition, common practice often seems to reflect acceptance of the statement contained in the declaration adopted by the International Labour Conference at Philadelphia in 1944—and which seemed quite bold at the time—that "freedom of expression and of association are essential to sustained progress".[3] The link between freedom of association and economic development is further confirmed by the machinery for participation in planning that has been introduced in many countries at the national, sectoral, regional, local and enterprise level.[4]

At first blush, therefore, it would seem to be an established principle of social philosophy, embodied in such concepts as equal representation, consul-

[1] Eighty countries had ratified the Freedom of Association and Protection of the Right to Organise Convention, 1948 (No. 87), compared with only 36 countries at the time of a previous general survey in 1959. Similarly, between 1959 and 1973, the number of States that had ratified the Right to Organise and Collective Bargaining Convention, 1949 (No. 98), had risen from 40 to 93. By the end of 1975, Conventions Nos. 87 and 98 had been ratified by 82 and 96 countries respectively.

[2] This is the case, for example, in Colombia (article 44 of the Constitution), El Salvador (article 191), the United States (First, Fourth and Fourteenth Amendments), Haiti (article 24, paragraph 1, and article 32), Indonesia (article 28), Morocco (article 9), Turkey (article 46), Venezuela (article 72) and Zaire (article 17). In other countries, while not having constitutional force, freedom of association is recognised, albeit with occasional restrictions, in the Labour Code: this is the case in Iraq (article 159), Malaysia (Trade Unions Ordinance, 1959, and Industrial Relations Act, 1967), Singapore (article 17 of Employment Act, 1968, and articles 78 and 79 of Industrial Relations Ordinance, 1960), and Zambia (Industrial Relations Act, 1971). Consequently, a number of countries which have not as yet ratified Conventions Nos. 87 and 98 do nevertheless apply their provisions to a large extent.

[3] The active and constructive role of employers' and workers' organisations in economic and social development has been recognised in a whole series of international instruments and standards: the Consultation (Industrial and National Levels) Recommendation, 1960 (No. 113), for example, advocates the consultation and co-operation of such organisations "with a view to developing the economy as a whole or individual branches thereof, improving conditions of work and raising standards of living" (Paragraph 4); in the resolution concerning the concept of democratic decision-making in programming and planning for economic and social development, which the International Labour Conference adopted in 1964, it made the same point when it considered that "in developing countries economic and social programming and planning, in conformity with the specific conditions and requirements of each country", was "essential for their rapid economic growth and social advancement" and that "an indispensable condition for achieving the goals of democratic programming and planning for economic development and social advancement" was "the establishment, in accordance with the principles and aims of the International Labour Organisation, of effective machinery and procedures for active consultation with and participation of free and independent employers' and workers' organisations in the formulation and implementation of such programmes"; the resolution concerning social participation in the development process, adopted by the Ninth Conference of American States Members of the ILO, held in Caracas in 1970, and that concerning freedom of association for workers' and employers' organisations and their role in social and economic development, adopted by the Seventh Asian Regional Conference, held in Teheran in 1971, are along the same lines.

[4] ILO: *Employers' and workers' participation in planning* (Geneva, 1973), especially pp. 61-138.

tation and participation, that development must be the subject of open debate wherein agreement can be reached between freely organised employers and workers.

Points in dispute

However, a closer look at everyday events shows that agreement is less complete than it seems, where principles are concerned, and much shakier still as regards their practical implications. A few examples will make this clear.

To start with, certain theorists make no bones about their conviction that, at any rate in the underdeveloped countries, freedom of association may be a hindrance to economic development. Leaving aside for the time being various arguments which will be taken up in greater detail later and which purport to back up this assertion, the main point that is made is that there is a conflict between the requirements of economic growth and those of democracy, or in other words that freedom of association should be curtailed in countries whose governments want to promote economic development. [1] The governments of developing countries should accordingly restrict freedom of association or the right to bargain collectively, or both, and to that extent depart from the provisions of Conventions Nos. 87 and 98.

Furthermore, while they do not question the validity of principles to which they have subscribed, the governments of certain developing countries are anxious to avoid any dispersal of the national development effort and to conduct the process of economic growth as efficiently as possible. They feel that they must therefore control freedom of association, either because of the peculiarities of some social or occupational group or else to ensure that this freedom does not come to pose too great a threat to the long-term economic interests of the nation. As a result, the right to establish trade unions and the exercise of trade union rights may sometimes be curtailed. [2] Because they are mainly concerned with such problems as capital formation, expansion of entrepreneurial activity, market development and control and the stabilisation of prices and wages, governments may somewhat neglect their obligations in the field of industrial relations and fail to appreciate the full extent of their commitments in that respect. This would seem to be what is meant when it is said that, in a sense, the more a government is devoted to development, the less it can afford to pay special attention to organised labour. [3]

---

[1] K. de Schweinitz: "Industrialization, labor controls and democracy", in *Economic Development and Cultural Change*, July 1959, pp. 385-404.

[2] ILO: *The ILO and human rights*, Report of the Director-General (Part I), International Labour Conference, 52nd Session, Geneva, 1968, p. 37.

[3] F. J. Deyrup: "Organized labor and government in underdeveloped countries: Sources of conflict", in *Industrial and Labor Relations Review* (Ithaca, New York, Cornell University), Oct. 1958, p. 108.

These implicitly or explicitly controversial issues, which are aired in specialised publications, are clear evidence of the need for a closer look at the relationship between freedom of association and economic development. That need is confirmed by the fact that almost a third of the member States of the International Labour Organisation have not yet ratified Convention No. 87, and by the complaints of real or alleged violations of the principle of freedom of association brought before the ILO Fact-Finding and Conciliation Commission on Freedom of Association and before the Committee on Freedom of Association of the Governing Body.

Definition of the problem

It has been pointed out that consultations between governments and employers' and workers' organisations are no longer limited to working conditions, labour legislation and labour-management relations but increasingly embrace the broad questions of general economic policy which determine the levels of employment and incomes. [1] It is precisely at the level of the broad questions of general economic policy that the problem of the relationship between freedom of association and economic development arises, for at least two fundamental reasons.

First of all, freedom, which is the very lifeblood of the ILO, is indivisible. Accordingly at its 54th Session, in 1970, the International Labour Conference unanimously recognised that the absence of civil liberties removed all meaning from the concept of trade union rights and called upon all member States which had not done so to ratify and apply the United Nations Covenants on Civil and Political Rights and on Economic, Social and Cultural Rights. [2]

Secondly, economic development, which was for a long time the main political problem in the most advanced countries, has now become a major concern of all countries and even, since the adoption by the United Nations General Assembly on 24 October 1970 of the International Development Strategy for the Second United Nations Development Decade, of global policy. By pledging themselves "to pursue policies designed to create a more just and rational world economic and social order in which equality of opportunities should be as much a prerogative of nations as of individuals within a nation", the member States of the United Nations proclaimed that, for most people, freedom was meaningless if divorced from its economic and social context.

---

[1] ILO: *Prosperity for welfare: Social purpose in economic growth and change*, Report of the Director-General (Part I), International Labour Conference, 58th Session, Geneva, 1973, p. 61.

[2] Resolution concerning trade union rights and their relation to civil liberties. See also ILO: *Trade union rights and their relation to civil liberties*, Report VII, International Labour Conference, 54th Session, Geneva, 1970.

However, although freedom may be associated with development in declarations of intent and in people's conscience, those desiderata are less easy to reconcile at the practical level. The difficulty of reconciling the two concepts is the subject of this study.

APPROACH

If the findings of this study are to be of any use, the subject will have to be approached in accordance with a number of principles, of which three seem to be of prime importance, namely a well defined geographical scope, a sufficiently broad historical range and a diversified methodology. As is explained below, this study is limited to the industrialisation processes currently under way in the developing countries, and is based on an interdisciplinary approach to labour-management relations.

Geographical scope

To begin with, from the geographical point of view it is important not to fall into the trap of regarding as typical the conditions obtaining in one's own country, and of using as one's yardstick a system of industrial relations which, although undoubtedly prevailing in the dominant economic system, applies as yet to only a very small minority of the world's working population. It will be useful, then, to establish a classification [1] of industrial relations, [2] by endeavouring to identify four sets of problems of industrial relations (the regulation of the production and distribution of incomes and welfare, the social integration or possible marginality of various sections of the population, the regulation of the extent and quality of participation in decisions having to do with industrial relations, and the legitimacy of the industrial relations system and the general acceptability of its procedures), in the light of four basic criteria (the technological context, the relative power of employers and workers respectively in view of the degree of worker organisation, the level of decision-making, and the relationship to the political system), some allowance being made also for the quality of industrial relations (paternalistic, contractual or inspirational). According to this classification 11 broad types of industrial relations systems can be distinguished:

(1) The subsistence system, which is characteristic of peasant economies in which family units produce mainly for their own consumption, by primitive

[1] From Robert W. Cox, Jeffrey Harrod and others: *Future industrial relations: An interim report* (Geneva, International Institute for Labour Studies, 1972); see also Robert W. Cox: "Approaches to a futurology of industrial relations", in the *Bulletin* of the International Institute for Labour Studies, 1971, No. 8, pp. 139-164.

[2] In the very broad sense of social relations in production.

technology, and independently of the monetised economy. This system is to be found in Africa and in some parts of Asia and Latin America, and covers about 8 per cent of the world labour force.

(2) The "peasant-lord" system under which technology is also primitive but workers are subject to superiors whose power may be tempered by an ethic of paternal obligation. The State does not intervene in the relationship between lord and peasant, except to extract some of the product. A form of this system, which covers about 15 per cent of the world labour force, exists on the big estates in some Latin American countries and in some rice-producing areas of Asia.

(3) The primitive labour market system, which comes into existence when landless peasants become mobile wage earners with no labour organisations. The State does not enter the work relationship. This system can be observed among the urban marginal population in many developing countries, and covers about 10 per cent of the world labour force.

(4) The enterprise labour market system under which, in the absence of any effective intervention by the State, the enterprise is the only domain of meaningful decision-making. The system exists in small manufacturing enterprises which form part of the modern sector in developing countries, as well as on plantations and in commercial establishments. Trade unions may exist in a nascent state; the employers tend to be paternalistic. This system covers about 7 per cent of the world labour force.

(5) The enterprise-corporatist system, which is a fairly accurate description of the lifetime commitment of Japan, in which the worker is guaranteed employment security and welfare by the employer, and of the white-collar labour market of American and European undertakings. The trade unions tend to operate at the enterprise level, and the system covers about 5 per cent of the world labour force.

(6) The bipartite system, under which the workers are specialised, skilled and mobile, bargaining between the trade unions and the employer is direct and the State plays a minimum role. This system is to be found in Canada and in the United States, and covers about 3 per cent of the world labour force.

(7) The tripartite system, under which the government plays a more active role, being a major employer concerned with the possible influence of industrial relations on its economic policy objectives. The system has come into being in a number of Western European countries, in particular, and covers about 6 per cent of the world labour force.

(8) State corporatist systems whose ideologies place a high value on consensus and peaceful labour relations. Such systems are made up of semi-autonomous organisations of employers and workers under the tutelage of the

State, whose influence is decisive, and they cover about 2 per cent of the world labour force.

(9) The mobilising system found in China and in other developing countries where it is often somewhat unstable. It enables a political élite to mobilise the hitherto non-participating segments of society and those not assimilated into modern production through mass movements while at the same time restraining the tendency of trade unions towards "economism". [1] Owing to the enormous population of China, this system covers 24 per cent of the world labour force.

(10) The socialist system, which is often the eventual outcome of the previous system; trade unions and management are functionally related agencies co-operating in the implementation of a planned economic policy. This system covers about 12 per cent of the world labour force.

(11) The self-employed system (for example, artisan-type work), operating in a modern technological context, covers about 8 per cent of the world labour force.

There is of course room for argument on whether this classification is really appropriate, but as far as the presentation of the issues to be dealt with here are concerned it does at least serve to define the geographical scope of this book. It shows that the systems in which no significant employers' and workers' organisations exist (the first four categories in the list above) involve about 40 per cent of the world labour force, those of developed market economy countries 9 per cent and the socialist systems 12 per cent, and that systems associated with rudimentary economic development account for 23 per cent of the world labour force, those associated with economies in which development is under way for 41 per cent and those associated with modern societies 36 per cent.

This book deals essentially with the developing countries. All kinds of facts and figures will accordingly be marshalled in the following pages in order to shed as much light as possible on the problem as it affects those particular countries, which otherwise do not have a great deal in common. Consequently, reference to developed-economy and socialist countries has been deliberately avoided except where it may be useful to clarify certain aspects or to introduce possible points of comparison. The geographical area in question can be seen more clearly as that contained in the box in table 1.

[1] This is a Marxist term denoting the behaviour of trade unions which are concerned only with advancing the interests of their own members and thus come to forget their political commitments under the "transmission belt" theory formulated by Lenin.

Table 1. Regional distribution of industrial relations
(Total labour force in thousands and *percentage distribution*

Region	Gross national product (GNP) per head in US$ at 1970 prices		Percentage share of industry in the GNP around 1965-70	Kind of system			
	Circa 1970	1985		Subsistence (106 States)	"Peasant-lord" (56 States)	Primitive labour market (118 States)	Enterprise labour market (122 States)
Africa	100	150-180	12	71 188 *56* (1)	5 299 *4* (6)	15 897 *12* (2)	9 274 *7* (4)
Middle East	200	350	15	2 350 *7* (6)	2 350 *7* (5)	7 720 *23* (1)	4 364 *13* (4)
Latin America	400	600	18	7 934 *9* (6)	12 342 *14* (3)	26 447 *30* (1)	8 816 *10* (5)
Asia [1] (slow economic growth)	150	200	15	31 808 *9* (3)	183 769 *50* (1)	81 282 *22* (2)	14 136 *4* (5)
Asia [1] (rapid economic growth)	450	850	23	1 612 *2.5* (7)	19 350 *30* (1)	10 965 *17* (3)	8 385 *13* (4)
China	—	—	—	—	—	—	—
Japan	1 500	4 000	30	—	—	4 177 *8* (4)	8 354 *16* (2)
Oceania	1 900	3 000	27	152 *1.9* (5)	—	8 *0.1* (6)	640 *8* (4)
Socialist countries	1 100	2 600	50	—	—	—	—
North America	3 800	5 400	27	—	—	3 587 *4* (5)	33 176 *37* (1)
Western Europe	1 900	4 000	35	—	141 *0.1* (8)	2 821 *2* (7)	12 553 *8.9* (4)

[1] Excluding China, Japan, and the Asian part of the USSR.

Source: Cox, Harrod and others, op. cit., pp. 16, 18, 65, 71; classification of countries in regions on pp. 78-79.

system, in terms of members of the labour force concerned
***in region;* rank order of systems for each region in parentheses)**

Enterprise-corporatist (79 States)	Bipartite (26 States)	Tri-partite (91 States)	State-corporatist (28 States)	Mobilising (17 States)	Socialist (13 States)	Self-employed (146 States)	All systems (146 States)
3 842 *2.9* (7)	132 *0.1* (10)	6 624 *5* (5)	2 650 *2* (8)	2 650 *2* (9)	—	11 923 *9* (3)	132 479 *100*
2 350 *7* (7)	—	2 013 *6* (8)	6 042 *18* (2)	671 *2* (9)	—	5 706 *17* (3)	33 566 *100*
793 *0.9* (10)	88 *0.1* (11)	3 526 *4* (7)	10 579 *12* (4)	882 *1* (9)	1 763 *2* (8)	14 986 *17* (2)	88 156 *100*
7 068 *2* (7)	2 121 *0.6* (9)	4 948 *1.4* (8)	—	14 050 *4* (6)	—	28 272 *8* (4)	371 934 *100*
1 935 *3* (6)	322 *0.5* (8)	—	4 515 *7* (5)	—	—	17 415 *27* (2)	64 499 *100*
—	—	—	—	351 797 *100* (1)	—		351 797 *100*
30 235 58 (1)	5 222 *10* (3)	—	—	(1) —	—	4 177 *8* (4)	52 215 *100*
1 040 *13* (2)	—	5 441 *68* (1)	—	—	—	720 *9* (3)	8 001 *100*
—	—	—	—	—	174 785 *94* (1)	11 156 *6* (2)	185 941 *100*
17 933 *20* (3)	24 120 *27* (2)	2 690 *3* (6)	—	—	—	8 070 *9* (4)	89 666 *100*
12 695 *9* (3)	9 874 *7* (5)	69 110 *49* (1)	9 732 *6.9* (6)	141 *0.1* (9)	—	23 879 *17* (2)	141 050 *100*

Historical range

From the chronological point of view it would be a mistake to consider only the more topical issues. These are often largely determined by the social situation in the economically dominant countries and, even though they may sometimes take on a similar form in the developing countries, their importance is not the same as elsewhere. To take just one example, the issue of freedom of association in the public service [1] has come to the fore only because of the very recent growth in union membership and the changes currently taking place in legislation or collective agreements in the United States. [2] Individual problems and particular aspects must be placed in a sufficiently wide historical context so that their real significance can be properly appreciated. As regards the developing countries and the particular subject dealt with here—the relationship between freedom of association and development—the historical context is that of the process of industrialisation. There are at least three fundamental aspects of industrialisation that need to be looked at more closely: the nature of the governing élite, whose policies simultaneously affect the way in which industrialisation takes place, the likelihood of freedom of association and the form it takes; the response of the workers' organisations to the challenge which they face and which, because of the influence it has on worker protest, provokes a greater or lesser degree of social tension; and the web of rules which evolves in the course of such labour disputes as there may be and under which freedom of association has a different place and takes a different form according to the circumstances. To put it differently—

> all industrializing societies . . . create managers and industrial workers and labor organizations. These societies also develop and define the arrangements among managements, labor organizations, and governments which in turn establish, change, and administer the growing body of rules of the work place. Industrialization requires an industrial jurisprudence at the work place and in the work community. In short, each industrializing society creates an industrial relations system.
>
> Industrial relations systems reflect both uniformities and diversities. All industrial relations systems serve the functions of defining power and authority relationships among managements, labor organizations, and government agencies; of controlling or channelling worker protest; and of establishing the substantive rules. Uniformities are also found in the substantive rules themselves. Even under different rule-making arrangements, it is not unusual to find similar rules where common technologies and market conditions prevail.
>
> If uniformities emerge from common challenges and problems, diversities in industrial relations systems derive from the significantly different or unique backdrops against which they are fashioned. In different societies, these systems have been started at different historical periods, each of which has left its indelible mark. They have

---

[1] ILO: *Freedom of association and procedures for staff participation in determining conditions of employment in the public service*, Report II, Joint Committee on the Public Service, First Session, Geneva, 1970.

[2] See, for example, J. P. Goldberg: "Changing policies in public employee labor relations ", in *Monthly Labor Review* (Washington, US Department of Labor), July 1970, pp. 5-14.

started from different degrees of economic backwardness. They also differ at the present moment of time since they reflect different stages and speeds of economic development. They contend with quite dissimilar pre-industrial cultures. And . . . the industrializing societies are under the command of different élites with different visions, programs, and tasks for their emerging industrial relations systems. [1]

Methodology

From the methodological point of view, a study of this subject must look beyond the legal problems of freedom of association or the economic aspect of development. Instead, a conscious effort must be made to maintain an interdisciplinary approach so as to overlook none of the political considerations or ideological aims that may be involved, nor the institutional peculiarities of the countries concerned, nor even the philosophical overtones of a subject in relation to which the clash of systems of values is sometimes decisive. In other words the interdisciplinary nature of this study should be precisely that which colours industrial relations, which have been described as "a crossroads where a number of disciplines have met—history, economics, government, sociology, psychology and law". [2]

OUTLINE

The apparent consensus that exists on the acceptance of the principle of freedom to organise trade unions and the necessity of economic development, on the one hand, and the implicit or explicit controversies that arise in connection with the actual exercise of freedom of association and the different views that are held of the actual process of economic development, on the other, are clear enough evidence that the two concepts are far from meeting universal approval. The first step will therefore be to define the terms "freedom of association" and "economic development", so as to pinpoint the real issues that are at stake.

Secondly it would be as well to establish the pertinence of the arguments put forward by examining them in the context in which they were advanced. (This seems necessary irrespective of whether it is felt once the arguments have been analysed that freedom of association must be curtailed in order to satisfy the requirements of economic development or, on the contrary, that freedom of association and economic development are not only not mutually exclusive but in fact closely related, or whether the answer is thought to lie somewhere in between.)

---

[1] Clark Kerr, John T. Dunlop, Frederick Harbison and Charles A. Myers: *Industrialism and industrial man* (New York, Oxford University Press, second edition, 1964), pp. 192-193.

[2] J. T. Dunlop: *Industrial relations systems* (Southern Illinois University Press, 1970), p. 6.

Having dissected the arguments and bearing in mind that they are largely a matter of conjecture and hypothesis, it is then essential for the student to consider what practical implications they have for an industrial relations policy. For this one can adopt a behaviourist approach and take the view that, ultimately, the only way to resolve a dispute is to understand how it came about [1] by analysing the factors that caused it, the form it has taken and the way it fits into the general pattern of industrial conflict, [2] or one can prefer the "institutional" approach of an "Oxford school" [3] which considers that the central task of a theory of industrial relations is to explain why particular rules have been established. [4] In either case one's thinking is likely to be clarified, if only because it will be more up to date, and one can then try to find out what fundamental socio-economic relationship develops between the much vaunted principle of freedom of association and the desired objective of economic development.

The definition of the concepts involved, the examination of the theories advanced and the consideration of the implications entailed are therefore the three main stages of a study in which the framework is established in the first chapter, the issues identified in the second and their practical implications deduced in the third. [5]

---

[1] C. J. Margerison: "What do we mean by industrial relations: A behavioural science approach", in *British Journal of Industrial Relations*, July 1969, pp. 273-286.

[2] R. Williams and D. Guest: "Psychological research and industrial relations: A brief review", in *Occupational Psychology* (London), Vol. 43, Nos. 3 and 4, pp. 201-211.

[3] So-called because based on the work of Allan Flanders, Senior Lecturer in Industrial Relations at the University of Oxford, which provided the theoretical basis for the recommendations of the Donovan Commission, whose findings were used in drafting the United Kingdom's Industrial Relations Act of 1971.

[4] "The central task of a theory of industrial relations is to explain why particular rules are established in particular industrial-relations systems and how and why they change in response to changes affecting the system" (Dunlop, *Industrial relations systems*, op. cit., pp. viii-ix).

[5] Editorial note: within individual chapters, the arrangement of the text has been altered for English-speaking readers.

DEFINITIONS 1

Only on a superficial view do the expressions "freedom of association" and "economic development" have a clear meaning: even a rapid study of legal or economic texts suffices to show that the meaning attached to those expressions varies quite considerably from one author to another. It will therefore be necessary to pick out the various definitions, to place them in their context and to ascertain whether, irrespective of their immediate differences, a few simple underlying notions can be distilled from them for the purposes of this study and in accordance with the approach described in the introduction.

FREEDOM OF ASSOCIATION

Freedom of association entails, in particular, the right for workers and employers, without distinction whatsoever, to establish and to join organisations of their own choosing without previous authorisation. To this right, as defined by Article 2 of the Freedom of Association and Protection of the Right to Organise Convention, 1948 (No. 87), the Convention adds the exercise of a certain number of supplementary rights as regards the free functioning of the organisations constituted in this way, affiliation with international organisations, and protection against anti-union discrimination. [1] Since the essential purpose of trade unions is to defend and promote the interests of their members, freedom of association also implies freedom to bargain collectively, possibly after or simultaneously with strike action, and the participation of workers and employers in various private or public bodies. Quite obviously, too, there

[1] Similar provisions are to be found in other international labour standards, listed in the appendix to this chapter, paras. 1-4, pp. 28-29.

can be no freedom of association without a number of civil liberties (notably the right of assembly, freedom of expression and the right to security of the person). [1]

A definition such as this is too broad, however, to give any immediate idea of all the implications. Fortunately, in addition to a number of legal works of a doctrinal nature, [2] interpretative texts or quasi-judicial decisions [3] can be found which specify the actual mode of application, and thereby illustrate the scope, of the concept of freedom of association. In addition to the international surveys contained in the McNair report and those of the Committee of Experts on the Application of Conventions and Recommendations, [4] a very large number of articles have been published in the *International Labour Review*, and provide abundant information on the trade union situation in the various countries. However, the practical content of the concept of freedom of association still has to be determined. The task has been greatly simplified by a resolution concerning trade union rights and their relation to civil liberties, which was adopted unanimously by the International Labour Conference at its 54th Session (1970), and calls upon the Governing Body of the International Labour Office "to instruct the Director-General to publish and distribute widely in a concise form the supplementary decisions taken by" the Governing Body's Committee on Freedom of Association. The publication which resulted from this decision [5] helps to identify the various elements of the concept of freedom of association, [6] which will now be described.

---

[1] A resolution concerning trade union rights and their relation to civil liberties, adopted by the International Labour Conference in 1970, places special emphasis on the following civil liberties, as defined in the Universal Declaration of Human Rights, which are essential for the normal exercise of trade union rights: *(a)* the right to freedom and security of person and freedom from arbitrary arrest and detention; *(b)* freedom of opinion and expression and in particular freedom to hold opinions without interference and to seek, receive and impart information and ideas through any media and regardless of frontiers; *(c)* freedom of assembly; *(d)* the right to a fair trial by an independent and impartial tribunal; and *(e)* the right to protection of the property of trade union organisations.

[2] Especially Georges Spyropoulos: *La liberté syndicale* (Paris, Librairie générale de droit et de jurisprudence, 1954); C. Wilfred Jenks: *The international protection of trade union freedom* (London, Stevens and Sons, 1957); *The right to organise and its limits: A comparison of policies in the United States and selected European countries* (Washington, Brookings Institution, 1950); Ernst B. Haas: *Human rights and international action: The case of freedom of association* (Stanford, California, Stanford University Press, 1970).

[3] By the bodies discussed in the appendix, paras. 5-9, pp. 29-30.

[4] See the appendix, para. 5, p. 29.

[5] ILO: *Freedom of association: Digest of decisions of the Freedom of Association Committee of the Governing Body of the ILO* (second edition revised, Geneva, 1976). For the exact reference to the texts of the reports themselves, see the bibliography at the end of this volume.

[6] G. von Potobsky: "Protection of trade union rights: Twenty years' work by the Committee on Freedom of Association", in *International Labour Review*, Jan. 1972.

Practical content

Freedom of association implies the right of workers and employers without distinction whatsoever to establish and join organisations of their own choosing. The words "without distinction whatsoever" mean that there must be no discrimination of any kind on the basis of such criteria as occupation, sex, colour, race, belief, nationality, or political opinion. The ILO standards lay down that workers and employers should be able to form their organisations in full freedom; this principle has three fundamental implications. In the first place, although Convention No. 87 is not intended to make trade union diversity an obligation, it does require that such diversity should at least remain possible at all times. Consequently, the institution of a trade union monopoly established by law, whether at the level of the undertaking, of the economic sector or at the national level, is to be condemned, whereas a situation in which organisations in fact join together voluntarily is perfectly consistent with the provisions of the Convention. Secondly, to be consistent with the provisions of the Convention, the privileges granted to the most representative organisations must not go beyond according them priority in terms of representation for purposes of collective bargaining, consultation by governments or designation of delegates to international institutions; in particular, they should not deprive minority organisations of the essential means whereby they may defend the occupational interests of their members. Thirdly, union security clauses of various kinds are quite consistent with the provisions of Convention No. 87 provided they are the outcome of collective bargaining. It must be possible to establish organisations without previous authorisation. The registration of trade unions, which is a normal statutory requirement in many countries, does not inherently constitute an infringement of Convention No. 87, provided that it is no more than a formality, that the conditions of registration are clearly specified in the legislation and do not run counter to the guarantees laid down by the Convention, and that a refusal to grant registration is subject to a right of appeal to the courts.

Trade unions must be able to operate in full freedom. This means, first of all, that they must be free to draw up their Constitutions and rules without interference, even though they may base the text on specimen Constitutions proposed by the administrative authorities, provided that there is no obligation to accept a model. Secondly, it entails the right freely to elect, [1] dismiss

[1] ILO: *Eligibility for trade union office* (Geneva, 1972) contains a detailed study of the various provisions relating to the principle laid down on this particular point by Article 3 of Convention No. 87. Legislation can be said to restrict the right of workers and employers freely to elect their representatives if it refers to *(a)* qualifications based on nationality or citizenship; *(b)* residential qualifications; *(c)* racial disqualifications; *(d)* disqualification on political grounds; *(e)* age qualifications; *(f)* qualification according to the sex of the person concerned; *(g)* educational qualifications; *(h)* qualifications based on the occupa-

(footnote concluded overleaf)

or suspend trade union leaders. Consequently any intervention by the authorities in the various stages of the election (such as approval of the list of candidates, presence of public servants during the vote or approval of the results of the vote) and provisions requiring all trade union leaders to be engaged in the occupation to which the trade union devotes its activities (which, in the event of the dismissal of a trade union leader, might well jeopardise the freedom of action of the organisation) are therefore to be condemned. Measures for the dismissal, suspension or disqualification of trade union officials as a penalty provided by law should not become enforceable except on the basis of a firm sentence on the part of the competent judicial authority. The free functioning of trade unions also entails their right to organise their administration and activities and to formulate their programmes, and if necessary to undertake political action as a means towards the advancement of their economic and social objectives, provided their action is not of such a nature as to compromise the continuance of the trade union movement or its social or economic functions. In particular, measures of supervision over the administration of trade union funds should only be employed to prevent abuses and to protect the members of the union themselves; financial independence is a fundamental aspect of freedom of association. [1] Freedom of association also includes the right of workers and employers to establish federations and confederations and, if necessary, to affiliate with international organisations.

To prevent these rights from remaining a dead letter, it is not sufficient merely to introduce legislation prohibiting anti-union discrimination: measures of this kind must be supported by efficient machinery for ensuring their practical application, particularly with regard to such matters as dismissal, transfer, demotion and pensioning off; the machinery must operate swiftly; and if trade union officers are to be able to perform their duties without any interference they must be given special protection, for example by means of clauses specifically safeguarding them against dismissal either during their term of office or for a certain length of time after its completion. [2]

tional status of the persons concerned; *(i)* disqualification of supervisory employees; *(j)* disqualifications based on incompatibility with the holding of other union or non-union office; *(k)* disqualifications based on conduct while holding previous union office; *(l)* disqualification from re-election; *(m)* disqualifications resulting from various types of legal disability or personal circumstances; or *(n)* disqualifications based on the penal record of the person concerned (p. 3).

[1] Legislation on the subject deals mainly with the submission of reports at specified intervals, official supervision and information to be supplied to the authorities on request, rules for the keeping of trade union accounts, approval of budgets, of certain financial operations and of trade union investments, and administration of the trade unions by the authorities. See ILO: *The public authorities and the right to protection of trade union funds and property* (Geneva, 1974).

[2] ILO: *Protection and facilities afforded to workers' representatives in the undertaking*, Report VIII (1), International Labour Conference, 54th Session, 1970. In 1971 the Conference adopted the Workers' Representatives Convention (No. 135) and Recommendation (No. 143).

As defined by Convention No. 98, the right to bargain collectively raises several problems in connection with the relations between the contracting parties, on the one hand, and the attitude of the public authorities on the other. As regards relations between the parties, a refusal to bargain, or the adoption by one of the parties of an uncompromising attitude during the negotiations, cannot be looked upon as an infringement of trade union rights. As to the attitude of the authorities, statutory provisions whereby the validity of an agreement is subject to prior approval by a government authority, or modifying the conditions of work laid down in the collective agreement or preventing the parties from negotiating such conditions as they may consider desirable, may constitute infringements of the right of the parties to bargain collectively. Stabilisation measures rendering it impossible for wage rates to be settled freely through collective bargaining should be introduced in exceptional circumstances only; they should be restricted to a reasonable period and kept to the minimum. That the parties should, in their negotiations, voluntarily take account of considerations relating to economic policy and to the defence of the general interest, is possible; that they should be obliged to do so, on the other hand, is apt to constitute an infringement of the right to bargain collectively.

The international Conventions adopted by the ILO do not make any explicit reference to the exercise of the right to strike. However, inasmuch as the right to strike is one of the essential means through which workers and their organisations may promote and defend their occupational interests, it is a necessary extension of freedom of association and of the right to bargain collectively. In certain cases, of course (the public service, essential services), the exercise of the right to strike may be restricted, provided that the workers' interests are adequately safeguarded, for example through appropriate conciliation and arbitration machinery, and provided above all that the definition of essential services is not so broad as to constitute a serious and unjustified limitation on the freedom of action of the unions. While prerequisites (prior notification, for example) or temporary restrictions (prohibition of strike action in breach of collective agreements, for example) are consistent with the exercise of the right to strike, the same cannot be said of general provisions prohibiting strike action in all sectors of employment.

In addition, a free trade union movement cannot develop unless fundamental rights are respected. This means that a trade union must be entitled to hold meetings on its own premises and, if necessary, to organise public meetings and demonstrations (on 1 May, for instance). It also implies the free circulation of information, opinions and ideas: the censorship of publications, their seizure or the withdrawal of licences by administrative decision can constitute serious interference in trade union affairs. Trade union premises should not be occupied or searched without a warrant issued by the ordinary judicial authority. In the event of the arrest of trade union officials, it is the responsibility of the government to prove that the action taken has nothing to do with the trade union activities of the persons concerned. In any case, even when trade unionists are charged with political or criminal offences, it is important that they should be brought to trial as quickly as possible before an independent and impartial judiciary.

Individual freedom of conscience and the right to bargain collectively

Many authorities on labour law [1] consider that freedom of association has an individual aspect—in the sense that it is recognised as the personal right of each member of an occupation—and a collective aspect—in the sense that it is a civil liberty. This dualism corresponds to two different phases of historical development: for example in France in 1884 freedom of association was established by the legislature along the lines of an individual freedom, inasmuch as the law merely stated that trade unions might be formed freely, whereas subsequently, especially after the First World War, freedom of association came to be looked upon as a fundamental aspect of the relations between the employers' and workers' organisations and the public authorities and between the unions and management. The dualism further corresponds to two contradictory rather than complementary ways of looking at trade unionism. Both the debate that preceded the passing of the law on trade union branches at the level of the undertaking in France in December 1968 [2] and the history of the movement in other countries provide ample proof that for some people freedom of association is merely an offshoot of freedom of conscience, while for others it is more a right to organise, and it accordingly implies the recognition of trade unions and the right of such organisations to play a part in society and to negotiate with others.

If freedom of association is regarded merely as an individual right which finds its expression in the personal act of giving support to a movement or joining it, which from the economic and social point of view is ultimately

---

[1] For example, G. H. Camerlynck and G. Lyon-Caen: *Droit du travail* (Paris, Dalloz, 6th edition, 1973), pp. 448 ff.

[2] In his *Le syndicat dans l'entreprise* (Paris, Editions du Seuil, 1967), pp. 61-64, H. Lesire-Ogrel argued that the employers' attitude was to reject trade unionism in the undertaking but—with not a few exceptions—to recognise that everyone had the right to freedom of association, provided that right was not exercised at the workplace. He pointed out that in such circumstances freedom of association was gagged and robbed of any meaning. One could not talk about freedom of association if there were no trade union rights. Freedom of association was first and foremost a collective right. Just as freedom of the press was not simply a question of being free to write and peddle a manuscript, the tradition of freedom of association found its expression in its necessary instrument, the trade union, and the effective enjoyment of that freedom was to be assessed in those terms. The author concluded by asking what was left of such a freedom if it was not allowed expression in the places where there was a need for it.

Table 2. Worker protest and the élites

Industrialising élite	Organising principle of group protest	Forms of group protest	Attitudes of élites toward conflict
Middle class	Job control	Organised economic strikes	Affirmative role for limited conflict
Dynastic	Class consciousness	Demonstrations and political strikes	Inconsistent with paternal society
Revolutionary intellectuals	Self-criticism	Diffused and suppressed, except for occasional outburst	Inconsistent with ideology and rapid industrialisation
Colonial administrators	Anti-colonialism	Demonstrations for independence, often violent	Inconsistent with role of mother country
Nationalist leaders	Nationalism	Demonstrations, ordinarily peaceful	Inconsistent with nationalist ideal and economic development

Source: Kerr, Dunlop, Harbison and Myers, op. cit., pp. 182-183.

no more than a way of exercising freedom of thought, it will hardly interfere with economic development. Seen from this angle, the link between economic development and freedom of association is not significantly unlike its link with any ideology, whether or not it sets out to mobilise people or to transform society. [1]

However, freedom of association can also be looked upon as a collective right that is intimately bound up with the demand for more power over the employment relationship and that is only as valid as the goals it seeks to attain. Seen in this light, the link between freedom of association and economic development is of an altogether different nature: development is no longer influenced only indirectly by an ideology but directly by economic pressure groups whose policies, objectives and means of action differ widely. If freedom of association were merely an individual right, then the groups responsible for economic development could compare the ideologies professed by workers' (and employers') organisations, assess their degree of compatibility with the development objective, and accept or reject the ideologies in question; but if it is a collective right, they have to consider the conflicts that can stem from the existence of organisations whose activities may jeopardise the development

[1] Freedom of association can then be regarded as an idea or a system of values with various components that can be discussed and compared with those that underlie ideologies of the industrialising élites, as they emerge, for example, from the works of P. Sigmund: *The ideologies of the developing nations* (London, Praeger, 1967); Y. Bénot: *Idéologies des indépendances africaines* (Paris, Maspéro, 1972); L. Garrucio: *L'industrializzazione tra nazionalismo e revoluzione — le ideologie politiche dei paesi in via di sviluppo* (Bologna, Società editrice Il Mulino, 1969).

process. In other words, on the one side there is freedom of association as a specific manifestation of freedom of thought and, on the other, freedom of association as a form of active intervention by workers' and employers' organisations which effectively undertake to defend and promote the interests of their members. It is therefore as a form of group protest that the problem of freedom of association can best be tackled. Table 2 illustrates the points raised above in the form of a classification to which reference will frequently be made as a working hypothesis.

ECONOMIC DEVELOPMENT

Like "freedom of association", the expression "economic development" has been interpreted in various ways. Recent interest in such matters as the quality of life and the pollution of the environment and of nature sometimes puts the case for "Better" rather than the "More" which Samuel Gompers once proclaimed as the objective of the trade union movement in the United States. That interest therefore sheds some light on the real issues involved.

A distinction that springs to mind immediately is that while growth is undoubtedly necessary for development, the two are not synonymous. The point has of course already been made:

> Economic growth, i.e. an increase in output and income, is probably the most basic objective and the most significant single indicator of progress in the development of the Asian countries. The attainment of other common development objectives —such as stepping up the rate of capital formation, achieving a satisfactory balance on external account, self-sufficiency in food supplies, the maintenance of price stability, rising living standards, the reduction of income disparities between social groups or different parts of a country—is closely related to and is often conditional upon achieving an adequate rate of growth. [1]

Although growth is almost invariably necessary for development, it is not the same thing, for several reasons. The growth of the gross domestic product per head of the population is a very unreliable indicator, often erroneously regarded as measuring something of unchanging composition, owing to an inability to apprehend developments otherwise than through the distorting mirror of monetary values. Bertrand de Jouvenel, [2] along with many others, has pointed out that there is a mistaken tendency to regard the product as something concrete: what is generally called growth of the real product is in fact only the growth of a monetary value which has been deflated as far as

---

[1] ILO: *Human resources development: Objectives, problems and policies*, Report of the Director-General, Sixth Asian Regional Conference, Tokyo, 1968, p. 9.

[2] " Sur la croissance économique ", in Lionel Stoléru (ed.): *Economie et société humaine*, ... exposés et ... débats des Rencontres internationales du Ministère de l'Economie et des Finances, ... Paris, ... 20, 21 et 22 juin 1972 (Paris, Denoël, 1972), pp. 47-48.

possible; it is a highly abstract and not at all a physical concept; consequently, it is a serious mistake to refer to it as a "growth in volume", for it has nothing to do with physical volume—growth may well take the form of a miniaturisation of goods, or a "vapourisation" resulting from their use without ownership, in the form of services. The monetary approach ignores a number of factors such as the assets bestowed freely by nature and public assets not subject to an assessment in market terms. All of them are items whose destruction, while harmful to the welfare of the community, is sometimes the counterpart of steady, measurable growth. Consequently, what is significant about growth is not so much what it indicates as the terms of reference it uses. Economic growth cannot and must not be looked upon otherwise than as the abstract expression of the growth of supplies corresponding to the changing way of life of the nation as its structure and mores evolve. Observers must concentrate their attention on the direction which that evolution takes, and they must not do so passively, so as to foresee it, but actively, so as to influence it. [1]

In some cases at least, growth and development may actually be contradictory. At best, all that can be said [2] in favour of the growth of the gross national product is that it suggests a probability, but no more, that the economy is changing for the better, is bringing greater welfare. The highest growth rates may be obtained at the expense of a more equitable distribution of income by means of a reduction in employment: in that case growth and welfare do not go hand in hand.

Thanks to the distinction between growth and development that has been explained above, some of the principal features of development can now be identified. The resolution adopted unanimously by the United Nations General Assembly on 24 October 1970 and setting forth the International Development Strategy for the Second United Nations Development Decade can be useful here. As far as economic growth, savings and international trade are concerned, the goals and objectives of the Strategy are defined in quantitative terms: the average annual rate of growth in the gross product of the developing countries as a whole should be at least 6 per cent and the average annual rate of growth of gross product per head about 3.5 per cent, which would double the average income per head in the course of two decades; the average annual expansion of agricultural output should be 4 per cent, and of manufacturing output 8 per cent; there should be an average annual expansion of 0.5 per cent in the ratio of gross domestic saving to the gross product, somewhat less than

[1] ibid., p. 58. Bertrand de Jouvenel's statement was in answer to the first of two questions framed by the Minister who organised the meetings: "Is the goal of a systematically high growth rate in industrialised societies the best way of satisfying contemporary man's every requirement?" (ibid., p. 29).

[2] Statement by S. El-Naggar, Director of the United Nations Economic and Social Office in Beirut, at a regional seminar on development and environment held in Beirut in 1971.

7 per cent in imports and somewhat more than 7 per cent in exports. The resolution also proposes a number of social objectives which, unlike the economic objectives, are not defined quantitatively: it states that development means bringing about a more equitable distribution of income and wealth for promoting both social justice and efficiency of production, raising substantially the level of employment, achieving a greater degree of income security, and bringing about qualitative and structural changes that must go hand in hand with rapid economic growth. More precisely, the resolution states—

> Each developing country should formulate its national employment objectives so as to absorb an increasing proportion of its working population in modern-type activities and to reduce significantly unemployment and underemployment. . . . Housing facilities should be expanded and improved, especially for the low-income groups and with a view to remedying the ills of unplanned urban growth and lagging rural areas. . . . The full participation of youth in the development process should be ensured [and] the full integration of women in the total development effort should be encouraged. [1]

It is recognised in the resolution that these objectives are both determining factors and end-results of development and that they should therefore be viewed as integrated parts of the same dynamic process, since "the ultimate objective of development must be to bring about sustained improvement in the well-being of the individual and bestow benefits on all. If undue privileges, extremes of wealth and social injustices persist, then development fails in its essential purpose." [2] In connection with this resolution the point has been made that "the unanimous recognition by the General Assembly of the United Nations that development is a complex process involving far more than an acceleration of economic growth is a welcome refutation of earlier theories that social progress should to a greater or lesser extent be sacrificed by one or more generations for the purpose of accelerating economic development through increased savings and investment". [3]

This awareness of the qualitative dimension of development is in fact a recent one, although it does now appear to be widespread both among academic economists and among those responsible for framing economic policy. [4]

---

[1] Para. 18 of the resolution.

[2] Para. 7.

[3] ILO: *Freedom by dialogue: Economic development by social progress—The ILO contribution*, Report of the Director-General, Part 1, International Labour Conference, 56th Session, Geneva, 1971, p. 7.

[4] This could be demonstrated by any number of references. To realise the progress made in this direction, however, it may be more useful for the reader to compare two volumes which appeared 15 years apart. The differences between *The economics of underdevelopment*, edited by A. N. Agarwala and S. P. Singh (Oxford University Press, 1958) and *Underdevelopment and development: The Third World today*, edited by H. Bernstein (Harmondsworth, Middlesex, Penguin Books, 1973), are not only apparent from the field they cover (strictly economic in the first case and very much socio-economic in the second) or from their approach to the problems (essentially analytical in the first case, with more attention to political implications in the

In the case of economic theory, a radical change has visibly taken place over the past decade. In 1955, in the very first lines of his book, Arthur Lewis described his subject matter as the growth of output per head of population, going on to note—

"Growth of output per head of the population" is rather a long phrase to repeat over and over again in a book. Most often we shall refer only to "growth" or to "output", or even occasionally, for the sake of variety, to "progress" or to "development". Whatever the short term used, "per head of the population" should be understood, unless total output is clearly specified or clearly intended by the context. [1]

On the other hand, Benjamin Higgins, in a classic and extremely promising work, felt able four years later to widen the concept and give it a dynamic context by stating that the essential problem of economic development was "launching a take-off into sustained growth", which he defined as "a discernible rise in national and per capita real income, widely diffused throughout the population, that continues for two or more generations". [2] Even ten years ago no clear distinction was drawn between growth and development, at least in Anglo-Saxon intellectual circles, whereas by then François Perroux, in France, in a whole series of works, had proposed drawing a series of distinctions between—

(a) expansion, which is the temporary and possibly reversible accretion of economic quantities attributable mainly to cyclical movements;

(b) growth, which is the increase over a long period, marked by structural changes, of significant quantities that can be measured by means of certain indicators;

(c) development, which is the over-all transformation of mental and institutional structures that provides the backing for growth; and

(d) progress, which is a sort of model put forward as the end result of the process of development.

Generally speaking, development is a prerequisite for growth since the latter is the combination of the mental and social adjustments of a nation that enable it to ensure the cumulative and durable growth of its real total product. [3] However, development also requires—as implied in the concept of

---

second), but also from the kind of authors included (Western and above all Anglo-Saxon authors in the first case, maximum coverage of experts from developing countries such as Celso Furtado, T. dos Santos, R. Stavenhagen, F. H. Cardoso and C. V. Vaitsos in the second). Finally, the differences in terminology, which in the second book is geared to quite different preoccupations, are an illustration of how the developing countries have acquired a growing awareness of their own problems.

[1] Arthur Lewis: *The theory of economic growth* (London, Allen and Unwin, 1955), pp. 9, 10.

[2] Benjamin Higgins: *Economic development: Principles, problems and policies* (New York, Norton and Co., 1959), p. 21.

[3] François Perroux: *L'économie du XXe siècle* (Paris, Presses universitaires de France, 1961), p. 155.

progress—an economic ideology: full employment on a world scale of all material and human resources, promoted with a view to ensuring that each person will have the material means considered necessary in scientific terms for complete fulfilment. [1] A similar point of view was held around the same time by L. J. Lebret, who considered that as an activity, development was a co-ordinated series of transitions towards a society more favourable to the actualisation of human potential; and as a state of affairs, the outcome of such transitions. [2]

This distinction between growth and development is now generally recognised in economic works, as can be seen in more recent publications. According to D. F. Dowd, "growth is a quantitative process, involving principally the extension of an already established structure of production, whereas development suggests qualitative changes, the creation of new economic and non-economic structures". [3] The terms are similarly defined by C. K. Wilber, who states that "a distinction should be made between economic growth, analyzed in terms of changes in the value of economic parameters in given institutional conditions, and economic development, when changes in the value of economic parameters are accompanied or even preceded by institutional changes". [4] Again, for Dudley Seers, development transcends economic growth and incorporates such factors as social justice in the form of equal opportunity, full employment, generally available social services, equitable distribution of income and basic political liberties. [5]

The evolution of economic theory regarding the definition of development that has been outlined broadly above parallels the trend in international economic policy. In its earliest studies devoted to the underdeveloped countries the United Nations was concerned essentially with growth [6] as defined above, considering that it could best be promoted by two sets of vital measures, industrialisation [7] and agrarian reform. [8] For the First United Nations Development Decade, the goal for developing countries as a whole was an annual

[1] François Perroux: *L'économie du XXe siècle*, op. cit., p. 163.

[2] L. J. Lebret: *Dynamique concrète du développement* (Paris, Les éditions ouvrières, 1961), p. 41.

[3] D. F. Dowd: "Some issues of economic development and of development economics", in *Journal of Economic Issues* (East Lansing, Michigan State University), Sep. 1967, p. 153.

[4] C. K. Wilber: *The Soviet model and underdeveloped countries* (University of North Carolina Press, 1969), p. 8.

[5] Dudley Seers: "The meaning of development", in *International Development Review* (Washington, Society for International Development), Dec. 1969, pp. 2-6.

[6] United Nations: *Measures for the economic development of underdeveloped countries* (New York, Sales No. 1951.II.B.2).

[7] idem: *Processes and problems of industrialisation in underdeveloped countries* (New York, Sales No. 1955.II.B.1).

[8] idem: *Land reform: Defects in agrarian structure as obstacles to economic development* (New York, Sales No. 1951.II.B.3).

growth rate of 5 per cent. However, the achievement of this economic goal in the developing countries taken as a whole, if not in each individual country, left no doubt in the mind of even the least informed observer that, in many cases, development in such a limited economic sense had accentuated rather than attenuated inequalities and had done nothing to eliminate poverty, hardship, hunger, sickness and ignorance. In other words, at the same time as the developed countries were discovering that poverty could continue to exist in spite of expansion, and even because of it,[1] the developing countries were reaching a similar conclusion about the type of growth of which they had been both the beneficiaries and the victims. A complete rethinking was called for.

This fundamental shift of emphasis in the international attitude towards the social objectives of development was a long time coming. The ILO did much to hasten it. In fact, the past history of the Organisation placed it in a very good position to do so: looking backwards, one need only recall the economic and social philosophy of the first Director of the International Labour Office, Albert Thomas, the underlying message of reports of the second, Harold Butler, in the 1930s or the basic principles that led to the framing of the declaration which was adopted by the International Labour Conference at its 26th Session, held in Philadelphia in 1944, and which affirms that—

(a) all human beings, irrespective of race, creed or sex, have the right to pursue both their material well-being and their spiritual development in conditions of freedom and dignity, of economic security and equal opportunity;

(b) the attainment of the conditions in which this shall be possible must constitute the central aim of national and international policy.

The recognition of social objectives as an integral part of development is now common currency.[2] Consequently it is unnecessary to reproduce a long series of quotations all of which point in the same direction, and it is easy to appreciate that "the ILO challenge of a generation ago to the conventional wisdom has now become the conventional wisdom".[3] The new outlook which now prevails among the practical promoters of development is given particular force in the International Development Strategy for the Second United Nations Development Decade, which was unanimously adopted by the General

[1] See, for example, M. Harrington: *The other America: Poverty in the United States* (New York, Macmillan, 1962); P. M. de la Gorce: *La France pauvre* (Paris, Grasset, 1965); K. Coates and R. Silburn: *Poverty: The forgotten Englishmen* (Harmondsworth, Middlesex, Penguin Books, 1970); Gunnar Myrdal: *The challenge of world poverty: A world anti-poverty program in outline* (New York, Pantheon Books, 1970).

[2] As is amply demonstrated by statements by the Secretary-General of the United Nations, the Administrator of the United Nations Development Programme, the President of the World Bank and the Secretary-General of the United Nations Conference on Trade and Development, quoted in ILO: *Prosperity for welfare: Social purpose in economic growth and change*, op. cit., p. 2 (footnote).

[3] ILO: *Prosperity for welfare: Social purpose in economic growth and change*, op. cit., p. 1.

Assembly on 24 October 1970 and which declares, as already stated, that "the ultimate objective of development must be to bring about sustained improvement in the well-being of the individual and bestow benefits on all. If undue privileges, extremes of wealth and social injustices persist, then development fails in its essential purpose."

MEANINGS CONSIDERED IN THIS STUDY

These somewhat lengthy reflections on the nature of development and the meaning it should be given should help to identify the links that can logically be established between freedom of association and development. As long as development continues to be improperly identified with growth, which in turn is associated with the upward movement of an indicator (generally gross national product per head) over time, the issue is a very simple one. As has been seen above, the two essential aspects of freedom of association are the right to join a trade union and to put forward certain union claims with regard to terms of employment. If the objective is merely the highest possible growth rate, all that is needed is to consider whether those rights are a constraint that has to be taken into account and, if necessary, reduced, or whether they constitute an instrument that might serve a useful purpose within the framework of the economic policy pursued. However, when development is taken in the wider sense, the situation changes altogether and becomes far more complex. In this case, development, quite apart from the structural changes it entails—and therefore the shifts in inter-related variables which a single growth indicator cannot hope to reflect—raises questions of quality and has to be assessed by reference to the systems of values of a particular society. Of course there is not always the incompatibility between growth and development that was suggested in the discussions of the Club of Rome and in the Massachusetts Institute of Technology model, and which, if taken to extremes, would mean that genuine development could be accompanied by zero growth. However, such studies, like many others, do at least avoid the pitfall of confusing a highly unreliable indicator (growth of the gross national product per head) with the chosen objective of development, which implies the implementation of a complex set of measures which are precisely those listed in the annex to the ILO Constitution [1]—full employment and the raising of standards of living, the employment of workers in the occupations in which they can have the satisfaction of giving the fullest measure of their skill and attainments, the possibility for all of enjoying a just share of the fruits of progress, the co-operation of management and labour in the continuous improvement of productive efficiency and in the preparation and application of social and economic measures, the extension

[1] The ILO Declaration of Philadelphia, also cited on pp. 2, 25 and 29 (para. 4).

Table 3. Possible combinations of the concepts of freedom of association and development

Freedom of association	Economic development
(1) As a liberty of the individual	(3) As the quantitative growth of an indicator
(2) As a collective right	(4) As qualitative factor changes

of social security measures, protection for the life and health of workers, and the assurance of equality of educational and vocational opportunity. Seen in this light, the issue of freedom of association and economic development takes on yet another meaning since it must now be viewed as a confrontation of different social objectives.

The meanings to be attached to the terms used in the title of this study have been defined in the foregoing pages. Freedom of association has been examined successively in terms of the international standards concerning it, of the reports on the way in which it is actually applied in different countries and of the legal procedures that have been established to safeguard it and which show up its practical aspects. It would seem that freedom of association can be looked upon as an individual freedom, a collective right, or both. [1] Development, which for a long time was somewhat confused with economic growth, can now be seen, both through the writings of economic theorists and through the statements of those responsible for framing economic policy, to be a matter of quantity but also, and above all, of quality.

A simple permutation of the different concepts of freedom of association and economic development (table 3) show the four possible combinations: 1-3, 1-4, 2-3 and 2-4. Although theoretical argumentation and political debate have so far tended to regard freedom of association as a collective right and have pitted it against the goal of pure economic growth (hypotheses 2-3) and although this is the combination that needs analysing above all, it would be wrong to overlook the other aspects of the subject altogether.

[1] The distinction drawn here is not always as clear-cut in the legislation on the subject. The point has been made, for example, that French positive law relating to trade unions is the outcome of a variety of successive initiatives, and does not hang together very well, being something of a patchwork: under the basic legislation, which has hardly been amended, the trade union was a strictly private body representing the interests of its members; numerous subsequent provisions recognised the authority of the trade union to speak on behalf of workers or employers collectively in individual occupations and thus to represent wider interests; thereafter, further provisions were introduced, step by step, to build up a whole structure of trade union functions at all levels of economic and social life. As a result, the basis of this legislation is still the concept of an individual freedom that finds its fulfilment in the personal act of joining a union, whereas the functions attributed to the trade union are to some extent powers of public authorities and reflect the collective aspect of the right to organise, which embodies a right to take action as much as a right of association. (J. M. Verdier: *Syndicats* (Paris, Dalloz, 1966), pp. XIII-XIV.)

APPENDIX: INTERNATIONAL STANDARDS CONCERNING FREEDOM OF ASSOCIATION

1. In addition to the Freedom of Association and Protection of the Right to Organise Convention, 1948 (No. 87), the relevant Conventions are the Right of Association (Agriculture) Convention, 1921 (No. 11), the Right of Association (Non-Metropolitan Territories) Convention, 1947 (No. 84), the Right to Organise and Collective Bargaining Convention, 1949 (No. 98), the Workers' Representatives Convention, 1971 (No. 135), and the Rural Workers' Organisations Convention, 1975 (No. 141).

2. Unlike an international labour Convention (which is a kind of international treaty adopted at the International Labour Conference by a two-thirds majority with a view to establishing international labour standards but whose provisions the States Members of the ILO formally undertake to apply only if they become parties to the Convention by ratifying it), an international labour Recommendation—which is another kind of international instrument adopted by a two-thirds majority—is not subject to ratification but is communicated to all member States for their consideration with a view to its implementation through national legislation or in some other way; these Recommendations are fundamentally intended to provide guidelines for national action. A number of these Recommendations relate more or less directly to the theme of freedom of association. Examples of such instruments are the Consultation (Industrial and National Levels) Recommendation, 1960 (No. 113), which reiterates the principles of non-discrimination, freedom of association and the right of collective bargaining; the Termination of Employment Recommendation, 1963 (No. 119), which stipulates that union membership or participation in union activities outside working hours or, with the consent of the employer, within working hours, should not constitute valid reasons for termination of employment; the Communications within the Undertaking Recommendation, 1967 (No. 129), which recognises the importance and role of trade union representatives in promoting the acceptance and effective application of "communications policies"; the Examination of Grievances Recommendation, 1967 (No. 130), which provides for the association of workers' organisations in the establishment and implementation of grievance procedures and the participation of workers' representatives during the examination of grievances; the Workers' Representatives Recommendation, 1971 (No. 143), which establishes the principle that workers' representatives in general, including trade union representatives, should enjoy effective protection against any act prejudicial to them, including dismissal, based on their status or activities as workers' representatives or on union membership or participation in union activities and recommends that facilities in the undertaking should be afforded to workers' representatives as may be appropriate in order to enable them to carry out their functions promptly and efficiently; and the Rural Workers' Organisations Recommendation, 1975 (No. 149), which contains numerous provisions designed to encourage the growth of organisations of rural workers.

3. A number of resolutions adopted at various meetings of the International Labour Organisation also have a bearing on freedom of association. Such resolutions include those adopted by the International Labour Conference concerning the independence of the trade union movement (1952), the protection of trade union rights (1955), the abolition of anti-trade-union legislation in the States Members of the ILO (1957), freedom of association and the protection of the right to organise, including the protection of representatives of trade unions at all levels (1961), freedom of association (1964), workers' participation in undertakings (1966), action by the International Labour Organisation in the field of human rights and in particular with respect to freedom of association (1968), and trade union rights and their relation to civil liberties (1970). These subjects are also dealt with in resolutions adopted by regional conferences and meetings; for example, by conferences of the American

States Members of the Organisation, resolutions concerning freedom of association and protection of the right to organise and to bargain collectively (Mexico City, 1946), freedom of association (Montevideo, 1949), freedom of association (Petropolis, 1952), defence of trade union rights (Havana, 1956), social policy and economic development (Buenos Aires, 1961), and social participation in the development process (Caracas, 1970); by Asian regional conferences, resolutions concerning freedom of association in Asia (Tokyo, 1968), and freedom of association for workers' and employers' organisations and their role in social and economic development (Teheran, 1971); by African regional conferences, a resolution concerning freedom of association and protection of the right to organise (Lagos, 1960). Resolutions along similar lines have also been adopted on numerous occasions by the ILO's industrial committees: the Inland Transport Committee (1961); the Iron and Steel Committee (1946); the Textiles Committee (1968); the Petroleum Committee (1966); and the Joint Committee on the Public Service (1970).

4. The principle of freedom of association is particularly important in the ILO, where it is looked upon as a kind of customary rule which has become part of the common heritage of man in the twentieth century, independently of the provisions of international labour Conventions. [1] The principle of "the effective recognition of the right of collective bargaining" is included in a "declaration of the aims and purposes of the International Labour Organisation and of the principles which should inspire the policy of its Members", adopted by the International Labour Conference at its 26th Session (Philadelphia, 1944), and annexed to the Constitution of the ILO. It is accordingly felt that freedom of association should "be observed by the States Members by reason of their membership in the Organisation" (resolution on freedom of association and industrial relations in Europe, unanimously adopted by the Second European Regional Conference of the ILO in January 1974), and the principle is one of the bases of the special supervisory procedure which was introduced by the ILO in 1950 to protect freedom of association, and under which complaints can be examined even against countries that have not ratified the Conventions on freedom of association.

5. On five occasions, in 1953, 1956, 1957, 1959 and 1973, the ILO Committee of Experts on the Application of Conventions and Recommendations has examined reports submitted by governments, at the request of the Governing Body, in accordance with article 19 of the Constitution of the Organisation, on the position of the law and practice in their respective countries in regard to the matters dealt with in Conventions on freedom of association which they had not ratified, or in the Recommendations on the same subject. The reports which the Committee of Experts submitted to the International Labour Conference in those years provide a picture of the situation in respect of freedom of association in the various countries, and thus supplement and bring up to date the inquiry into the trade union situation in the States Members of the ILO conducted in 1956 by a committee on freedom of employers' and workers' organisations, known as the McNair committee, [2] and the factual surveys into conditions relating to freedom of association in various countries carried out by study missions in accordance with a decision taken by the Governing Body in 1958. The reports of the Committee of Experts provide an insight into the way the problem of freedom of association arises in actual fact throughout the world and, more particularly, in the geographical area of the developing countries as defined in the introduction.

[1] As may be inferred from ILO: *The trade union situation in Chile: Report of the Fact-Finding and Conciliation Commission on Freedom of Association* (Geneva, provisional edition, 1975), p. 108, para. 466.

[2] The report of that committee was published in the *Official Bulletin* of the International Labour Office (Vol. XXXIX, 1956, No. 9).

6. The Conventions, Recommendations and resolutions adopted by the ILO define a right. The reports of the Committee of Experts on the Application of Conventions and Recommendations are mainly concerned with the legislation of the various countries, on which they offer a number of observations. The gap between the reality and the right is sometimes so great that accepted commitments are held to have been violated. Consequently, a dual procedure for protecting freedom of association has been introduced. [1]

7. The function of the Fact-Finding and Conciliation Commission on Freedom of Association, provided for in 1950 and composed of nine members selected for their competence and independence, is to carry out an impartial examination of any complaints that may be referred to it by the Governing Body of the ILO. To be receivable, these complaints must emanate from workers' or employers' organisations or from governments. The Commission is essentially a fact-finding body, but is authorised to discuss with the government concerned the possibilities of securing the adjustment of difficulties by agreement. Except in the cases covered by article 26 of the ILO Constitution, which relate to the examination of complaints in respect of ratified Conventions, it may consider a case only with the consent of the government concerned. To date, four cases (concerning Japan, Greece, Lesotho and Chile) have been dealt with in this way. [2]

8. The tripartite nine-member Committee on Freedom of Association set up by the Governing Body in November 1951 considers all complaints of infringement of freedom of association submitted to the ILO. When a complaint is received, it is communicated to the government concerned for its observations, while the complaining organisation is allowed a stipulated period in which to supply further information in substantiation of its complaint. Once in possession of all this information, the Committee makes its recommendations to the Governing Body. The same rule of receivability of complaints applies for the Governing Body Committee on Freedom of Association as for the Fact-Finding and Conciliation Commission. Since it was set up in 1951, the Committee has dealt with more than 800 cases. Although the decisions of the Committee are taken in the light of the special circumstances prevailing in each case, reasoning by analogy plays a major role. When certain situations present some similarity, the Committee regularly refers to previous decisions. In this way, a continuity as regards the criteria employed in reaching its conclusions results in the creation of a kind of case law.

9. In addition to the special machinery described in the last two paragraphs, a commission of inquiry established by the Governing Body and composed of independent persons can be set up to consider certain complaints of infringement of the Conventions on freedom of association when such complaints are submitted against a country that has ratified the Conventions in question. This procedure, which is provided for in the ILO Constitution, is applicable to all international labour Conventions. The complaints may be brought by a State Member of the ILO that has itself ratified the Convention concerned; the procedure can also be set in motion by the Governing Body, either on its own initiative or acting on a complaint lodged by a delegate to the Conference. [3] So far, only one case, concerning Greece, has been examined in connection with freedom of association. [4]

---

[1] This procedure is described in paragraphs 7 and 8. See also ILO: *The impact of international labour Conventions and Recommendations* (Geneva, 1976), pp. 69-73.

[2] See the *Official Buletin*, Vol. XLIX, No. 1, Special Supplement, Jan. 1966; No. 3, Special Supplement, July 1966; document GB.197/3/5, June 1975; and *The trade union situation in Chile*, op. cit.

[3] See articles 26 ff. of the Constitution.

[4] See the *Official Bulletin*, Vol. LIV, No. 2, Special Supplement, 1971.

THE ISSUES

2

The stimulating article by Karl de Schweinitz to which reference has already been made [1] has the advantage of presenting a concise summary of the basic arguments of a number of other authors regarding the problems raised by the principle of freedom of association in the developing countries: [2] because, unlike the modern developed countries at the time of their industrial revolution, underdeveloped countries nowadays have trade unions, their propensity to consume is increased and their capital formation jeopardised. Of course, such a categorical statement raises several problems; for example, at the theoretical level, that of the social structures in economic development [3] and, at the practical level, that of controlling a trade union move-

[1] de Schweinitz, op. cit.

[2] J. T. Dunlop: "The role of the free trade union in a less developed nation", in *American labor's role in less developed countries*, report on a conference held at Cornell University, October 12-17, 1958; E. J. Berg: "Major issues of wage policy in Africa", in A. M. Ross (ed.): *Industrial relations and economic development* (London, Macmillan, 1966), pp. 185-208; H. A. Turner: *Wage trends, wage policies, and collective bargaining: The problems for underdeveloped countries* (Cambridge University Press, 1965); W. Galenson: *Labor in developing economies* (Berkeley, University of California Press, 1962). Leaving aside minor variations from one author to another, the broad views of this school of thought have been summarised very well by Paul Fisher: "As a matter of policy, John Dunlop once suggested 'not to have any trade union, at least for a time, or to have a controlled union'. Karl de Schweinitz left us with a choice between permitting some measure of effective unionism and delaying economic growth, or suppressing democracy altogether for the sake of maximum development, and between permissive or totalitarian methods of dealing with labor unions. Walter Galenson . . . speaks of a 'balance' which 'must be struck which both satisfies the requirements of the economic planner and the minimum demands of the industrial worker'. Sturmthal suggested the nature of such a compromise: union leaders should delay the struggle for a wage increase, accept postponement of the effective date to give the economy time 'for the initial investment push . . .'. Where this is not feasible, he identifies the delay in capital formation as 'the price to be paid to avert a further deterioration of the prospect for economic growth' caused by political or social upheavals" ("Unions in the less developed countries: A reappraisal of their economic role", in E. M. Kassalow (ed.): *National labor movements in the postwar world* (Evanston, Illinois, Northwestern University Press, 1963), pp. 104-105).

[3] In his article, "Sous-développement, industrie, décolonisation: Perspectives et questions", published in *Esprit* (Paris), Oct. 1961, J. Cuisenier argues that for a sociologist the main issue

(footnote concluded overleaf)

ment regarded as a menace to economic growth. [1] Those problems will be left aside for the time being, and the subject of this chapter will be the issues discussed by de Schweinitz.

THE RECORD

In the often shifting terminology used by the authors whose views will be quoted in this chapter, analogies appear to be assumed between such expressions as "industrial revolution", "primitive accumulation" and "take-off". [2] These assumptions merit detailed consideration, but are accepted here for argument's sake, and the expressions in question will all be regarded as denoting merely the starting point of a process of industrialisation, [3] even though it may be necessary later to question their appropriateness. To undertake a comparison between the past state of countries now developed and the present situation of the developing countries, a more careful scrutiny must now be made of the institutional and economic history of the countries involved.

Institutional history

At first sight, the history of institutions seems to confirm de Schweinitz's assertions: in many now industrialised countries, the combination of workers or employers, not to mention permanent workers' or employers' organisations, were for a long time prohibited.

In France, an early Act of 2-17 March 1791 to abolish the guilds and proclaim freedom of work and industry was rapidly followed on 14 June 1791 by a second, known as the Le Chapelier Act, providing a legal framework for

---

seems to be what kind of social structure is most conducive to the industrialisation of production (p. 368). Yet one is bound to admit that the study of the structures that are conducive to economic progress, as found in such works as those of McClelland and Perroux, is still in its infancy.

[1] A. Sturmthal poses the problem in the following terms: "Effective unions, whatever else they may do, . . . tend to delay, reduce, or prevent altogether the growth of investment. If maximum growth is to be obtained, they must be suppressed by totalitarian methods and replaced by bodies which, in the guise of labor unions, are in fact agencies of a growth-conscious government rather than representatives of the workers" ("Unions and economic development", in *Economic Development and Cultural Change* (Chicago), Jan. 1960, p. 199).

[2] The meaning of these expressions is examined in the appendix to this chapter.

[3] This was suggested by C. Fohlen, who considers that "the links between the concepts of 'industrial revolution', 'economic growth' and 'development' are obvious. The first term denotes a phase, the critical phase, of the second. It is here that the notion of 'take-off' can be extremely useful to historians who are familiar with qualitative problems but somewhat less so with quantitative interpretations. These are not the only differences: historians are more concerned with long-term developments as a means of discovering the mechanism behind the take-off, and the economist more with the short-term developments. The fact remains that recent economic research has provided historians with invaluable material for interpreting a past which is still somewhat shrouded in mystery." (op. cit., p. 68).

capitalism which was to remain virtually unchanged for almost a hundred years. Because of its fundamental importance, it is worth giving a translation of this not very well known text, which illustrates particularly clearly the individualistic and liberal ideas of the legislators of the French Revolution:

1. In as much as the total abolition of all forms of corporations of citizens of the same trade or profession is one of the fundamental principles of the French Constitution, it shall be forbidden to revive them in practice, under any pretext and in any form whatsoever.

2. Citizens of the same trade or profession, employers, shopkeepers, workmen and journeymen of any craft whatsoever shall not, when gathered together, appoint presidents, secretaries or committees, nor shall they keep records, take decisions or adopt resolutions, or draw up rules in defence of their alleged common interests.

3. All administrative or municipal bodies are prohibited from accepting any address or petition in the name of a trade or profession or giving any reply whatsoever to any such address or petition; and they are further enjoined to declare null and void such resolutions as may be adopted in such a manner and to take care to ensure that no action is taken on them.

4. Should citizens belonging to the same occupations, arts and crafts adopt resolutions or reach agreements among themselves contrary to the principles of liberty and of the Constitution so as to refuse as a body, or to grant only at a fixed price, the fruit of their industry or their labours, such resolutions and agreements, whether sworn or not, shall be declared unconstitutional, a violation of liberty and of the Declaration of the Rights of Man and null and void; administrative and municipal bodies shall be required to declare them as such. The authors, leaders and instigators responsible for promoting or drawing up such resolutions or agreements, or for presiding over their discussion, shall be liable to the imposition by the police of a fine of 500 livres and shall be suspended for one year from the exercise of all the rights of active citizens and from admission to primary assemblies.

5. Under pain of their members' being called to account on their own behalf, all administrative and municipal bodies are prohibited from employing, recognising or permitting the recognition of such employers, workmen or journeymen as may have promoted or signed the said resolutions or agreements, save in the event of their having presented themselves of their own volition to the clerk of the police court to retract or repudiate them.

6. Should the resolutions or convocations, posters or circulars contain any threat against employers, craftsmen and workmen or against those who might accept a lower wage, all the authors, instigators and signatories of the records or writings shall be punished by a fine of 1,000 livres each and three months' imprisonment.

7. Persons who utter threats or use violence against workers exercising the freedom accorded to work and industry under the constitutional laws shall be liable to criminal prosecution and shall be punished with the full rigour of the law as disturbers of the public peace.

8. All gatherings of craftsmen, workmen or journeymen, or gatherings of persons incited by them to interfere with the free exercise of industry and labour (which right pertains to every kind of person under whatever conditions may be mutually agreed upon) or with the action of the police and the execution of sentences rendered in this respect, or with the public auction and adjudication of various undertakings, shall be deemed to be seditious gatherings and, as such, shall be dispersed by the police in conformity with legal orders, and punishment shall be inflicted with all the rigour of the law on the originators, instigators and leaders of such gatherings and on all persons guilty of assault and battery and other acts of violence.

The principles referred to are particularly clear. As Le Chapelier stated, it was by free and mutual agreement between individuals that the daily wage of each workman should be determined. Thereafter, it was up to the workman to observe the agreement he had made with his employer. The individualism thus underlying labour relations might appear impartial, since it outlawed combinations of employers and workers alike. However, this formal equality concealed a relationship of economic and social domination, and did not withstand the test of time: not only were employers' chambers of commerce legally authorised but, very rapidly, a whole series of repressive laws were introduced. The reintroduction of the workbook by an Act of 12 April 1803 was both a police measure designed to enable the administrative authorities to keep track of the movements of workmen and a means of coercion in the hands of employers since, to quote the author of the report on the proposed legislation, it was intended to "protect workshops from absenteeism and contracts from being violated"; articles 1780 and 1781 of the Civil Code governing contracts for hire made the payment of wages subject to the good faith of the employer; and articles 414 to 416 of the Penal Code laid down different penalties for combinations of workers and employers respectively.

The example of France was followed by most European countries which had adopted, with suitable adjustments, the provisions of the Napoleonic Code on combinations of workers and employers.

This was so of Belgium, the Netherlands, Luxembourg, the Scandinavian countries, Spain, Italy and the various States of the German Confederation. Articles 181 to 184 of the Prussian regulations of 1845 on crafts, for example, prohibited all agreements, banned all gatherings of workers not authorised by the police and made the breaking of a contract punishable by law. In Great Britain, the Combination Acts of 1799 and 1800 declared to be illegal "all contracts ... between any journeymen manufacturers or other workmen ... for obtaining an advance of wages ... or for lessening or altering their ... hours ... of working ... or for preventing any person or persons from employing whomsoever" they should "think proper to employ in their manufacture, trade or business, in the conduct or the management thereof". In the United States the tribunals took their lead from English common law, and specifically from the criminal conspiracy doctrine. Workers' organisations were banned not only in countries such as Belgium (article 2 of the 1831 Constitution) which had recognised the right of association, but in those such as Great Britain, Norway, Sweden and the United States, which had traditionally accorded it to all categories of people.

The philosophy underlying the legislation described above can be summarised as follows. When capitalism came to the fore, its ideology included two basic principles contrary to the recognition of group interests. The first principle is that of political individualism and the rejection of intermediaries, and was espoused by Rousseau:

> So long as a number of men in combination are considered as a single body, they have but one will, which relates to the common preservation and to the general well-being. . . . But when the social bond begins to be relaxed and the State weakened, when private interests begin to make themselves felt and small associations to exercise influence on the State, the common interest is injuriously affected and finds adversaries; unanimity no longer reigns in the voting; the general will is no longer the will of all; opposition and disputes arise, and the best counsel does not pass uncontested. [1]

The second principle is that of economic laissez-faire, whereby the best possible economic situation will result from the free interplay of individual interests. Long before Bastiat and his economic harmony, [2] Adam Smith expressed this viewpoint in a famous passage:

> . . . Every individual necessarily labours to render the annual revenue of the society as great as he can. He generally, indeed, neither intends to promote the public interest, nor knows how much he is promoting it. By preferring the support of domestic to that of foreign industry, he intends only his own security; and by directing that industry in such a manner as its produce may be of the greatest value, he intends only his own gain, and he is in this, as in many other cases, led by an invisible hand to promote an end which was no part of this intention. . . . By pursuing his own interest he frequently promotes that of the society more effectually than when he really intends to promote it.[3]

It may seem a far cry from these general quotations from works of political or economic philosophy to the attitude adopted by the public authorities towards workers' and employers' organisations. Yet it is precisely on these two principles that Le Chapelier, a barrister, relied when he was appointed by the Constituent Assembly, in 1791, to report on a dispute between the carpenters of Paris and their employers. The conclusions which he placed before the Assembly on 14 June 1791 owe something to Rousseau:

> There is no longer any place for corporations in the State. There is room only for the specific interests of each individual and the general interest. Nobody may foster an intermediate interest among citizens or separate them from the common weal by fomenting a corporative spirit.

They also take into account the unwelcome economic consequences that workers' organisation would engender:

> The object of these assemblies which are springing up throughout the kingdom and which have already established links among themselves is to oblige the contractors, the afore-mentioned master carpenters, to raise the price of a day's work, to prevent the workmen and the individuals employing them in their workshops from arriving

[1] *Du contrat social*, Book IV, Ch. 1.

[2] Frédéric Bastiat: *Les harmonies économiques* (1850).

[3] *Inquiry into the nature and causes of the wealth of nations*, Book IV, Ch. 11.

at agreements on their own, and to make them undertake in writing to accept the wage established by these assemblies and other rules which they may take upon themselves to draw up. They do not even stop short of violence to impose their rules.

Many years were to go by before this doctrine was modified and before the law was changed so as to recognise agreements and understandings that had hitherto been deemed to constitute combination or conspiracy, and before recognition was therefore accorded to the legitimacy of a concerted and collective refusal to work—in other words, of resorting to strikes and lockouts. The Parliament of the United Kingdom repealed the Combination Acts in 1824, but combinations themselves were not fully legalised until the passing of the Trade Union Act, 1871, which recognised that "the purposes of any trade union shall not, by reason merely that they are in restraint of trade, be unlawful so as to render void or voidable any agreement or trust", and the Conspiracy and Protection of Property Act, 1875, which provides that "an agreement or combination by two or more persons to do or procure to be done any act in contemplation or furtherance of a trade dispute between employers and workmen shall not be indictable as a conspiracy if such act committed by one person would not be punishable as a crime". In France, an Act of 25 May 1864 repealed former article 414 of the Penal Code which made combination an offence. Belgium followed suit in 1866, the North German Confederation in 1869, Austria-Hungary in 1870, the Netherlands in 1872, Italy in 1890. Nevertheless, most countries continued to uphold legal provisions making attacks on the freedom of work and industry a special offence. [1]

This rapid survey of institutional history in the major industrialised countries of today suggests that the thesis under consideration—that there were no employers' and workers' organisations when their industrialisation gathered momentum—may have some basis in fact. It is interesting to see whether it stands up to closer examination. To begin with, to say that in the initial stages of industrialisation there were no workers' organisations is meaningless unless it is explained exactly what time in history is referred to. Primitive accumulation occurred in fact at a time when employers and workers were organised in guilds. As regards the Industrial Revolution, until the Second World War this was generally held in Great Britain to have taken place between 1750 (with the development of the steam engine by Watt) and 1802 (with the first Factory Act); since then the period has been described as starting earlier—J. U. Nef goes right back to the sixteenth century [2] so as to take in the period of pri-

[1] Act of 1825 in the United Kingdom; new articles 414 and 415 of the Penal Code introduced by an Act of 25 May 1864 in France; article 310 of the Belgian Penal Code of 1867; article 153 of the Industrial Code of 1869 of the North German Confederation.

[2] J. U. Nef: *Cultural foundations of industrial civilisation* (Cambridge University Press, 1958).

mitive accumulation—and as lasting longer, right up to 1830 according to T. S. Ashton, [1] or even 1850 according to Beales. Actually the duration of the Industrial Revolution varied, taking somewhat longer in France and somewhat less time in the United States and in Japan. Consequently, depending on the period chosen, it may well coincide with the emergence of the trade union movement. [2] But this is perhaps a little too vague to be of any practical use. Take-off, which covers a shorter period in time, can be more easily dated, since W. Rostow tells us that it took place in Great Britain between 1783 and 1802, in France between 1830 and 1860, in Belgium between 1833 and 1860, in the United States between 1843 and 1860, in Germany between 1850 and 1873, in Sweden between 1868 and 1890, in Japan between 1878 and 1900, in Russia between 1890 and 1914, and Canada between 1896 and 1914, and that the take-off started in Argentina in 1935, in Turkey in 1937, and in China and India in 1952. Taking these dates, the claim that there were no trade unions loses much of its force; at best it can fit the first countries in the list above, but certainly not the others. In the United States, for example, the National Trade Union (which implies the notion of interoccupational association) was established in 1830; in Germany the trade unions [3] set up by the liberals Hirsch and Dunker and the Workers' General Union [4] of the disciples of Lassalle came into being as soon as the ban on combinations was lifted (in 1861 in Saxony, in 1869 in the North German Confederation); in the Scandinavian countries the first trade unions made their appearance in 1880; and in Russia the workers were already highly organised at the turn of the century. Furthermore, not only did trade unions develop but the denial of the existence of group interests, which may have had some basis as long as the workers, being employed in small firms, were in direct contact with their employer, gave way to another doctrine altogether which left room for the defence and promotion of group interests inasmuch as it recognised the legitimacy of temporary combinations of workers and employers and subsequently the legitimacy of permanent workers' and employers' organisations.

Particularly if it is not restricted to the traditional example of Great Britain, institutional history therefore tells us that take-off occurred whether or not trade union organisations existed, that their establishment sometimes accompanied industrialisation and sometimes preceded it, but that however approximate the chronological correspondence it would be difficult to claim that there

---

[1] Ashton, op. cit.

[2] This is the view taken by W. O. Henderson: *The industrialisation of Europe*, 1780-1914 (London, Thames and Hudson, 1969); and idem: *The Industrial Revolution on the Continent: Germany, France, Russia*, 1880-1914 (London, Frank Cass, 1967); and in Rioux, op cit.

[3] *Gewerkvereine*.

[4] Allgemeine Deutsche Arbeiterverein.

is no link between the trade union movement and industrial development, as most authorities on the labour movement (e.g. Commons, Cole, Perlman, Polanyi, Clapham) have agreed. If there are really causal relationships between the two, it is unlikely that they can be severed today without causing more harm than good. [1]

Statistics

While institutional history is not as conclusive as some authors would like to think, the statistical record may well have other surprises in store. One of the assumptions of the thesis discussed here is that, unlike the underdeveloped countries of today, modern developed countries benefited during their period of capital accumulation from the absence of workers' organisations. This assumption has to be put to the test, difficult though this may seem. The fact is that, while standard econometric studies may argue about the greater or lesser relevance of the variables employed, the problem here is essentially one of obtaining suitable statistical series. However, though they may be few and far between and their reliability often questionable, certain series do exist that may be useful.

Date of legal establishment of trade unions

A first statistical test is to see whether economic growth curves rose less sharply after the recognition of the right to organise. To begin with Great Britain, the cradle of the Industrial Revolution, the writings of practitioners of "political arithmetic" (Petty, Graunt, King, Young) include statistical series from very early on which, although they may be rudimentary by modern standards, do at least, thanks to the efforts of Phyllis Deane, [2] provide usable

[1] "The promotion of freedom of association constantly encounters fresh problems. The new demands of efficiency, for example, may create genuine difficulties in this respect. This applies not only to developing countries but also to those that are economically advanced, where increased association of occupational organisations with major decisions of general economic and social policy involves greater concentration of efforts on their part. Whatever the difficulties we must not forget that the unions have a vital part to play in society in broadening and reinforcing the democratic system. It is all the more necessary that they should provide a genuine forum for all workers in a world where conflicts of interest between individuals and groups, and between these interests and those of society at large, show no signs of disappearing. While the denial of trade union rights invites violence, limitations on the freedom of individuals leads sooner or later to discontent with the trade union movement itself—which can only be harmful to the workers themselves and, in the long run, to society as a whole." (ILO: *The ILO and human rights*, op. cit., p. 38.)

[2] P. Deane: "The implications of early national income estimates for the measurement of long-term economic growth in the United Kingdom", in *Economic Development and Cultural Change* (Chicago), Nov. 1955; "Contemporary estimates of national income in the first half of the nineteenth century", in *Economic History Review*, Apr. 1956; and "Contemporary estimates of national income in the second half of the nineteenth century", ibid., Apr. 1957.

Table 4. England and Wales: National income, 1688-1846

Year	Total national income at current prices (millions of pounds)		Population of England [1] (thousands)	National income of England [1] per head at current prices (pounds)	Price index (1865 and 1885 = 100)	National income in England [1] at constant prices	
	England [1]	Great Britain				Total (millions of pounds)	Per head (pounds)
1688	48	.	5 500	8.7	96	50	9.1
1770	130	.	7 100	18.5	97	134	19.1
1798	200	.	9 000	22.2	144	139	15.4
1812	290	330	10 500	27.6	194	149	14.2
1822	262	288	12 200	21.4	122	214	17.5
1831	374	424	13 900	26.9	109	340	24.4
1841	395	445	15 900	24.8	119	332	20.8
1846	414	467	16 800	24.6	108	383	22.8

[1] Including Wales.
Source: Paul Bairoch: *Révolution industrielle et sous-développement* (Paris, Société d'édition d'enseignement supérieur, 1963), p. 271.

data that Paul Bairoch was quick to seize upon. [1] Two sets of figures can accordingly be drawn up, one for England and Wales and the other for Great Britain. For England and Wales, the series reconstituted by Bairoch to cover the period 1688-1846 [2] are shown in table 4.

From this table the following deductions can be made: between 1688 and 1770 the anual average growth rate of the total income was 1.2 per cent and that of income per head 0.9 per cent; between 1770 and 1822 total income expanded at an annual rate of 1 per cent whereas income per head declined as a result of an annual population growth rate of 1.05 per cent; after 1822 and up to 1846 the annual growth rate of the national income was 2.5 per cent and that of income per head 1.1 per cent. Far from confirming the assumptions of de Schweinitz, the statistical data would thus seem instead to invalidate them since—always assuming, of course, that there is some causal relationship between trade unions and economic growth—the economic growth rate reached its peak after the repeal of the Combination Acts in 1824. The national income figures for the United Kingdom, which are given in table 5, [3] lead to

[1] P. Bairoch: *Révolution industrielle et sous-développement* (Paris, Société d'édition d'enseignement supérieur, 1963).

[2] ibid., p. 271. Deane's sources for her estimates of national income are: G. King (1688), A. Young (1770), Colquhoun (1812), Lowe (1822), Pebrer (1831), Spackman (1841) and Smee (1846); for the population estimates, J. Brownlee and G. T. Griffith for the period up to 1801, census figures thereafter. Her price indexes are taken from E. B. Schumpeter for the period up to 1822 and P. Rousseaux from 1822 onwards.

[3] Bairoch, op. cit., p. 272. The sources used by Deane are: Pitt, Beck and Bell (1800). Colquhoun (1812), Lowe (1822), Pebrer (1831), Spackman (1841), Smee (1846), Levi (1851), Mulhall (1866, 1870, 1880 and 1889) and Giffen (1902); the price indexes are taken from Rousseaux.

Table 5. United Kingdom: National income, 1800-1902

Year	Total national income at current prices (millions of pounds)	Population (thousands)	National income per head at current prices (pounds)	Price index (1865 and 1885 = 100)	National income at constant prices	
					Total (millions of pounds)	Per head (pounds)
1800	297	15 745	18.9	157	189	12.0
1812	405	18 367	22.1	194	209	11.4
1822	358	21 339	16.8	122	294	13.8
1831	533	24 135	22.1	109	489	20.3
1841	556	26 751	20.8	119	467	17.5
1846	562	28 002	20.1	108	520	18.6
1851	588	27 393	21.5	97	606	22.1
1860	938	28 778	32.6	116	809	28.1
1870	961	31 257	30.7	113	850	27.2
1880	1 156	34 623	33.4	100	1 156	33.4
1889	1 285	37 179	34.6	84	1 530	41.1
1902	1 750	41 893	41.8	86	2 035	48.6

Source: Bairoch, op. cit., p. 272.

similar conclusions. The right to organise newly acquired as a result of the Trade Union Act of 1871 and the Conspiracy and Protection of Property Act of 1875, far from leading to a decline in the rate of economic expansion, actually coincided with an increase in income per head, which grew at an annual rate of 1.4 per cent during the period 1851-1860 to 1889-1902, and in total income, which grew at an annual rate of 2.2 per cent.

It will be interesting now to see whether the picture was any different in France, which is the second historical example frequently quoted. Table 6 [1] is based on data drawn from J. Marczewski's [2] cliometric studies.

In the eighteenth century (1701-1710 to 1781-1790), the annual growth rate of the total volume of production was 0.65 per cent, compared with an annual increase per head of 0.35 per cent. Similar growth rates recurred during the revolutionary period and under the First Empire. Thereafter, expansion was more rapid, especially during the period 1825-1834 to 1835-1844 when the take-off really began. Table 7 is based on the calculation of the volume of

[1] Population figures taken from Reinhard and Armengaud, Labrousse, and Bourgeois-Pichat. The findings of F. Perroux: "Prises de vues sur la croissance de l'économie française, 1780-1950", in *Income and Wealth*, Series V (London, 1955) tend to confirm the interpretation given here.

[2] J. Marczewski: "Y a-t-il eu un 'take-off' en France?", in *Cahiers de l'Institut de science économique appliquée*, Supplement No. 111, Series AD, No. 1, Mar. 1961; "Some aspects of the economic growth of France, 1660-1958", in *Economic Development and Cultural Change*, Apr. 1961.

Table 6. France: Volume of output, 1701-1904

Period	Total volume of output [1] at constant prices (millions of francs at 1905-1913 prices)	Population (millions)	Volume of output [1] per head (francs)
1701-1710	2 818	20.0	141
1781-1790	4 760	26.8	178
1803-1812	5 693	29.0	196
1825-1834	7 458	32.6	229
1835-1844	9 047	34.2	264
1845-1854	10 405	35.8	291
1855-1864	12 308	37.4	329
1865-1874	14 052	36.1	389
1875-1884	15 360	37.7	408
1885-1894	17 037	38.3	444
1895-1904	20 377	39.0	523

[1] Gross national product minus services, i.e. total value of output of goods (neglecting depreciation).
Source: Bairoch, op. cit., p. 346.

Table 7. France: Annual growth rate of the volume of output [1] at various stages in the history of the trade union movement

Period	Annual growth rate	
	Over-all	Per head
Prohibition of combinations	1.7	1.2
De facto tolerance	1.2	1.2
Legal recognition	1.6	1.0

[1] Gross national product minus services, i.e. total value of output of goods (neglecting depreciation).

output, over-all and per head, during the twenty years leading up to the Act of 1864 (after which combination was no longer illegal), during the following twenty years up to the adoption of the Act of 21 March 1884 (when tolerance led up to official recognition of the trade union movement), and during the period following the passing of that Act.

After the transition from prohibition to tolerance, there was a decline in the growth rate of total output but not in that of output per head. Legal recognition coincided with an expansion of total output, similar to that of the earlier period, while the growth of output per head slowed down. Here, therefore, the figures are less conclusive than in the case of Great Britain, but it is still difficult to claim that they lend any special credence to de Schweinitz's assumptions.

Table 8. United States: Ten-yearly growth rate and share of capital formation in the gross national product, 1834-1953

(Percentages)

Period from—	Period to—	Ten-yearly growth rate (at 1860 constant prices) Total	Ten-yearly growth rate (at 1860 constant prices) Per head	Share of capital formation
1834-43	1844-53	63	20	9
1839-48	1849-58	70	25	11
1844-53	1854-63	.	.	13
1849-58	1859-68	.	.	14
1854-63	1864-73	.	.	.
1859-68	1869-78	.	.	.
1864-73	1874-83	.	.	.
1869-78	1879-88	65	27	22
1874-83	1884-93	50	19	21
1879-88	1889-98	36	9	22
1884-93	1894-1903	36	13	26
1889-98	1899-1908	51	25	28
1894-1903	1904-13	49	23	27
1899-1908	1909-18	35	12	28
1904-13	1914-23	28	11	.
1909-18	1919-28	38	20	.
1914-23	1924-33	29	11	.
1919-28	1929-38	4	—5	.
1924-33	1934-43	17	9	.
1929-38	1939-48	50	44	.
1934-43	1944-53	52	33	.

Source: Gallman, op. cit., p. 27.

Table 9. United States: Long-term growth rate of the real gross national product, over-all and per head, 1800-1953

(Percentages)

Period	Over-all	Per head
1800-1835	4.28	1.22
1835-1855	4.40	1.30
1835-43 to 1894-1903	4.80	1.60
1894-1903 to 1944-53	3.40	1.60

Source: David, op. cit., p. 48; Gallman, op. cit., p. 27.

The United States is the third example, and here Simon Kuznets, [1] updated by R. E. Gallman [2] and P. A. David, [3] provides a wealth of statistics that have been used in table 8.

The most immediately striking feature is the generally cyclical nature of growth in the United States during the period dealt with, which means that, if comparisons are to be significant, long-term trends must be consulted rather than the figures corresponding to any particular cycle. Instead of indulging in statistical adjustments which are always rather delicate, it should suffice to take periods sufficiently long to avoid short-term anomalies, if not the longest cycle. The result is table 9.

The last period was marked by the Great Depression; if that period is left aside, it will be seen that the long-term growth rate of the real gross national product increased steadily. The creation of the National Labour Union in Baltimore in 1868 and the establishment in 1869 of the Knights of Labor (a dissident branch of which later became the American Federation of Labor in 1886) do not therefore appear to have affected the growth rate in the United States any more than did government support for collective bargaining (the Erdman Act of 1898), which was the first effort to compensate for the hostile attitude of the courts [4] in their use of injunctions against trade unions. In fact, the last column of table 8 shows that the share of capital formation in the gross national product during the period examined grew steadily over the years, which runs counter to the thesis that the advent and growth of trade union organisations slow down the accumulation of capital.

Trade union membership figures

However, the foregoing first statistical test—an all-or-nothing kind of test—is an oversimplification, since the question asked was simply whether the growth rate was higher in the absence of a trade union movement than once labour organisations had been legally established. It may be useful to rephrase the problem in less trenchant terms and to consider whether, by

[1] Kuznets has published a series of articles in *Economic Development and Cultural Change* since 1956 under the general title "Quantitative aspects of the economic growth of nations". See also Simon Kuznets, assisted by Elizabeth Jenks: *Capital in the American economy: Its formation and financing*, National Bureau of Economic Research, Inc., Studies in Capital Formation and Financing, No. 9 (Princeton University Press, 1961).

[2] R. E. Gallman: "Gross national product in the United States, 1834-1909", in P. Temin (ed.): *New economic history* (Harmondsworth, Middlesex, Penguin Books, 1973), pp. 19-43.

[3] P. A. David: "New light on a statistical dark age: US real product growth before 1840", in *American Economic Review*, May 1967, pp. 294-306, reprinted in Temin, op. cit., pp. 44-60.

[4] As evidenced in the following passage from the judgement in the Philadelphia cordwainers' case (1806): "A combination of workmen to raise their wages may be considered in a twofold point of view; one is to benefit themselves . . ., the other is to injure those who do not join their society. The rule of law condemns both."

taking a quantitative indicator such as the membership of trade unions as a measure of freedom of association and the annual expansion of the product as a measure of growth, an inverse relationship can be established between the two curves that will support the thesis under discussion, namely that the history of the Industrial Revolution provides clear evidence for the under-developed countries of today that in order to maximise economic growth rates they must limit the development of the trade unions. The fact that trade union membership figures are sometimes unavailable even long after freedom of association has been recognised and that such figures are occasionally unreliable even when available poses a statistical problem. However, because this study is more concerned with detecting underlying trends than with calculating precise ratios, it is a difficulty that can be overlooked.

In the case of Great Britain in figure 1 the vertical axis represents on a convenient scale the membership of trade unions, on the one hand, and growth indicators, on the other. [1] It will be seen that during the period in question, although the correlation that can be discerned between the two curves is not absolutely symmetrical, it does tend to be positive rather than negative. This does not fit in with the thesis advanced by de Schweinitz.

In the case of France (figure 2), for the General Confederation of Labour (CGT) alone, the long-term trend in union membership, which was obtained by collating a number of different sources, [2] shows that the history of the labour movement is marked by a series of surges in union membership (1918-21, 1934-38, 1944-47, 1966) followed by declines to levels that are higher each time. To give an exact idea of the real long-term trend, the Force Ouvrière, with about 700,000 members, and the Federation of National Education (FEN), with around 400,000 members, both of which broke off from the CGT in the split that took place in 1947, should also be included. Once again the correlation is fairly tenuous, as might be expected in the light of the vagaries of the French trade union movement, but again, as in the previous example, there is

[1] The figures for trade union membership are taken from A. Flanders: *Trade unions* (London, Hutchinson University Library, 1960), p. 8; those for the average national output per head at constant 1912-14 prices from S. Pollard and D. W. C. Rosley: *The wealth of Britain* (London, Batford Ltd., 1968), p. 258.

[2] For the period 1913-20 the membership figures are taken from M. Labi: *La grande division des travailleurs: Première scission de la CGT, 1914-1921* (Paris, Les éditions ouvrières, 1964), p. 246; for the 1921-37 period, from A. Prost: *La CGT à l'époque du Front populaire* (Paris, Colin, 1964), p. 35; for the 1947-51 period, from G. Lefranc: *Le mouvement syndical de la libération aux événements de mai-juin 1968* (Paris, Payot, 1969); for the period 1922-36 the membership of the CGT and of the CGTU have been combined. The data on economic activity are taken from A. Sauvy: *Histoire économique de la France entre les deux guerres (1918-1931)* (Paris, Fayard, 1965), p. 465, and idem (1967), p. 528; and from J. J. Carré, P. Dubois and E. Malinvaud: *La croissance française* (Paris, Editions du Seuil, 1972). In both statistical series the Second World War caused a break that did not occur in the series for Great Britain or the United States. The two parts of each curve must therefore be looked upon as being relatively independent of one another rather than directly comparable.

Figure 1. Great Britain: Trade union membership and output per head, 1900-60

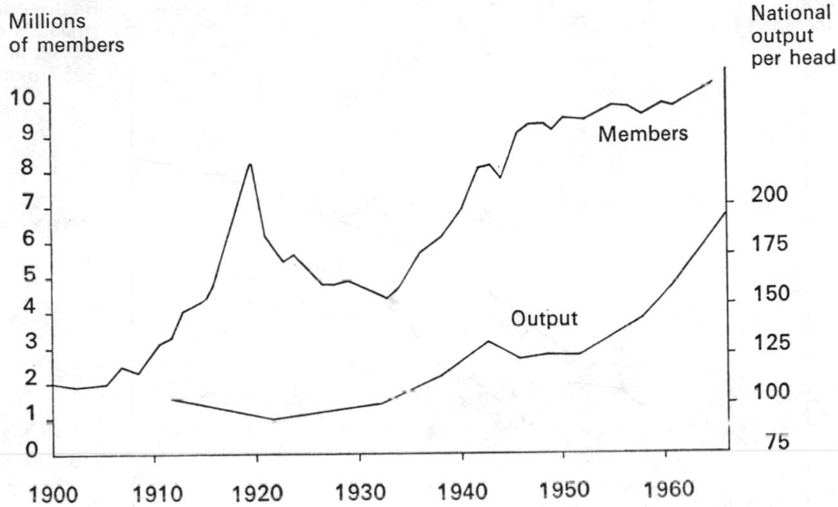

Figure 2. France: Trade union membership and gross domestic product (GDP), 1910-70

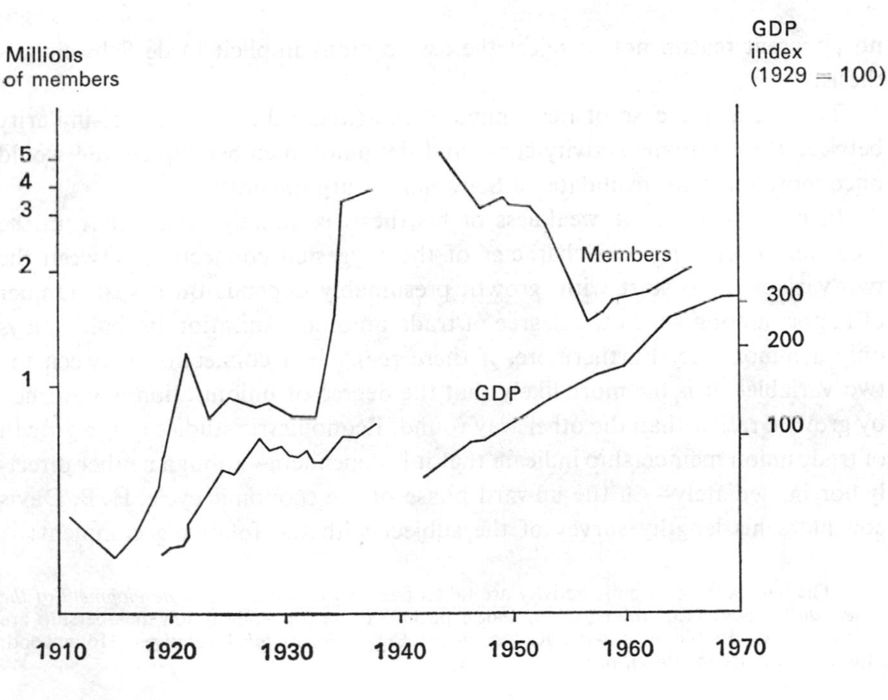

Figure 3. United States: Trade union membership and real output, 1910-65

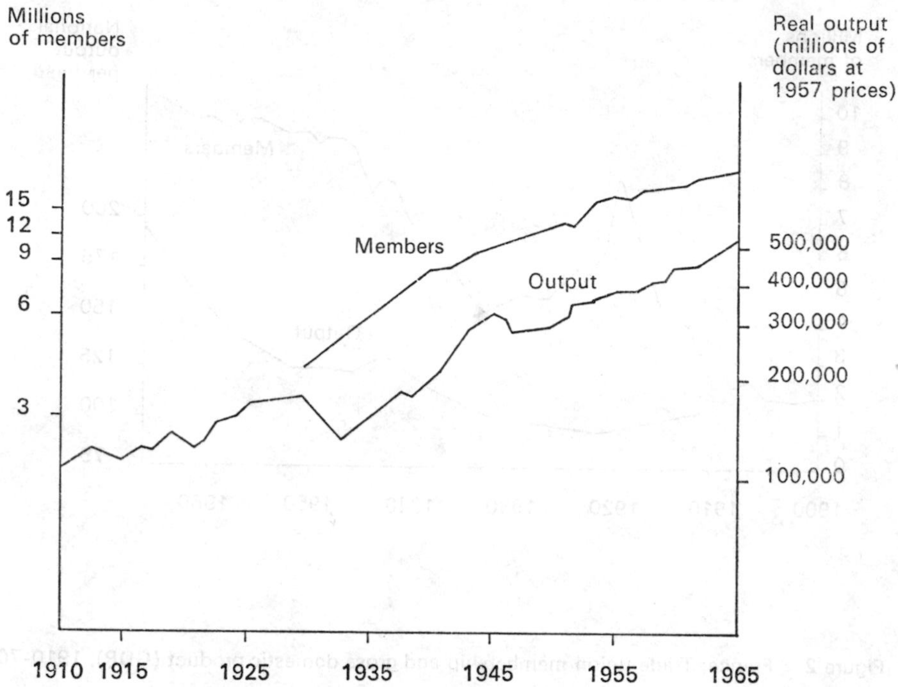

no apparent reason not to reject the assumptions implicit in de Schweinitz's thesis.

Thirdly, in the case of the United States (figure 3), the relative similarity between the economic activity curve and the union membership curve [1] would once more seem to invalidate de Schweinitz's argument.

In point of fact, the weakness of his thesis is already apparent from the loose and over-simplified character of the suggested connection between the two variables. To start with, growth presumably depends on a vast number of factors among which the degree of trade union organisation probably plays only a minor role. Furthermore, if there really is a connection between the two variables, it is far more likely that the degree of unionisation is governed by growth, rather than the other way round. Econometric studies of the growth of trade union membership indicate that it is dependent—though neither directly nor immediately—on the upward phase of the economic cycle. H. B. Davis concludes his lengthy survey of the subject with the following comment:

[1] The figures for economic activity are taken from A. C. Bolino: *The development of the American economy* (Columbus, Ohio, 1968), p. 564; those for trade union membership are taken from G. F. Bloom and H. R. Northrup: *Economics of labor relations* (Homewood, Illinois, R. D. Irwin, 1969), p. 68.

Table 10. England, France, Germany, the United States: Trade union membership and business conditions [1]

Number of years of business—		Number of years during which trade union membership—		
		rose—		fell
		sharply [2]	slightly [3]	
Recession and depression	49	14	10	25
Revival	20	16	2	2
Prosperity	61	42	4	15
Total	130	72	16	42

[1] Dates: England, 1891-1925; France, 1890-1914, 1917-1919 and 1921-1925; Germany, 1890-1925; United States, 1897-1936. [2] More than 3 per cent. [3] Less than 3 per cent.
Source: Davis, op. cit., p.615.

Union growth proceeds by waves which are not closely synchronized with those of the business cycle. These waves indicate that there is considerable inertia in the movement of union membership. A major wave of growth, if not brought on by a war, will nearly always be found to have been preceded by an accumulation of wage earners' grievances, as during a major depression, while the accumulation of employer resistances during a wave of growth is a factor in the ensuing period of absolute or relative decline. [1]

The figures given in table 10 support the author's reasoning and the ideas he advances.

THEORY

Since by and large neither institutional history nor statistical records seem to support the factual assumption on which the theory of a link between freedom of association and economic development is based, an attempt will now be made to get down to the root of the problem by economic analysis. Being logical in structure, economic theory does not lend itself to taking a correlation for a causal relationship, which is the danger incurred by a misuse of statistics, or to a subjective overestimation (or underestimation) of the significance of any particular factor, which is a hazard besetting the institutional historian. Economic analysis can take two forms that are possibly complementary: it can stay at the level of macro-economic reasoning based on highly aggregated quantities or it can take more account of structural factors, thus calling on the other social sciences.

[1] H. B. Davis: "The theory of union growth", in *Quarterly Journal of Economics*, Aug. 1941, p. 632.

Consumption and investment

Keynesian macro-economic theory links the formation and distribution of income. Wage earners, whose propensity to consume is taken as being close to unity, are regarded as being essentially consumers, whereas entrepreneurs have a propensity to invest. The distribution of income is therefore not entirely independent of the process of capital formation. It is this concept that is at the heart of de Schweinitz's thesis, which has been summed up extremely well by R. Freedman: [1]

> The author's central argument is that political democracy means strong trade unions; strong trade unions redistribute income from profits to wages; laborers have a higher propensity to consume than entrepreneurs; *ergo*, savings decline, consumption rises, and accelerated investment rates are rendered impossible.

This basic argument is then taken a step further:

> By analogy, it is argued, the underdeveloped world now is willy-nilly in the position of the USSR of the 1920s and 1930s for three reasons: (1) the cost of investment has risen; (2) the "gap" between the developed and underdeveloped world has grown, requiring greater effort; and (3) the "demonstration effect" has put added pressure for a diversion of scarce resources to immediate consumption.

It will be convenient to take the arguments put forward by de Schweinitz in the reverse order, viz. arguments (3), (2), (1) in the last quotation, followed by the main argument as summed up in the quotation before that.

To begin with the demonstration effect, it is known to encourage consumption and to increase as a result of the switch from a subsistence to a market economy. De Schweinitz makes reference to a fact that is well known to historians of the trade union movement in underdeveloped countries when he adds that the demonstration effect also extends to wage claims. Because of the limited capacity of the system of production, wage claims were moderate when the Western countries embarked upon their process of industrialisation. "The Industrial Revolution in Great Britain was a response to preferences for historically given wants. The labor force, therefore, was motivated in terms of these wants and could not be irritated by a consciousness of a more dazzling standard which similar groups in other countries had attained". [2] It was thus possible to maintain the standard of living at a fairly low level, [3] whereas this is generally unthinkable today in the developing countries. This argument about

---

[1] R. Freedman: "Industrialization, labor controls and democracy: A comment", in *Economic Development and Cultural Change*, Jan. 1960, p. 192.

[2] De Schweinitz, op. cit., p. 395.

[3] De Schweinitz does, however, point out (p. 395, footnote 13) that historians do not agree on this point. For some (Engels, the Hammonds, Toynbee, Hobsbawm), wages were greatly reduced; others on the contrary (Ure, Bowley and Woods, Clapham, Ashton), find evidence of an increase in wages in the period following the Napoleonic wars. Wherever the truth may lie, it is undeniable that the standard of living of workers was very low, as can be seen from the reports of factory inspectors in England.

the demonstration effect seems fairly unimpeachable since both the organisation and the ideology of the labour movement imitate those prevailing in the dominant countries. However, the same can hardly be said of the other two accessory arguments.

As regards the gap between developed and underdeveloped countries, it is argued that it has widened in the industrial relations field mainly because the population explosion has led to an increase in the supply of labour: when the population expands more rapidly than the demand for labour, the result is higher unemployment, and hence greater discontent, whereas for a long time emigration provided a kind of outlet that no longer exists. [1] It must be pointed out, however, that the automatic correlation between the growth of the population and the growth of the supply of labour becomes manifest only in the long term. In addition, the argument seems circular. Although it may be true, as de Schweinitz says, [2] that "to the extent that economic growth induces a decline in mortality rates prior to a decline in fertility rates, the unemployment potential grows with the increasing size of the labor force", it is hard to see how this development can be accompanied by the existence of a powerful trade union movement pushing up the level of wages, especially if, as certain authors believe, the supply of labour is perfectly elastic. [3] Is there not a danger that this "industrial reserve army", to use the Marxist term, will by its mere presence induce the trade unions to be more reasonable and moderate in their demands?

As regards the cost of investment—accessory argument (1)—de Schweinitz accepts as fact that it is higher or, to be more precise, that the capital intensity ratio has risen. This assumption leads to the inevitable conclusion that there can be no individual solutions to worker discontent and that the need to

[1] Thus, "one might conjecture that the allegedly more bitter resistance to industrialization among English workers than among German workers was in part explicable by the greater ease with which Germany could shed potential dissidents to America than England" (de Schweinitz, op. cit., p. 399). Emigration from Great Britain did not start until after 1860, by which time its process of industrialisation was complete, while in the case of Germany, although emigration did not start until 1880, 117,000 departures were recorded from the very start (L. Dollot: *Les migrations humaines* (Paris, Presses universitaires de France, 1958), p. 29).

[2] De Schweinitz, op. cit., p. 388.

[3] "There is, in fact, reason to believe that we have in West Africa, for the unskilled labor which makes up much of the wage-earning labor force, a kind of labor market in which the assumptions of the classical model of labor allocation are at least as closely approximated as they ever were in Europe: a (migrant) labor force which is homogeneously unskilled and transferable between employments, great physical and occupational mobility, and widespread knowledge of and sensitivity to alternative employments and rewards. In such a labor market the quantity of labor flowing to any employer, industry, territory, sector (wage earning or sharecropping), or country (French West Africa or Ghana) is directly related to the rates of return and working conditions offered; the supply curve of migrant labor is positively sloped." (E. J. Berg: "French West Africa", in Walter Galenson (ed.): *Labor and economic development* (New York, Wiley, 1959), p. 197.)

promote rapid growth necessarily entails a restriction on the exercise of freedom of association. Whereas in the nineteenth century it was relatively easy for a worker to set up in business on his own when he found his subordinate position in a factory or industry too disagreeable, nowadays "advancing technology increases the height of the capital and knowledge barriers which entrants into industry must surmount, thus restricting the scope of competition and the individualistic response to labor discontent". [1] Moreover, the presence of this advanced technology in industrialised Western countries places the underdeveloped countries of today in the following dilemma:

> If they proceeded according to neo-classical optimality criteria and maximized output from currently available resources, they would have developed light industry and industrialized labor-intensive methods of production; but then they might not have been able to accelerate the rate of growth enough to reduce the gap between their own economic strength and that of the more mature economies in the West. But if they tried to leap the technological gap and adapt the capital-intensive production methods of the West, they would perhaps accelerate the future growth of new supplies of resources, but at the cost of a repressed labor force and of limited opportunities for spontaneous participation in the organization of production. [2]

Some readers will feel that here de Schweinitz is on particularly weak ground, or at least that he has not found a clinching argument to round off satisfactorily a study whose statistical findings are inconclusive, to say the least, and still highly debatable. Certain data would in fact suggest that the volume of capital per person employed in similar conditions is much lower in such countries as Mexico, Colombia and India than in the United States, and show that there is at any rate a good deal of flexibility in capital-labour ratios. [3] Besides, as a critic has pointed out, there is no evidence that the cost per unit of output has risen, even though capital intensity may have increased. [4] In Higgins's opinion, for example, the capital-output ratio in China, India, Pakistan and the Philippines is low; [5] and similar conclusions have been reached by Adler. [6]

Coming now to de Schweinitz's main argument—that capital formation suffers—this can be illustrated in two respects which, though closely interrelated, can be distinguished for the purposes of analysis. In the first place, the trade union movement is against any reduction of wages or fringe benefits for the purpose of promoting forced saving in order to finance economic

[1] De Schweinitz, op. cit., p. 393.

[2] ibid., p. 394.

[3] Higgins, op. cit., p. 671.

[4] Freedman, op. cit., p. 195.

[5] Higgins, op. cit., pp. 646-649.

[6] J. H. Adler: "World economic growth—Retrospect and prospects", in *Review of Economics and Statistics*, Aug. 1956.

development. Many authorities consider that "all economic development is based on the exploitation of the labour force, whether recognised in times of monetary stability or disguised in periods of 'secular' inflation by means of the monetary illusion and forced saving". [1] Development presupposes a wage level below that of average current productivity, since otherwise there could be no profit, no net investment and no development. If these premises are accepted, it follows that the trade union movement will prevent growth. This it will do partly by rejecting the sacrifices which it is sought to impose on the working class and which, in the nineteenth century, made possible the economic development of the Western world. In addition, through its propaganda, militancy and educational activities, it will help its members to see through the monetary illusion, either by demanding that wages should be brought into line with price increases that have already taken place, or by reacting violently to the spectre of inflation and therefore putting forward claims that would forestall future price increases. Put more bluntly, the activities of the trade unions highlight the conflict between the welfare state and growth.

In the second place, if the trade union movement wants "everything, now", to use everyday language, it interferes with the growth mechanism by fostering a situation in which there will be a structural excess of global demand. The trade unions really do try to achieve a redistribution of national income in favour of wages and at the expense of profits. The truth of the matter is that workers have a very high propensity to consume, which is further accentuated by a demonstration effect that leads to a desire for new goods. The demonstration effect becomes increasingly strong as trade union propaganda acquires a wider audience. Over-all consumption rises, savings decline, and the high investment rates that are needed for take-off prove unattainable. As a result, growth comes to a halt. The point might also be made that like the cost increases to which it gives rise, trade union pressure on total demand reduces the basic possibility of financing development in developing countries. In Berg's view, for example, the granting of high wages in African countries has a whole

[1] P. Dieterlen: "La monnaie, auxiliaire du développement. Contribution à l'étude de l'inflation séculaire", in *Revue économique* (Paris), July 1958, p. 517. The author later spells out what the conciseness of his formula left unsaid (p. 524-525): "In monetary economies, in other words in all developed countries, monetary policy cannot avoid the following alternative:

(1) Either one refuses to go along with the 'monetary illusion', and one cuts back nominal wages to the precise extent that is intended to produce a surplus for investment. In this way development is made possible by means of what could be described as 'wage deflation' without monetary inflation. The exploitation is open, and the currency is stable, is assumed to be sound and is not an instrument of policy.

(2) Alternatively, one can rely on the monetary illusion, resort to disguised exploitation, allow nominal wages to rise and offset this increase by a more than proportional expansion of credit, in other words by a more than proportional inflation which will have the effect of reducing wages to the extent necessary for the development effort."

series of negative effects: it reduces government services and capital formation; it reduces employment or slows its increase; it increases strains on the balance of payments; and it restricts the expansion of peasant agriculture by redistribution of income from peasants to wage earners. [1]

This anti-consumption thesis, which has a large number of adepts, can be summed up as follows:

(i) The trade unions, in order to attract and hold members, must find ways of satisfying workers' demands for higher pay and a higher standard of living (i.e. more food, better clothing, more adequate housing, new consumption goods); (ii) since domestic savings are the main—in some cases the only—source of investment funds, the propensities of the unions to increase consumption interfere with capital formation; (iii) since the trade union demands for a higher real income for workers endanger the efforts to increase the rate of investment, the solution is to curb these demands. Although the argument is generally made in terms of the consequences of an increase in wages, strike activity on the part of the trade unions presents a similar problem. On the one hand, strikes may be necessary to achieve trade union objectives; on the other hand, strikes tend to decrease productivity and make investment less attractive to foreign investors. [2]

It is from this central thesis that de Schweinitz draws economic policy conclusions entailing the curtailment of freedom of association. Once again, however, a different view can be taken. In the first place, trade unions in the developing countries are very likely to be too weak to impose a redistribution of national income to their advantage. The banning of trade unions is by no means a necessary condition for economic growth. If the object is simply to divert sufficient financial resources from consumption into savings, this can quite well be done at the expense of other social classes or other economic categories than wage earners alone—oil companies with petroleum concessions, hereditary nobility, landowners with conspicuous consumption habits who place any savings they may make abroad or uselessly hoard scarce resources that could be usefully invested in the national industry. De Schweinitz's premise is that consumption and investment are mutually exclusive, and yet one can easily imagine cases in which wage increases would not necessarily be accompanied by a rise in consumption: for example, the economic power may be in the hands of landed interests that endeavour to meet the demand of foreign countries by keeping the standard of living of wage earners at the lowest possible level of consumption, or the wage increases may be channelled not into imports of beer, cigarettes, and so forth (as the argument based on the demonstration effect assumes) but (either spontaneously or, more likely, by means of heavy taxation) into the construction of schools, hospitals, and so on.

---

[1] Berg, "Major issues of wage policy in Africa", op. cit., p. 201.

[2] A. Warner: *Factors that foster or hamper progress in the field of labour relations in developing countries: A trends report surveying selected relevant documentation* (Geneva, ILO, 1970; internal document IR 47/1970, mimeographed), p. 106.

Freedman, who makes this point, adds: "I choose my examples—schools, hospitals, education, etc.—deliberately to indicate that many of the items which labourers are likely to purchase may not be consumer items at all, but expenditures which improve 'human capital'." [1]

Even if the long-term productivity of social investments is not a valid criticism within the framework of de Schweinitz's own thesis, his conclusions would be invalidated if the mechanical and static model he uses were dropped in favour of a dynamic one. Union pressure on wages, for example, could work to further development: because of the danger of a reduction in profit margins, it might encourage more efficiency in a system of production that is often monopolistic and protected by external tariffs—provided, of course, that the increase in wage costs could not be passed on too easily to the consumers and did not discourage enterprise. [2]

In short the main criticism that can be levelled against the theses under discussion is not so much that they lead to false conclusions as that they apply to all underdeveloped countries findings reached through observations or reasoning applying to only a few. It therefore seems less important to establish the implications of the model analysed here than to draw attention to its limitations. To sum up the main criticisms that can be made of such theses, their most serious shortcoming could be said to lie in their lack of method. The approach is mechanical and purely economic. Myrdal is probably right to suggest that causal relationships of a mechanical nature should be replaced by an approach based on the concept of "circular causation"; [3] that a theoretical analysis which is restricted to the interactions of "economic factors" alone and which is therefore closely related to the equilibrium assumption is entirely unrealistic; and that a distinction between "relevant" and "irrelevant" factors, or "more relevant" and "less relevant" factors, should be drawn instead. [4]

Applying strictly de Schweinitz's own logic, it can in fact be argued that, in the orthodox Keynesian thinking to which he subscribes, the propensity to consume and the inducement to invest are not as contradictory as he suggests, since expansion through a growth of real demand can be achieved if either or both of the instrumental variables are modified. Moreover, the model chosen loses much of its relevance through being transposed to the long term from the short term for which it was designed. Furthermore, modern economic

[1] Freedman, op. cit., p. 194.

[2] Sturmthal, op. cit., p. 205.

[3] Gunnar Myrdal: *Economic theory and underdeveloped regions* (London, Duckworth, 1957). Myrdal describes the concept as follows: "The variables are so interlocked in circular causation that a change in any one induces the others to change in such a way that the secondary changes support the first change, with similar tertiary effects upon the variable first affected, and so on" (p. 17).

[4] ibid., p. 10.

analysts are inclined to the view that models are operational only once they have been "deglobalised" so as to make allowances for both economic structures and patterns of social behaviour. This, however, implies a slightly different kind of analysis which is at once more specific and more diversified. What it gains in empirical observation and in the flexibility of positive recommendations, however, it loses in clarity. It can take several forms.

Labour cost and employment

Whereas the foregoing analysis followed in the footsteps of Keynesian theory and made the opposition between consumption and investment the main issue, the present approach, which derives rather from classical economics, emphasises the influence of an increase in the cost of labour on the volume of employment. This is implicit, for example, in the statements of J. Tinbergen. Tinbergen begins by stressing the importance of the unemployment problem in developing countries:

> As long as there are so many unemployed or underemployed in the developing countries, the reduction of unemployment is more important than increases in wages. [1]

This observation, which might at first sight have appeared to be mainly inspired by a sense of social justice, is subsequently supported by a basically economic argument:

> The priority to be given to employment is not an easy task for trade unions in developing countries. It implies that they should not press too hard for wage increases, as long as there is still high unemployment. This implies a task of educating their own members in a sense of solidarity with their unemployed brethren. [2]

Implicitly or explicitly, the argument that is often used by economists in the United States to the effect that a trade union monopoly constitutes a threat to the optimum allocation of resources keeps recurring. A graph (figure 4) can be used to illustrate that argument. Let D_1, D_2, D_3 be the demand for labour in activities 1, 2 and 3, with corresponding initial wages of W_1, W_2, and W_3 and quantities of labour actually demanded at current wage levels of L_1, L_2 and L_3. If, as a result of trade union pressure, an increase in wages is obtained which raises them to the new levels of W'_1, W'_2, and W'_3, the new demand for labour will then be only L'_1, L'_2 and L'_3. As this example shows, the extent of the reduction in employment on account of a given increase in wages depends on the elasticity of the undertaking's demand for labour. Working from analyses of this kind, L. G. Reynolds and P. Gregory reached the conclusion

---

[1] International Confederation of Free Trade Unions [ICFTU]: *Economic development and the free trade unions* (Brussels, 1971), p. 44.

[2] ibid., pp. 45-46.

Figure 4. Labour demand and wage increases

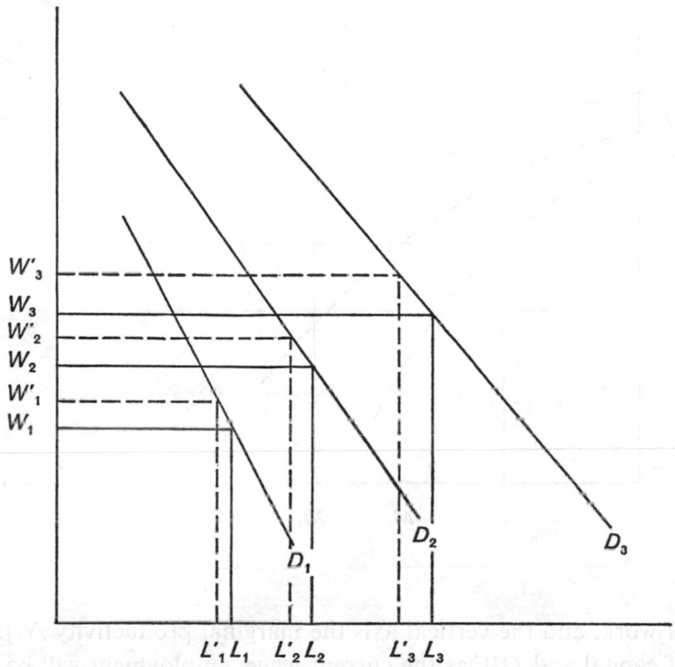

that, had wages not risen, about 29,000 extra jobs would have been created in Puerto Rico between 1954 and 1958. [1]

From the theoretical point of view, there would seem to be two reasons why this reasoning cannot be applied to the developing countries. To start with, it presupposes the perfect mobility of labour that is a characteristic of perfect competition in a market economy. Yet one of the factors which is often taken into account in analysing underdeveloped economies is the dualism that inevitably arises when a modern sector is established and develops side by side with the former traditional economy, with which, by its very nature, it can have only the most tenuous connection, if any. [2] Secondly, it is often assumed that the supply of labour at current wage levels is unlimited: take for example Lewis's hypothesis. [3] Let the horizontal axis of a graph represent the

[1] L. G. Reynolds and P. Gregory: *Wages, productivity, and industrialization in Puerto Rico* (Homewood, Illinois, R. D. Irwin, 1965), p. 305.

[2] R. Bastianetto: *Essai sur le démarrage des pays sous-développés* (Paris, Cujas, 1968), p. 91.

[3] A. Lewis: "Economic development with unlimited supplies of labour", in *The Manchester School of Economic and Social Studies*, May 1954. It is irrelevant at this point whether the supply of labour comes from disguised unemployment, women looking for work or population growth.

Figure 5. Displacement of the marginal productivity curve in the event of reinvestment of profits, on the assumption of an unlimited supply of labour

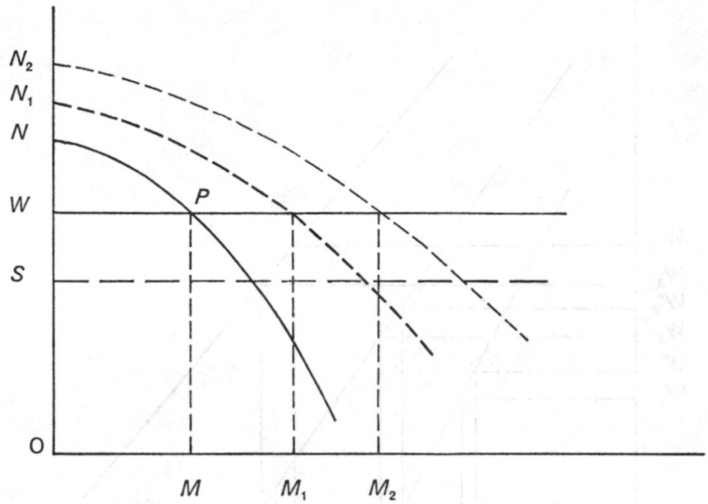

volume of work, and the vertical axis the marginal productivity. With a given volume of capital and *OW* as the current wage, employment will be *OM*, and the surplus (profits) accruing to the capitalist *NWP*. *OW* is greater than *OS* (living wage), the difference between them representing, for example, the psychological cost of transferring the manpower from one sector to another. If the capitalist reinvests his profits, the marginal productivity curve moves upwards and the surplus and employment increase. So long as there is a substantial reservoir of manpower that employers can tap, they can easily resist trade union pressure in favour of higher wages.

Of course these models and their various derivatives [1] are debatable and have many limitations. [2] This is not the place to argue the point. It should suffice to note that the conclusions drawn from them are incompatible with the view that there is a negative relationship between wage increases and the volume of employment. Not only is this argument somewhat shaky at the

---

[1] For example, the models of J. C. H. Fei and G. Ranis: *Development of the labor surplus economy: Theory and policy* (Homewood, Illinois, R. D. Irwin, 1964.). or of D. W. Jorgenson: "Surplus agricultural labour and the development of a dual economy", in *Oxford Economic Papers*, Nov. 1967, pp. 288-312.

[2] See for example, J. Gaude: "Agricultural employment and rural migration in a dual economy", in *International Labour Review*. Nov. 1972, pp. 475-488—summary of an econometric study by the same author: *Emploi agricole et migrations dans une économie dualiste* (Geneva, Droz, 1972).

theoretical level; its practical validity is also challenged by the workers' organisations concerned:

It has been said that wage restraint will help to solve the problem of unemployment. We had wage restraint in India and the unemployment problem has not been solved. It is not only a case of India. At the end of the First Development Decade it is a case of almost all the developing countries and some of the developed countries also. It is not at all automatic that because you have wage restraint you solve the problem of unemployment, even to a limited extent. [1]

In the course of the same debate, another speaker added:

I will mainly deal with the draft statement and programme of action, where it says: "Trade unions in developing countries must appreciate that since economic and social progress implies sacrifice, they must press their governments for the establishment of a machinery for the equitable distribution of income and further ensure"—this is the part to which I would like to refer—"that in formulating their wage demands they should avoid creating too much of a gap between their incomes and those of the rural population. . . ." This is the argument usually used by employers and sometimes by governments to keep the wages of the workers in the developing countries down; that you must think of the 80 per cent of the population in the rural sector and should not demand anything. I think this will give a handle to that argument. We have felt and we have experienced that there are natural circumstances which depress the wages of workers in industries, and no further argument in this respect is necessary. We have found that when the wages of the workers in industries go up, it brings some prosperity even to the rural population. There has always been an upward movement in the rural sector whenever the wages of the industrial workers have gone up. Therefore we should not have this kind of argument, which will be a handle further to depress the wages in the industrialised sector. Rather, they should be treated as the pace setter, not only for workers in other depressed industries, but also for the rural population. [2]

Economic role of trade unions

An even more sophisticated theory endeavours to reconcile productivity for development, a high level of savings and a free trade union movement. [3] This represents an attempt to depoliticise trade unions by restricting their activity to claims disputes alone:

Fighting the elections on specific issues, forming the Government or the opposition, agitation and propaganda on political problems and similar issues should be left outside the trade union field. . . . These aspects could be tolerated in a colonial economy for political reasons, but trade unions in a free democratic country on its path of economic development can hardly afford such activities. [4]

---

[1] M. V. Kulkarni, of the Hind Mazdoor Sabha, in ICFTU: *Economic development and the free trade unions*, op. cit., p. 84.

[2] M. K. Mehta, of the Indian National Trades Union Congress, in ICFTU: *Economic development and the free trade unions*, op. cit., p. 55.

[3] G. B. Baldwin: "Labor problems in a developing economy", in *Current History* (Philadelphia), Aug. 1959, p. 92.

[4] A. Mehta: "The mediating role of the trade union in underdeveloped countries", in *Economic Development and Cultural Change*, Oct. 1957, pp. 20-21.

Seen in this light, freedom of association, which was seriously curtailed by de Schweinitz's thesis and somewhat less so by that of Tinbergen,[1] would seem to conform almost entirely to the principles laid down by the ILO Committee on Freedom of Association, whereby trade union organisations should have regard, in the interests of the development of the trade union movement, to the principles enunciated by the International Labour Conference in 1952 at its 35th Session;[2] of course it is not always easy to draw a clear line between what is of an occupational character and what is political in character, but the distinction must be drawn wherever feasible,[3] even though, when the frontier between political and genuinely trade union affairs is difficult to see, it is inevitable and sometimes usual for trade unions to take a stand on questions having political aspects as well as on strictly economic or social questions.[4]

Freedom of association is thus recognised, but the trade union movement itself is assigned quite specific objectives all of which are confined to the economic sphere:

The role the trade unions can most usefully play may be as follows:

1. Observing self-imposed wage restraint on all levels.
2. Educating their members to give up extra-spendthrift habits of the labor class.
3. Encouraging small savings among the classes.
4. Increasing the labor productivity through propaganda.
5. Settling the differences through the legally instituted machinery based on the principles of conciliation and/or arbitration.
6. Helping the displaced labor thrown out of employment as a result of rationalization by inducing them to take training in new skills in the institutions set up by the Government or State management.
7. Initiating co-operative action in the enforcement of minimum wages.
8. Inducing the labor class to effectively participate in social security and provident fund schemes.

---

[1] The first thesis is largely incompatible with the provisions of the Freedom of Association and Protection of the Right to Organise Convention, 1948 (No. 87). The second thesis accepts freedom of association but involves the placing of certain limitations on freedom to bargain. Some of these limitations are in fact recognised by the case law of the Committee on Freedom of Association. The Committee holds that if, as part of its stabilisation policy, a government considers that wage rates cannot be settled freely through collective bargaining, this restriction should be imposed as an exceptional measure and only to the extent that is necessary, without exceeding a reasonable period, and should be accompanied by adequate safeguards to protect workers' living standards (110th Report, Case No. 503, para. 46), and that ways can be found of persuading the parties to collective bargaining to have regard voluntarily in their negotiations to considerations relating to the economic or social policy of the Government and the safeguarding of the general interest, provided the objectives recognised as being in the general interest have been widely discussed by all parties, in accordance with the principles laid down by the Consultation (Industrial and National Levels) Recommendation, 1960 (No. 113) (85th Report, Case No. 341, para. 187).

[2] 12th Report, Case No. 75, para. 290. The resolution is reproduced in Appendix 2 of the present chapter.

[3] 14th Report, Case No. 101, para. 74.

[4] 112th Report, Case No. 528, para. 113.

9. Sharing in the profits on an acceptable basis which, while apportioning a significant percentage of profit to labor, will leave sufficient incentive to the management to plow the profits back into the industries they own.

The economic implications of such trade union behaviour are twofold: (1) to restrict consumption, and (2) to bring about an increase in the desired levels of production. [1]

There are any number of texts along similar lines. More or less detailed variations on Mehta's propositions have been advanced, for example, in the African countries; Kassalow points out that it is not unusual for political leaders in that continent to maintain that urban wage earners, particularly unionised groups, must not be allowed to extend their already advantageous position relative to the rural population. However, "whether this policy of holding stable or reducing the income gap between favoured urban or modern sector workers and those in the rural, traditional areas is consonant with effective development policy is at least debatable; but it is prevalent, and it heightens social tensions in Africa". [2]

As it can be interpreted from the quotations above, the programme of action of the trade unions [3] shows a profound wisdom which is unfortunately far from commonplace. The important thing is to consider whether the tendency of government officials and some trade union leaders to regard the labour movement "as an instrument of economic development in the interests of the whole nation, rather than as a class group" [4] will correspond to the way in

---

[1] A. Mehta: "The mediating role of the trade unions in underdeveloped countries", op. cit., pp. 18-19.

[2] E. M. Kassalow: "Trade unionism and the development process in the new nations: A comparative view", in S. Barkin and others (ed.): *International labor* (New York, Harper and Row, 1967), p. 72.

[3] As far as declarations of intent are concerned, the employers' organisations are not overlooked, either. For example, at a seminar on the role of workers' and employers' organisations in economic and social development in Africa, which was held in Addis Ababa from 3 to 10 December 1968, certain participants stressed that "in view of the needs of development, the role of employers' organisations should, in addition to their normal functions, cover the following aspects: (1) mobilisation of national talents, skills and experience and the training of personnel for the acceleration of economic and social development; (2) promotion of all measures of national self-help; (3) encouragement of measures calculated to improve all types of management-labour relations at all levels; (4) assistance in the preparation, execution and evaluation of national development plans, in particular through: *(a)* collection of adequate business and industrial data and information; *(b)* informing employees in all sectors of the need for and the aims, scope and expected advantages of national development plans; *(c)* promoting among the employers in particular and the business community in general a real sense of 'industrialisation consciousness'; *(d)* assuring best use of scarce national resources in relation to external aid, especially ILO technical assistance programme; *(e)* helping ILO technical experts as well as those of other aid-giving agencies in the fulfilment of their missions; and *(f)* assisting the national authorities in the evaluation of international technical co-operation projects; (5) encouragement and help to African entrepreneurs and co-operatives, especially in the field of setting up small industries." ILO: *Report of the Seminar on the Role of Workers' and Employers' Organisations in Economic and Social Development in Africa* (Geneva, 1969; document ILO/OTA/AFR/R.10), pp. 7-8.

[4] C. A. Myers: *Labor problems in the industrialization of India* (Cambridge, Massachusetts, Harvard University Press, 1958), p. 180.

which the situation will actually develop. Naturally one can take the view that a harmony of interests will establish itself automatically and that each of the parties needs the other and is quite aware of the fact; that the government has no desire to alienate the workers because they represent a considerable political force, whether potential or real, while the workers, since political aid is vital if their needs are to be met in the foreseeable future, do not want to act as the opponents of the government. Unfortunately, the real world does not seem to conform to this rosy picture. For instance, in spite of government support of the Indian National Trade Union Congress, in spite of the presence of trade union leaders in the Cabinet [1] and in spite of the solemn declaration that "in an economy which . . . is organised for planned production and distribution, aiming at the realisation of social justice and welfare of the masses, strikes and lock-outs have no place", [2] industrial peace cannot be said to have prevailed in India.

TENTATIVE CONCLUSIONS

The foregoing analysis appears to lead to three tentative conclusions.

First, the argument that freedom of association is an obstacle to development can be reversed; it is often closer to the truth to regard a lack of development as hampering the exercise of freedom of association. In underdeveloped countries freedom of association comes up against numerous barriers:

> . . . The multiplicity of small, scattered undertakings, with the result that the working class is widely dispersed; a high rate of labour turnover; open opposition by many employers to any strengthening of the workers' bargaining power; serious unemployment or underemployment, placing workers at their employer's mercy; illiteracy or a very low standard of education among the vast majority of workers, who are consequently unaware of their rights or of the value of combining in defence of their interests, and know little or nothing about the nature and aims of trade unions; lack of solidarity between urban and rural workers; scarcity of trade union leaders, and so on. In such countries freedom of association often lacks a fundamental element for its promotion—the initiative of the workers themselves—and the situation as a whole is marked by the weakness of the trade union movement and the inadequate development of collective bargaining. [3]

Secondly, a reassessment of the role of the trade union movement in developing countries would seem to be called for:

> The realities of the economic situation of most African countries have frequently been invoked to place severe limitations on the trade unions' wage-claiming function

[1] Before becoming Minister of Labour, Gulzari Lal Nanda had been General Secretary of the Textile Labour Association, and Khandubhai Desai, who had previously been Minister of Labour, became President of the Association. This kind of reshuffling of responsibilities is not peculiar to India; on the contrary, it is a common feature of several developing countries.

[2] *Labour Gazette* (Bombay), Aug. 1951, p. 1282.

[3] ILO: *The ILO and human rights*, op. cit., pp. 36-37.

and to oblige them to adopt policies contributing foremostly to the building up of the country's economy and to furthering social development without, at the same time, losing sight of their basic functions. While stressing their wage-claiming or "consumptionist" function, trade unions have constantly rejected a narrowing down of their activities to only such type of function. Instead these unions have insisted on their role in economic and social development. . . . While their role cannot be limited to the unpopular though necessary task of enforcing discipline and efficiency at the workplace, as it is sometimes suggested, trade unions can, if their positive role in development is duly recognised and supported and if assured of a fair share of benefits, bring out their potential in helping to increase productivity. [1]

Trade unions, then, can be regarded as pushing up productivity instead of acting as a brake on economic growth. It is a mistake to regard them as being no more than a disruptive factor in the labour market because of the strikes they call; they can also have a stabilising influence. Trade unions can in fact be regarded as a regulating factor. A union endeavours to establish a measure of control over the workers in their relationship with other workers and with the union as an institution; it does this by means of rules covering, among many other aspects, the pace of work, the timing and nature of labour claims, and the performance of its members. [2] Trade unions stabilise and assist in the recruitment of manpower, help to foster a sense of industrial commitment and discipline, develop workers' education, play an active role in social and economic reforms (agrarian reforms, nationalisation, planning), and enable the workers to feel that they are participating in vital economic decisions. This being so, the wisest policy for governments to adopt towards them is "support rather than control or suppression". [3]

A third conclusion, which follows from the first two, is that the relationship between freedom of association and economic development needs to be viewed in a new light:

If it is accepted that economic development has social objectives, trade unions will always have a proper role to play in it. There is no substitute for trade unions as the workers' own instrument for obtaining a more equitable share of the fruits of economic progress. Social discontent is perhaps inevitable in any society and there may be no possibility of entirely eliminating it. The real problem is to prevent it from leading to serious social unrest and grave labour troubles, which can threaten the political order or the stability of government and cause enormous economic losses. So long as workers can believe that their trade unions are doing a creditable job of defending and promoting their interests, they will depend on the unions for airing their desires, aspirations and grievances and for obtaining satisfaction, justice or redress through normal trade union methods. In this way, trade unions can be said to perform a vital role in preventing the danger of serious social unrest and in

[1] ILO: *Report of the Seminar on the Role of Workers' and Employers' Organisations in Economic and Social Development in Africa*, op. cit., p. 46-47.

[2] See C. Kerr and A. Siegel: "Industrialization and the labor force: A typological framework", in R. L. Aronson and J. Windmuller (ed.): *Labor management and economic growth*, Proceedings of a conference on human resources and labor relations in underdeveloped countries (Cornell University, 1954), p. 141.

[3] Fisher, op. cit., p. 113.

contributing to stable development and "sustained progress". . . . There is, however, no doubt that governments, especially in the developing countries, are seriously concerned about the effects of bad labour relations, industrial conflicts and work stoppages, and what they consider to be excessive or exaggerated trade union collective bargaining demands, in discouraging investment, hampering production and productive efficiency, and thereby slowing down the pace of economic growth. The real problem seems to be the desire of governments that trade unions should play a more constructive role in the system of labour relations, so that there will be less industrial disputes and strikes and more industrial peace, and a general climate of labour relations favourable to development. Are restrictions on trade union rights the most practicable way of attaining these objectives? Are there no possible alternatives to such restrictions, consistent with freedom of association, for accomplishing the same objectives? If it is desirable that trade unions should play a more constructive role, who should determine the conditions for such a role and what should be those conditions? [1]

Rather than discuss in absolute terms the question of the compatibility or incompatibility that may exist between the provisions of Conventions Nos. 87 and 98 and the economic demands that a developing country must meet, it will be useful to turn now to these more specific, but also more political questions.

APPENDIX 1: INDUSTRIAL REVOLUTION, PRIMITIVE ACCUMULATION AND TAKE-OFF

Industrial Revolution

The Industrial Revolution has often been identified with the advent of mechanisation. This was Engels' idea when he wrote:

> The history of the proletariat in England begins with the second half of this last century, with the invention of the steam engine and of machinery for working in cotton. These inventions gave rise, as is well known, to an industrial revolution, a revolution which altered the whole civil society; one the historical importance of which is only now beginning to be recognised. England is the classic soil of this transformation, which was all the mightier, the more silently it proceeded; and England is, therefore, the classic land of its chief product also, the proletariat. [2]

Marx subsequently indicated the extent of the changes wrought by the Industrial Revolution: "The revolution in the modes of production of industry and agriculture made necessary a revolution in the general conditions of the social process of production, i.e. in the means of communication and of transport." [3]

Among economic theorists, the expression "industrial revolution", which was a graphic way of describing the socio-economic upheaval that so impressed Marx's contemporaries, has gone through various phases. C. Fohlen points out that from a modest start in the early years of the nineteenth century right up to the present day, the expression "industrial revolution" has followed a chequered career, often

[1] ILO: *Freedom of association for workers' and employers' organisations and their role in social and economic development*, Report III, Seventh Asian Regional Conference, Teheran, 1971, p. 34.

[2] *The condition of the working class in England in 1844*, Introduction.

[3] *Capital*, Part IV, Ch. XV, section 1.

disappearing for a long time and then suddenly coming back to the fore. The notion, which originated among economic observers, subsequently came to be used only by historians before once again becoming the common property of all those who look to the past to explain the present and to the present to forecast the future. He suggests that these three stages in the acceptance of the term give a better idea of the scope and content of the Industrial Revolution. [1]

Nowadays there is some disagreement among historians as to the usefulness of the concept. Some accept it and use it, as does J. P. Rioux, who considers the Industrial Revolution as the starting point of a new type of growth characterised by technical innovations. By providing the impetus for a form of capitalism which was at last able to come into its own, the Industrial Revolution helped to establish fully capitalist production. It represents the decisive transition from an incomplete, pre-capitalist phase to a phase which bears the stamp of all the essential features of capitalism—constant technical progress, the mobilisation of capital for profit, a sharper distinction between a "bourgeoisie" which owns the means of production and the wage earners. [2] Others, meanwhile, deplore the inaccuracy of a concept which they agree to employ only because usage more or less obliges them to do so. This is the view of T. S. Ashton, who considers that the changes that took place were not just industrial but social and intellectual as well and that, in any case, the word "revolution" implies a suddenness that can hardly be used to describe an economic evolution. However, as he points out, such a long line of historians have talked about industrial revolution and the expression has become so commonplace that it would be rather pedantic to try to avoid it. [3]

Primitive accumulation

Primitive accumulation, in Marxist terms, represents the transitional phase between feudalism and capitalism:

> The process, therefore, that clears the way for the capitalist system, can be none other than the process which takes away from the labourer the possession of his means of production; a process that transforms, on the one hand, the social means of subsistence and of production into capital, on the other, the immediate producers into wage labourers. The so-called "primitive accumulation", therefore, is nothing else than the historical process of divorcing the producer from the means of production. It appears as primitive, because it forms the pre-historic stage of capital and of the mode of production corresponding with it. The economic structure of capitalistic society has grown out of the economic structure of feudal society. The dissolution of the latter set free the elements of the former. [4]

Having defined primitive accumulation as a transitional phase, Marx goes on to describe its basic features:

> The spoliation of the Church's property, the fraudulent alienation of the State domains, the robbery of the common lands, the usurpation of feudal and clan property, and its transformation into modern private property under circumstances of reckless terrorism were just so many idyllic methods of primitive accumulation. They conquered the field for capitalistic agriculture, made the soil part and parcel of capital, and created for the town industries the necessary supply of a "free" and outlawed proletariat. [5]

---

[1] *Qu'est-ce que la révolution industrielle?* (Paris, Laffont, 1971), p. 35.

[2] *La révolution industrielle, 1780-1880* (Paris, Editions du Seuil, 1971), p. 16.

[3] *The Industrial Revolution, 1760-1830* (London, Oxford University Press, 1958), p. 3.

[4] *Capital*, op. cit., Part VIII, Ch. XXVI.

[5] ibid., Part VIII, Ch. XXVII.

The discovery of gold and silver in America, the extirpation, enslavement and entombment in mines of the aboriginal population, the beginning of the conquest and looting of the East Indies, the turning of Africa into a warren for the commercial hunting of blackskins, signalised the rosy dawn of the era of capitalist production.[1]

Take-off

The definitions suggested by the originator of the concept of economic take-off, W. Rostow, have varied somewhat with his successive works. The following will serve the purpose:

(a) a rise in the rate of productive investment from (say) 5 per cent or less to over 10 per cent of national income (or net national product);

(b) the development of one or more substantial manufacturing sectors, with a high rate of growth;

(c) the existence or quick emergence of a political, social and institutional framework which exploits the impulses to expansion in the modern sector and the potential external economy effects of the take-off and gives to growth an ongoing character.[2]

The take-off has been described more succinctly by Rostow as "a convenient name for that short stage of development, concentrated within two or three decades, in which the economy and the society of which it is part transform themselves so that economic growth becomes more or less automatic."[3]

APPENDIX 2: RESOLUTION CONCERNING THE INDEPENDENCE OF THE TRADE UNION MOVEMENT,

adopted by the International Labour Conference at its 35th Session (1952)

Whereas the International Labour Conference at its recent session has formulated in international Conventions and Recommendations principles for the establishment of freedom of association and good industrial relations;

Whereas a stable, free and independent trade union movement is an essential condition for good industrial relations and should contribute to the improvement of social conditions generally in each country;

Whereas the relations between the trade union movement and political parties will inevitably vary for each country; and

Whereas any political affiliation or political action by the trade unions depends on national conditions in each country;

Considering nevertheless that there are certain principles which should be laid down in this regard which are essential to protect the freedom and independence of the trade union movement and its fundamental task of advancing the social and economic wellbeing of the workers,

The International Labour Conference at its 35th Session adopts this twenty-sixth day of June 1952 the following resolution:

1. The fundamental and permanent mission of the trade union movement is the economic and social advancement of the workers.

2. The trade unions also have an important role to perform in co-operation with other elements in promoting social and economic development and the advancement of the community as a whole in each country.

---

[1] *Capital,* op. cit., Part VIII, Ch. XXXI.

[2] "The take-off into self-sustained growth", in *Economic Journal*, 1956, p. 32.

[3] *The Economist*, 15 Aug. 1959.

3. To these ends it is essential for the trade union movement in each country to preserve its freedom and independence so as to be in a position to carry forward its economic and social mission irrespective of political changes.

4. A condition for such freedom and independence is that trade unions be constituted as to membership without regard to race, national origin or political affiliations and pursue their trade union objectives on the basis of the solidarity and economic and social interests of all workers.

5. When trade unions in accordance with national law and practice of their respective countries and at the decision of their members decide to establish relations with a political party or to undertake constitutional political action as a means towards the advancement of their economic and social objectives, such political relations or actions should not be of such a nature as to compromise the continuance of the trade union movement or its social and economic functions irrespective of political changes in the country.

6. Governments in seeking the co-operation of trade unions to carry out their economic and social policies should recognise that the value of this co-operation rests to a large extent on the freedom and independence of the trade union movement as an essential factor in promoting social advancement and should not attempt to transform the trade union movement into an instrument for the pursuance of political aims, nor should they attempt to interfere with the normal functions of a trade union movement because of its freely established relationship with a political party.

POLICY IMPLICATIONS 3

This chapter is not concerned with principles as such, nor with theoretical speculation on the compatibility or incompatibility of freedom of association and economic development. The two preceding chapters have already provided enough legal and economic background, and an attempt will now be made to ascertain how the problem arises in practice in the developing countries, for that is where it is most acute. As long ago as 1956 the McNair Committee made the following observation:

> In the countries which are less advanced industrially, it seems that organisations of workers and employers are not so strong vis-à-vis their governments as in the leading industrial countries, and the material summarised in this report shows that in many of the less advanced countries restrictions and limitations exist which would afford opportunities of domination and control to a government desirous of using them. [1]

---

[1] *Official Bulletin* (Geneva, ILO), No. 9, para. 343, p. 581. Listing some of these barriers, C. W. Jenks wrote: "While it is most unusual for previous authorisation as such to be required for the formation of employers' or workers' organisations, registration provisions exist in some 35 countries; their effect differs widely according to the extent to which registration is compulsory or optional, the extent to which registration which is optional in principle confers important privileges, the extent to which registration is discretionary or a matter of course if prescribed conditions are fulfilled, and the extent to which provision is made for any appeal against refusal to register. There appear to be some 25 countries in which there are restrictions upon the freedom of association of all or certain categories of public employees. There appear to be some 22 countries in which membership in employers' and workers' organisations is limited to the persons engaged in the occupation or economic activity or group of related occupations in connection with which the organisation is established, such limitations often being accompanied by territorial limitations; in some 11 countries all or some of the officers of an organisation must be actively engaged in the trade or occupation in respect of which it is formed. In some 18 countries organisations are prohibited from engaging in any or certain political activities, and in a further 8 countries there appear to be restrictions on the use of trade union funds for political purposes; in another 8 countries the trade unions appear to carry on their activities 'under the guidance of' the Communist Party. Restrictions upon the formation of federations and confederations appear to exist in some 20 countries. Provisions requiring the previous authorisation of, or the presence of a government official at, all or certain trade union meetings appear to exist in some 12 countries. In some 18 countries trade union elections appear to be subject to some measure of

(footnote concluded overleaf)

Seventeen years later, the ILO reported:

Governments in some of these countries consider that, in order to avoid any dispersal of the effort for national development, it is necessary to enforce certain restrictions on the free establishment of trade unions and the exercise of trade union rights. It is also contended in other circles that freedom of association acts as a restraint on economic and social development. [1]

Freedom of association can be curtailed in many ways:

The governments, anxious to avoid any dispersal of the effort for national development, strive to prevent a multiplicity of rival unions and to reduce the frequency of occupational disputes by taking various measures which at times may be incompatible with international labour standards. They may, for example, limit the right to establish organisations, dissolve some unions which already exist, force workers to join a single trade union organisation, supervise the choice of union leaders or the expenditure or other activities of trade unions, impose restrictions on the right of unions to join an international organisation, and so on. These are real problems which must be examined in the context in which they arise in the countries concerned. Once more, what is vital is the extent to which such arrangements leave the trade unions real freedom to express the views and defend the interests of their members. [2]

The real problem, therefore, is not a matter of the virtues of freedom of association as such or of economic development as such; nor can it be reduced to assessing their compatibility or incompatibility in absolute terms. On the contrary, the problem now has to do with possible derogations from a principle and with adjustments that it may be desirable to make to existing situations; in other words, it calls for policy decisions. Some light may be shed on this aspect [3] of the subject by considering one by one the specific implications of freedom of association for supply, demand and development itself.

---

governmental supervision. There appear to be some 25 countries in which workers' or employers' organisations receive either at the discretion of a public authority or in pursuance of the law financial payments of various types. Measures of financial control and supervision range from requirements for the proper auditing of accounts to provisions for detailed governmental supervision of financial administration and expenditure; provisions which go beyond requirements of proper auditing appear to exist in some 20 countries. The power of suspension or dissolution or cancellation of registration without previous application to a court of law appears to exist in at least 20 countries, in varying degrees." (*The international protection of trade union freedom*, op. cit., pp. 489-490.)

[1] ILO: *Freedom of association and collective bargaining*, op. cit., p. 3.

[2] ILO: *The ILO and human rights*, op. cit., p. 37.

[3] The best solution will therefore be to adopt the same approach—in a more restricted field, since it relates only to freedom of association and yet also on a bigger scale since, as was explained in the introduction, it includes the whole of the underdeveloped countries—as E. Córdova chose for an article on Latin America in which he stated: "In recent years attention has begun to be focused in Latin America on the study of the effects of labour legislation on the development process. Whereas in the past little thought was given to these effects, or they were regarded as being an integral part of the price that had to be paid for social progress, today there is a tendency to accord them more careful consideration. The emphasis on legislation for its own sake, which was formerly the predominating feature of the labour policy of the countries concerned, is beginning to give way to a broader outlook, which takes into account the various social and economic implications of the adoption of a labour

SUPPLY

Worker protest and the trade unions

The effect of freedom of association on supply is unquestionable: like lockouts, strikes, which are the expression of this freedom, reduce output. To take just one example, 16,562,000 working days were lost in 1947 in India, [1] and in 1950, in spite of the adoption of the Bombay Industrial Relations (Amendment) Act, 1949, a further 12,806,704 days of strikes were recorded. [2] However, strikes are not necessarily organised by trade unions, and wildcat strikes opposed by union leaders sometimes seriously disrupt production in the industrialised countries. [3] On the other hand, far from containing protest movements, the curtailment of freedom of association would seem more often to have the opposite effect:

> Although generalizations are hazardous, it does appear that strikes vary inversely with the acceptance of unionism as an institution by the society, and especially by the managerial classes. The more firmly the labor movement is institutionalized and "accepted", particularly in the sphere of labor-management relations, the greater the likelihood that there will be fewer strikes. [4]

Although strikes may be the most visible manifestation of worker discontent, they are only one of many signs of industrial conflict; a tendency for workers

standard. This new approach to the problem of labour law has coincided with governments taking an interest in evolving strategies for promoting integral or balanced development. The earliest labour provisions were enacted with purely social aims in mind, taking into consideration only the persons to whom they were directly applicable. This phase was followed by another, economy-oriented, phase in which stress was laid on the attainment of fixed over-all growth targets, and it was advocated in some quarters that all obstacles standing in the way of this objective should be swept away. Some authors have warned in this connection that development policy in Latin America is tending to become polarised into two equally dangerous trends—one concentrating essentially on investment and productivity and excluding or postponing consideration of social problems, and the other laying too much emphasis on the aspirations of the people and leading them on through the systematic improvement of social benefits, despite the fact that this drains away investment resources and causes inflation. It is obvious, however, that between these two positions the argument that there can be balanced development which reconciles the aspirations of social justice with the economic requirements of development has been gaining ground, and stress is even being laid on the advantages of making provision in plans for specified social objectives. This argument places special emphasis on the need to assess objectively all the implications of labour legislation. It would not be feasible, indeed, to advocate a balanced approach or to argue that certain provisions might hinder or facilitate development without knowing what repercussions the labour standards were likely to have or what role they could play in the development process." ("Labour legislation and Latin American development: A preliminary review", in *International Labour Review*, Nov. 1972, pp. 445-446.)

[1] *Indian Labour Gazette*, Sep. 1956, p. 266.

[2] ibid., Mar. 1957, p. 753.

[3] See G. Spitaels: *Les conflits sociaux en Europe: Grèves sauvages, contestation, rajeunissement des structures* (Bruges, Collège de l'Europe; Verviers, Editions Gérard et Cie; 1971).

[4] E. M. Kassalow: *Trade unions and industrial relations: An international comparison* (New York, Random House, 1969), p. 159.

to move from job to job, absenteeism, go-slow and sabotage are others that are found, particularly in undertakings in which there are no trade unions. "Strikes, labour turnover, absenteeism, etc., are in fact strategic variables having between them an inverse functional correlation." [1]

In developing countries, the dissatisfaction of individual workers is often expressed through absenteeism, leaving a job without notice, sleeping on the job, and passive or active insubordination [2] rather than a strike. In India there was an absenteeism rate of 71 per cent of the workforce among Bombay textile workers surveyed in 1953-54. [3] In the Ivory Coast a labour turnover of 80 per cent is not uncommon. In Dakar, in 1953, a textile factory had to recruit 908 people to fill 170 jobs. [4] In fact, a very high labour turnover is endemic wherever modern economic enterprise is dependent upon an indigenous social structure to give the worker security, or at least where management fails to make a sufficient effort to obtain the workers' total loyalty. [5]

Instead of the sequence freedom of association, strikes, reduced output, it would therefore be more accurate to talk of worker discontent, forms of resistance, declining product. The economic policy conclusions that might be drawn from the latter sequence should not lead to the curtailment of freedom of association in the interests of economic development. One should first endeavour to discover why certain forms of worker discontent emerge during the process of industrialisation, then try to gauge the capacity (or incapacity) of trade unions to express this discontent and, finally, determine the probable consequences of attempts to restrict the right to strike and what alternative policy might be suggested. This is the course that has been adopted in the following pages.

Industrial commitment among workers is a gradual and continuous process; the same is true of worker protest. At the risk of oversimplifying, the probable sequence can be described as in table 11.

---

[1] K. A. Zachariah: *Industrial relations and personnel problems: A study with particular reference to Bombay* (Bombay, Asia Publishing House, 1954), pp. 180-181.

[2] C. Kerr, J. T. Dunlop, F. H. Harbison and C. A. Myers: "The labour problem in economic development: A framework for a reappraisal", in *International Labour Review*, Mar. 1955, p. 233.

[3] Myers: *Labor problems in the industrialization of India*, op. cit., p. 44.

[4] E. J. Berg: "French West Africa", in Galenson (ed.): *Labor and economic development*, op. cit., p. 200; for a discussion of labour migration in West Africa, see W. Elkan: "Migrant labor in Africa: An economist's approach", in *American Economic Review*, May 1959.

[5] This recalls the well known comment that was made about the Wheatland labour disputes in California in 1913: "Resistance by the worker to an employer's labor policy takes one of two forms: either an open and formal revolt, such as a strike; or an instinctive and often unconscious exercise of the 'strike in detail'—simply drifting off the job" (C. H. Parker: *The casual laborer and other essays* (New York, Harcourt, Brace and Howe, 1920), p. 76).

Table 11. Forms of protest according to the degree of the worker's industrial commitment

Classification of workers by degree of commitment	Characteristic forms of protest
Uncommitted workers	Turnover Absenteeism Fighting Theft and sabotage
Semi-committed workers	Spontaneous stoppages Demonstrations and strikes
Committed workers	Plant and industry strikes Political protests and activity
Specifically committed workers	Grievance machinery, labour courts, and disputes settlement machinery, largely without stoppages Political party and organisational alliances

Source: Kerr, Dunlop, Harbison and Myers: *Industrialism and industrial man*, op. cit., p. 178.

This sequence of worker protest may, however, take a more or less alarming turn as far as the development process is concerned if it is influenced by a certain number of variables that can be said to work as follows:

The pace of industrialization, which is a central decision facing every élite, has a significant impact on the response of the emerging industrial workforce. The faster the pace, other factors being the same, the more sudden will be the transformations required of workers-in-process, the greater the impact of discipline and pace at the workplace, the greater the limitations on consumption, and the greater the dislocations in the community. The faster the rate of industrialization, with comparable resources, cultural settings, and historical periods, the greater will be the degree of latent worker protest. The faster the pace of industrialization in comparable settings, and the greater the pressures upon the managements of enterprises from the market, budgets, or directly from the élite, the greater will be the derived pressures and protest from the emerging workforce.

Similarly, the more drastic the methods used to structure the labor force, and the greater the adaptations required in the arrangements to recruit, hire, allocate, and train the labor force, the greater will be the latent protest in any period. Or, the greater the resistance of the traditional culture to industrialization and the more virile that pre-industrial culture, the greater will be the stresses and the latent protest involved in the industrial transformation. [1]

The trade union movement is intended to serve as a channel for the expression of worker discontent. The way it does so, however, is never a matter of pure and simple reproduction. As has been seen, the origins of industrial disputes are inevitably multidimensional; the reasons given by employers and workers themselves are usually little more than attempts to find some rational explanation for ill-defined sources of potential tension that already existed.

[1] Kerr, Dunlop, Harbison and Myers: *Industrialism and industrial man*, op. cit., p. 179.

It is the unions' task to draw attention to these sources of potential tension, warn the community that they are there, clarify anything that is still unclear, and formulate an appropriate policy. The conflict therefore exists before the strike, but the strike itself, which is in a sense the physical expression of the latent tension, brings it into the open by giving it a social dimension. The trade union, acting as a kind of catalysing agent, is also the agent through which the final break comes. The break, which occurs at the moment when what used to be dormant comes to life, is the product of three factors. In the first place, it marks the transition from an individual to a collective sentiment: a strike is by definition a form of joint action or inaction: there is no such thing as an individual strike; a strike is a collective refusal to work. [1] The motives for the discontent, then, have to be given a rationale and a justification; consequently, some authoritative person or body has to draw up a statement of claims. It is through the trade union that the compatibility of the claims are determined and through it, therefore, that the protest movement takes on its particular form. In the course of this process, the rank and file informs the leaders of what it believes that the leaders expect of it, and the leaders inform the rank and file of what they think it expects from them. [2] In other words, the trade unions really are the genuine spokesmen of the workers when they refer to the need for dignity and social justice, solidarity and freedom, but their demands relate to a set of social standards and, above all, involve precise and often quantified terms of comparison and reference as well as an order of priority. Inevitably, therefore, the representation of the rank and file by the leaders of a union is in a sense bound to be simultaneously adequate and inadequate, like the correspondence between an original text in one language and its translation into another. Another relevant point is that with the calling of a strike, the conflict potential is exposed in an open trial of strength. A collective, rationalised and open conflict such as that described here can ultimately take place only if the trade union movement serves as a channel for individual dissatisfaction. However, it remains to be seen whether in the developing countries the general process outlined here in highly abstract terms is not likely to come up against certain obstacles that are inherent in the very structure of the trade union movement.

At first glance, there would seem to be little scope for generalisations in this respect because of the apparent diversity of labour movements in the underdeveloped countries. This diversity is found, for example, at the ideological level: the All-India Trade Union Congress which was formed in 1918 at

---

[1] As pointed out in 1894 by Guesde, Jaurès and Sembat.

[2] M. Johan: "La CGT et le mouvement de mai", in *Les temps modernes* (Paris), Aug.-Sep. 1968, p. 367.

the instigation of the Congress Party derives its inspiration from Gandhi, [1] the Friendly Society, established in Japan in 1912, has its basis in Christian humanism, [2] the Latin American trade union movement grew out of small groups of anarchist or socialist militants fleeing from the repression in Germany, Italy or Spain at the end of the nineteenth century, [3] while trade unions in the former French colonies in Africa came under the ideological influence of the General Confederation of Labour (CGT) and the French Confederation of Christian Workers (CFTC). [4] This wide diversity of ideologies is accompanied by no less wide a diversity in the number of trade unions and union members from one country to another: in 1954 the Belgian Congo had only 7,538 union members; in 1955 Gambia had only 1,966; the same year there were just 1,942 in Uganda, [5] while there were 17 Jamaican trade unions with 93,285 members, [6] and in 1958 there were 268 Nigerian trade unions with 231,287 members. [7]

Union weakness in developing countries

Despite this obvious diversity, two general observations can be made about the trade union movement in the developing countries: because their possibilities of growth are limited by the small size of the capitalist sector of the economy, the trade unions will find it difficult to recruit enough members (a quantitative difficulty); because it is still in embryo, the working class will not find it easy to produce the kind of leaders it needs (a qualitative difficulty).

The main barrier is of course the small numerical size of the working class: in India, for instance, despite its huge territory and vast population, there were only 2.5 million industrial workers in 1957. Even including the workers employed on plantations, in mines and in the transport, construction and services sectors, the "industrial" labour force still amounted to barely 7 million workers. [8] In the same year, in the whole of former French West Africa, there were 169,000 African and 13,000 European wage earners employed in non-agricultural enterprises, and a total wage-earning labour force of 100,000 workers in public employment and 337,000 in private employment. [9] The scope for recruitment to the trade unions is therefore very limited.

[1] C. A. Myers: "India", in Galenson (ed.): *Labor and economic development*, op. cit.

[2] R. A. Scalapino: "Japan", in Galenson (ed.): *Labor and economic development*, op. cit.

[3] J. C. Neffa: *The Latin-American labour movement and its social strategy* (Geneva, International Institute for Labour Studies, 1969; doc. IEME 4071), p. 4.

[4] Berg: "French West Africa", op. cit.

[5] ILO: *African labour survey*, Studies and Reports, New Series, No. 48 (Geneva, 1958).

[6] United Nations: *Special study on social conditions in non-self-governing territories* (New York, 1958; Sales No.: 58.VI.B2).

[7] B. C. Roberts: *Labor in the tropical territories of the Commonwealth* (Durham, North Carolina, Duke University Press, 1964), p. 123.

[8] *Indian Labour Gazette*, Mar. 1957, p. 740.

[9] Berg: "French West Africa", op. cit., p. 201.

Moreover, the distribution of these workers by sector is hardly conducive to the best possible organisation: in the British West Indies, between 16 and 20 per cent of the labour force is employed in domestic services; [1] in Japan, up to 1920, 70 per cent of the manpower was female (the tradition of employing women from the age of 13 to 16 right up to their marriage and of housing them at the factory still exists today); with a few exceptions (Hong Kong and Singapore in Asia; Kenya, Zaire and Zambia in Africa, for example), the underdeveloped countries are basically agricultural. In Africa 80 to 90 per cent of the population lives in rural areas and mainly off the land; agriculture accounts for between one-third and two-thirds of the national product, whereas manufacturing generates less than 10 per cent. [2] As is well known, domestic servants, agricultural workers and women workers are traditionally rather difficult to organise. Table 12 shows these structural differences; the consequences they may have for union recruitment are obvious. The possibility of union organisation really exists only in a few particular sectors—government and public utilities (telecommunications and electricity and water supply), transport (especially railways, ports and docks, aviation), plantations (for example, rubber in Malaysia, sugar cane in Trinidad and Tobago or Jamaica), mining and petroleum. [3]

The labour force is usually unskilled. In former French West Africa only 18 per cent of workers were skilled. [4] Yet all industrial sociology studies agree

[1] W. H. Knowles: "The British West Indies", in Galenson (ed.): *Labor and economic development*, op. cit.; "Trade unionism in the British West Indies", in *Monthly Labor Review*, Dec. 1956.

[2] E. J. Berg: "Major issues of wage policy in Africa", op. cit., p. 187.

[3] B. C. Roberts, op. cit., pp. 337-364; and Kassalow: *National labor movements in the postwar world*, op. cit., p. 233. All surveys conducted under ILO auspices bear out these observations, as may be seen from the following articles published in the *International Labour Review:* J. A. Hallsworth: "Freedom of association and industrial relations in the countries of the Near and Middle East", Nov.-Dec. 1954; E. Daya: "Freedom of association and industrial relations in Asian countries", Apr.-May 1955; R. Vernengo: "Freedom of association and industrial relations in Latin America", May-June 1956.

[4] Berg: "French West Africa", op. cit. What R. Guillain wrote about Japan in 1959—a country which has "taken off" economically speaking and has a long-standing industrial tradition—could be applied to a good number of underdeveloped countries: "Altogether there are now 43 million workers in the country. The top 7 million of these, working in undertakings with more than ten employees, earn decent wages and enjoy substantial social benefits. The next 10 million, working in small undertakings, also receive a wage, albeit a meagre one, and work in worse conditions. Finally, after all those there are all the rest, a majority of 26 million non-wage-earners, 16 or 17 million of whom are peasants. The significance of this is fundamental. In Japan, the wage-earning classes do not occupy a central position in economic and social life. Instead, this position is occupied by the unorganised mass of family workers who are still steeped in family traditions that have barely evolved and are not remotely Western. From this it is obvious why trade union membership is not even 7 million: by and large, it corresponds to the first category I referred to above. In the following category the trade unions come up against the problem of trying to organise and unify the unending ramifications of family businesses. As to the non-wage-earners, the possibilities there are virtually nil." ("Le Japon éclate sur lui-même", in *Le Monde* (Paris), 10-17 Nov. 1959.)

Table 12. Distribution of labour force by economic sector, 1960 (Percentages)

Country	Agriculture, forestry, hunting and fishing	Mining and quarrying	Manufacturing	Construction	Commerce	Transport, storage and communication	Services
Developed countries							
European Free Trade Area	11.5	2.2	34.8	7.6	14.4	6.8	22.5
European Economic Community	20.5	1.8	32.1	8.5	13.0	5.4	18.8
North America	7.3	1.1	28.7	6.5	22.2	5.8	28.4
Developing countries [1]	*70.7*	*0.6*	*8.9*	*2.0*	*5.6*	*2.2*	*9.6*
Latin America	50.1	1.1	14.5	4.4	9.6	4.5	15.9
South and East Asia [2]	73.1	0.4	8.8	1.3	5.2	1.8	9.4
North Africa	69.6	0.5	7.6	2.2	6.3	2.3	11.4

[1] All countries of the world except Europe (including Turkey and the USSR); Canada and the United States; the Republic of South Africa; Australia and New Zealand; China, Japan, the Democratic People's Republic of Korea, Mongolia and the Democratic Republic of Viet-Nam. [2] Excluding China, Japan, the Democratic People's Republic of Korea, Mongolia and the Democratic Republic of Viet-Nam.

Source: P. Bairoch and J. M. Limbor: "Changes in the industrial distribution of the world labour force by region, 1880-1960", in ILO: *Essays on employment* (Geneva, 1971), pp. 30-31, 34-37.

that skilled workers are ideal recruits for trade unions and that a high proportion of them are potentially active members, whereas the mass of interchangeable labourers, when they have a job, hesitate to get mixed up in trade union activities for fear of dismissal and the subsequent difficulty of finding work. Another point is that in developing countries the industrial workers are often employed in very small undertakings, which are anything but conducive to trade union organisation. In Japan, for instance, 42.1 per cent of workers are engaged in undertakings with less than 30 employees.

These economic peculiarities are compounded by social factors that make trade union recruitment and organisation even more difficult. To begin with, the workers have no real sense of commitment and so they aim at keeping a job just long enough, for instance, to constitute a dowry, or—encouraged by the demonstration effect—to indulge in conspicuous consumption, or else to pay off their taxes. This situation has often been found to exist, even in places such as Singapore where trade union membership is fairly high. [1] The reasons include the illiteracy of the workers, ignorance of their rights, and lack of familiarity with industrial life. [2] In fact, in spite of rapid union growth the

[1] W. E. Chalmers: *Crucial issues in industrial relations in Singapore* (Donald Moore Press, 1967), p. 68.

[2] ILO: *Some aspects of labour-management relations in Asia*, Labour-management relations series, No. 3 (Geneva, 1958), pp. 11-12; S. C. Sufrin: *Unions in emerging societies: Frustration and politics* (Syracuse, New York, Syracuse University Press, 1964), p. 59; Ross (ed.): *Industrial relations and economic development*, op. cit., p. 359.

greatest obstacle to unionism is the apathy of workers. [1] Paternalism would seem to be a necessary and inevitable concomitant of modern industrial development, [2] for a variety of reasons. It may prove to be essential in order to maintain a stable industrial labour force, as in India—where the Tata Iron and Steel Company had to build the city of Jamshedpur, with 250,000 inhabitants, from scratch [3]—or in Egypt—where paternalism does not, however, extend beyond the gates of the factory; [4] or it may be a manifestation of old historical traditions, as in Japan, [5] or, more simply, of the employers' determination to control if not to influence the labour movement.

A great deal has been made of the origins of trade union leaders, which are very rarely working class; they tend to come either from outside the occupation represented or from a country other than the underdeveloped country in which the movement operates. In most Asian countries (India, Indonesia, Malaysia, Pakistan, Sri Lanka) the leaders are frequently politicians from the liberal professions (teachers, lawyers, doctors, civil servants) who are looking for popular support. [6] Although perhaps to a lesser degree, the same situation has been noted in Africa [7] and in Latin America. [8] As far as the workers are concerned, this is both an advantage and a drawback: it is an advantage in so far as they have access to outside skills in circumstances in which the legal or administrative machinery of the State can be used only by trained experts, [9] or simply because the jargon employed by the government

[1] W. H. Knowles: "Industrial conflict and unions", in W. E. Moore and A. Feldman (eds.): *Labor commitment and social change in developing areas* (New York, Social Science Research Council, 1960), p. 305.

[2] W. Galenson (ed.): *Labor and economic development*, op. cit., p. 5.

[3] C. A. Myers: "India", ibid., p. 29.

[4] F. H. Harbison: "Egypt", ibid., p. 158.

[5] R. Scalapino: "Japan", ibid.

[6] B. H. Millen: *The political role of labor in developing countries* (Washington, Brookings Institution, 1963), pp. 27-32; C. A. Myers: *Labor problems in the industrialization of India*, op. cit., pp. 76-80; E. M. Kassalow: *National labor movements in the postwar world*, op. cit., pp. 236-238; N. F. Dufty: *Industrial relations in India* (Bombay, Allied Publishers, 1964), pp. 82-85. For all their similarity, however, the viewpoints expressed by these authors relate only to a particular level. "It has often been pointed out that union leadership in most of the Asian countries is in the hands of 'outsiders' or persons who have had no connection with industry or experience as an employee. While there are various reasons for this, it is largely true only for the higher-level organisations and the main national federations; the officials of plant-level unions are generally employees in the undertakings where their unions operate." (ILO: *Freedom of association for workers' and employers' organisations and their role in social and economic development*, op. cit., p. 5.)

[7] B. C. Roberts: *Labor in the tropical territories of the Commonwealth*, op. cit., pp. 133-134; B. H. Millen, op. cit., p. 28.

[8] W. H. Knowles: "The British West Indies", op. cit.; H. Landsberger: "The labor elite: Is it revolutionary?", in S. M. Lipset and A. Solari (eds.): *Elites in Latin America* (New York, Oxford University Press, 1967).

[9] The Indian system of industrial relations, which attaches increasing importance to wage boards and industrial tribunals, means that the labour movement must often employ

authorities or employers is intelligible only to a minority of "intellectuals"; [1] it is a drawback in so far as the concerns of the leaders may well be different from those of the rank and file they represent. This point was made very forcefully by the Director-General of the ILO:

> The trade union movements of many Asian countries, and some in Latin America and Africa, could never have achieved their present status without the assistance of "outsiders", intellectuals, politicians, lawyers and other persons inspired by varying motives, who are not and never have been workers in the economic sector covered by the trade union. Their assistance is indispensable to the trade union movement, especially in the initial stages, when very widespread illiteracy among the workers makes it difficult to recruit qualified leaders from their ranks.
>
> ... The predominance of outsiders in union leadership has, however, created difficulties. Outside leaders who secured their position for political purposes have been responsible for much harmful inter-union rivalry, sometimes sacrificing the workers' interests to those of the party to which they belong. Another type of leader can do still more damage, namely the one who is in the movement for his own personal ends and who takes advantage of the workers' unfamiliarity with trade unionism and industrial relations. [2]

The main drawbacks of a situation that is often not properly appreciated by the workers—who attach little importance to it—are the danger that these leaders may be drawn into the governmental orbit, [3] the lack of contact between leaders and rank and file, [4] the accumulation of trade union responsibilities, [5] the tendency for trade unions to be taken over by careerists, [6] union rivalry, [7] and so on.

---

specialists. (See the report on a seminar on trade unions and politics in India, in *Indian Journal of Industrial Relations*, Jan. 1968, p. 320.) The same is true of Pakistan.

[1] Just as union leaders need to have a thorough grasp of English in India (V. D. Kennedy: *Unions, employers and government: Essays on Indian labour questions* (Bombay, Manaktalas, 1966), p. 85) and in parts of Africa formerly under British administration (B. C. Roberts, op. cit., p. 138), in the parts of Africa formerly administered by France it is essential to know French, which is the language still used for public business.

[2] ILO: *Labour relations: Existing problems and prospects for the future*, Report of the Director-General, Part I, International Labour Conference, 45th Session, Geneva 1961, p. 88.

[3] P. Kilby: "Industrial relations and wage determination: Failure of the Anglo-Saxon model", in *Journal of Developing Areas*, July 1967, p. 510.

[4] S. Fockstedt: *Trade unions in developing countries*, lecture given on 20 June 1966 at the International Institute for Labour Studies, Geneva (doc. ILO/INST/L.S.17, p. 6).

[5] In India one leader was president of 17 unions and secretary of 2 more, another was an office bearer of 20 unions, and another was president of 30 or more unions (K. N. Subramanian: *Labour-management relations in India* (Bombay, Asia Publishing House, 1967), p. 513).

[6] Whereas before Independence "the trade union field was largely a field of dedicated service with little expectations of any return or reward in the form of remuneration, patronage or prestige, ... Independence threw open the flood-gates of opportunism and patronage" (Subramanian, op. cit., p. 524).

[7] "Trade unions and politics in India", op. cit., pp. 320-321. This kind of rivalry, which is partly attributable to the politisation of national trade union confederations, is particularly prevalent in Asia; at the time of writing, there were four national organisations in India, seven in Pakistan, seven in Sri Lanka and twelve in Indonesia. In Africa, although there were five organisations in Nigeria, elsewhere the tendency, encouraged by the public authorities, was towards the constitution of a single union movement.

The implications are all too clear. If the survival of the trade union movement is dependent on the existence of a sufficiently large working class, adequate financial resources, stability of employment and an ability to maintain an independent bargaining position, the unavoidable conclusion is that these conditions do not normally prevail in the developing countries. This has at least three sets of consequences.

In the first place, the labour movement is often very weak and the dominant form of organisation is the plant-level union or the general workers' union; craft unions are rare because of the shortage of skilled workers, and there are few industrial unions because they presuppose a degree of solidarity that is still rather unusual.

The trade union movement in a number of countries (for example, Ceylon [Sri Lanka], India, Indonesia, Pakistan and the Philippines) is characterised by a high degree of fragmentation—the existence of a great number of unions with small membership, most of which are organised at the plant or enterprise level. The majority of these plant-level unions are probably members of industry-wide, regional or national federations, but the ties between the federations and their affiliates tend to be very loose. [1]

The same is true of Africa [2] and of Latin America, where most unions are organised at the enterprise level. [3]

Secondly, the weakness of the unions is due not only to the forms of organisation but also to the membership. In Africa and Asia the membership fluctuates widely. [4] This is the outcome of the lack of industrial commitment referred to above, but also of a whole set of cultural and social factors, three of which are fundamental:

(1) A large part of the labour force has been uncommitted to permanent wage employment; migration has been a major feature of the supply and seasonal employment a characteristic of the demand, especially for agricultural labour.

(2) Acceptance of the notion of belonging to a union as an essential function of employment in the modern sector only becomes a social norm after a lengthy period of time. Many unions have not been in existence long enough for workers to develop a close and continuous attachment. A new generation brought up to regard unions as a vital social necessity may well not be inhibited by this factor.

(3) Union rivalries, corruption, opportunistic leadership and failure to achieve promised goals have all contributed to a fluctuating membership. [5]

---

[1] ILO: *Freedom of association for workers' and employers' organisations and their role in social and economic development*, op. cit., p. 4.

[2] M. F. Neufeld: *Poor countries and authoritarian rule*, Cornell International Industrial and Labor Relations Report No. 6 (Ithaca, New York, Cornell University Press, 1965), pp. 142-143.

[3] Vernengo: "Freedom of association and industrial relations in Latin America", op. cit.

[4] ILO: *Report on the visit of a joint team of experts on labour-management relations to Pakistan and Ceylon*, Labour-Management Relations Series, No. 10 (Geneva, 1961), p. 14; *African labour survey*, op. cit., Ch. VII.

[5] B. C. Roberts and L. Greyfié de Bellecombe: *Collective bargaining in African countries* (New York, St. Martin's Press, 1967), pp. 30-31.

Of course it would be wrong to use typically Western criteria to judge union membership, since the distinction between members (who pay their union dues) and union followers (who are influenced by some union) is very hard to draw in the developing countries, where loyalty towards the union is often just a matter of voting for the workshop delegates and supporting strike action. It has been observed, for example, that many Africans look upon themselves as members of a trade union even though they may not have paid any dues for a long time. [1] One of the consequences of this state of affairs is the limited financial resources of trade unions in many parts of Asia (Pakistan, [2] India [3]) and Africa (Tanzania, Nigeria [4]). This shortage of funds creates a kind of vicious circle:

> Most of the unions are so poorly financed that they cannot afford full-time officers and staff members—which in turn makes it even more difficult to collect dues. Efforts to build a skilled cadre of leaders or carry out any program leading to the building of cohesive organizations are greatly hampered. [5]

It is also a powerful inducement to look for other sources of financing, even though they may compromise the union's independence: "The general pattern is financial dependency upon outside sources—government, political parties, philanthropists, private businessmen, individual politicians, and foreign or international labor movements." [6]

Thirdly, the politicisation of trade unions is often thought to be endemic in developing countries. The "political union" has a number of specific characteristics: [7] direct concern of the union leaders with political operations and discussions, ideological motivations of the leadership, frequent use of direct mass action in support of non-industrial objectives, tendency to give an improvement in the standard of living of the members second place to the capturing of political power, use of propaganda rather than collective bargaining by leaders who do not personally belong to the category of workers whom the union represents. This political unionism, which typifies labour organisations in Asia and Africa, is a product of the environment in which they operate. [8]

[1] Roberts and Greyfié de Bellecombe: *Collective bargaining in African countries*, op. cit., pp. 30-31.

[2] Sufrin, op. cit., p. 59.

[3] Kennedy, op. cit., p. 96.

[4] T. Yesufu: *An introduction to industrial relations in Nigeria* (London, Oxford University Press, 1962), p. 66.

[5] Millen, op. cit., p. 23.

[6] ibid., p. 24.

[7] On some of these see Millen, op. cit., p. 9.

[8] ibid., p. 53. According to W. Galenson "so strong is the presumption that [a highly political form of unionism, with a radical ideology] will be the prevailing pattern that, where it is absent, we may draw the conclusion that unionism is, in fact, subordinated to the employer or to the State, i.e. that we are dealing either with company unionism or a labor front" (*Labor and economic development*, op. cit., p. 8).

During the struggle for national independence, unionism evolves as an integral part of the nationalist movement and thus maintains close links with the political parties involved. Once national independence is achieved, a whole series of factors help to prolong this state of affairs: the need to create new political structures (wherein unionism serves as a counterbalance to religious, caste, tribal or linguistic forces), the redefinition of objectives in the direction of social reform, and the creation of ideologies and devising of themes capable of mobilising the masses. [1] This politicisation of the union movement aggravates the weaknesses referred to above by adding inter-union rivalries deriving from political commitments.

Restriction of the right to strike

As already stated, by acting as the vehicle for worker protest, the trade unions are able to influence over-all supply. In the developing countries there are naturally any number of obstacles to their doing so; some of them have already been mentioned. Nevertheless, in the interests of the economic development of the nation for which they are responsible, certain governments will be tempted in addition to restrict freedom of association. This they can do in several ways. Restricting the right to strike is the most radical measure open to governments that wish to achieve the largest possible volume of national product. Regulations along these lines may be more or less stringent and range from total prohibition to prohibition in certain sectors only or, without actually denying the right to strike, the introduction of delaying procedures.

The strict prohibition of strikes may be either absolute or limited to a given period. Until recently, there was strict prohibition of strikes in Spain. [2] A general prohibition that is apt to place a serious limitation on the freedom of action of trade union organisations is considered to be incompatible with the principles that are normally recognised in respect of freedom of association.[3] The second kind of prohibition—which numerous governments have had occasion to introduce—concerns any form of strike action in exceptional circumstances, such as war, a change of government following a coup d'état or a state of national emergency or crisis. A general prohibition of strikes,

[1] "With respect to trade unions it would appear that prior to their political functioning in an independent state, their role was important in Utopia building. Unions assisted in providing a popular myth regarding freedom for the members of the 'ideal' society which would follow independence. Once independence was secured, however, the functions of the trade unions became ideological, in the sense that immediate activities were undertaken which were not directly concerned with the ultimate myth and the value structure, but rather directed towards immediate, day-to-day operations" (Sufrin, op. cit., p. 46).

[2] ILO: *The labour and trade union situation in Spain* (Geneva, 1969), p. 223.

[3] Governing Body Committee on Freedom of Association, 17th Report, Case No. 73, para. 72; 25th Report, Case No. 136, para. 176.

which is often combined with requisitioning measures, [1] is an important restriction of one of the essential means by which the workers and their organisations can promote and defend their occupational interests; it must therefore be imposed exclusively as a transitory measure if it is not to constitute a violation of international standards. It is also significant that such measures are frequently just one aspect of a general policy that places trade unions in an extremely awkward position.

This struggle between decision-making centres with conflicting interests is reflected at the international level in the great number of complaints examined by the Governing Body Committee on Freedom of Association at the request of employers' and workers' organisations whose circumstances and very existence may be jeopardised from one day to the next as a result of a coup d'état. The history of Latin America is full of such examples; to mention just one, after the military take-over of 24 November 1948 the Government of Venezuela suspended constitutional guarantees, closed trade union premises, froze trade union funds, imprisoned or expelled from the country the best-known leaders of the workers' movement and dissolved by administrative action the Venezuelan General Confederation of Labour and most of the federations and trade unions which were affiliated to it. [2]

More common than a general prohibition of strike action is its prohibition in respect of certain sectors only. This can take two forms which may have quite different implications.

First, the ban on strike action may be directed at the public service. [3] Here the situation varies widely from one country to another in at least three respects. To begin with the prevailing doctrine, the justification for denying the right to strike is based on arguments that may be legal (incompatibility of strike action with the exercise of the sovereign power of the State, the undertaking of members of the public service to be loyal to the government), economic (non-profit-making nature of state monopolies, essential nature of public services) or social (action detrimental to the public interest). The contrary view, while refuting each of these arguments, stresses above all the fundamental importance of equity (equality of all workers before the law and economic equality in terms both of working and living conditions and of the

[1] Committee on Freedom of Association, 30th Report, Case No. 172; 36th Report, Case No. 192; 41st Report, Case No. 199; 46th Report, Case No. 208; 56th Report, Case No. 233; 71st Report, Case No. 273; 75th Report, Case No. 353; 86th Report, Case No. 438; 93rd Report, Cases Nos. 470 and 481; 110th Report, Case No. 561.

[2] Committee on Freedom of Association, First Report, paras. 119-129; Sixth Report, paras. 945-953, ILO: *Freedom of association and conditions of work in Venezuela*, Studies and Reports, New Series, No. 21 (Geneva, 1950).

[3] ILO: *Freedom of association and procedures for staff participation in determining conditions of employment in the public service*, op. cit.

nature of the jobs; certain private services are in fact just as vital to the national economy as public services while, conversely, certain public services are far less essential than certain private services). This contrary view seems to be steadily gaining ground. Next, as regards the attitude of labour organisations to strikes in the public service, a major change seems to have taken place in the last few years: whereas most trade unions were until recently loath to claim the right to strike, and even included an undertaking not to strike in their by-laws, recent research [1] points to the appearance of new trends. These came to the fore at the international level during a conference of Asian public service unions held in Tokyo in October 1969, which adopted a resolution calling on governments to grant all public service employees all trade union rights, including the right to strike. Changing attitudes actually seem to have been overtaken by events, since the number of strikes of public service employees during the past ten years has risen sharply in all countries whether industrialised (Canada, France, United States [2]) or underdeveloped (Benin, Sri Lanka). Lastly, the legal situation with regard to a strike of public service employees can take four main forms:

(*a*) explicit recognition of the right to strike of public service employees (Benin, Guinea, Ivory Coast, Madagascar, Mexico, Niger, Senegal, Togo, Upper Volta);

(*b*) no distinction for strike purposes between the public sector and other sectors of the economy (United Republic of Cameroon, Ghana, Malaysia, Mauritania, Mauritius, Nigeria, Sierra Leone, Singapore, Sri Lanka);

(*c*) no legislation, implying either the tacit recognition of the right to strike (Chad, Congo, Israel) or, on the contrary, its tacit prohibition (Algeria, Gabon, Iran, Pakistan); or

(*d*) prohibition of strikes in the public service (Bolivia, Brazil, Colombia, Costa Rica, Greece, Guatemala, Honduras, Kuwait, Lebanon, Peru, Philippines, Syrian Arab Republic, Thailand, Venezuela).

Here again, just as the doctrine on the subject and the practice of the trade unions are apparently evolving, the legislation is changing too. In Japan, for example, public service unions have intensified their efforts to obtain the right to strike, particularly since the ratification by the Japanese Diet of Convention

[1] A. M. Ross: "Public employee unions and the right to strike", in *Monthly Labor Review*, Mar. 1969; R. Blanpain: *Public employee unionism in Belgium* (University of Michigan, Institute of Labor and Industrial Relations, 1971).

[2] In the United States between 1958 and 1968 the number of government employee strikes per year rose from 15 to 254 and the number of workers involved from 1,700 to 202,000; the man-days of idleness increased from 7,500 to 2.5 million (S. C. White: "Work stoppages of government employees", in *Monthly Labor Review*, Dec. 1969, p. 29).

No. 87 in 1965; at the time of writing the matter was being examined by the Diet, along with other aspects of industrial relations in the public sector. [1]

Developments in these three directions would thus indicate that, while the provisions of Article 9 of Convention No. 87—to the effect that the extent to which the guarantees provided for in the Convention shall apply to the armed forces and the police shall be determined by national laws or regulations—are still entirely applicable, the distinction between the right to organise and the right to strike [2] has, by contrast, nowadays become somewhat less relevant to the civil service.

The partial prohibition of strike action can also be directed at workers in what are considered to be essential services, who may or may not be regarded as public service employees according to the country. [3] The danger is that the concept of "essential service" will be overworked. Of course it is difficult to define its scope in advance but, at the same time, its definition can hardly be left in each case to the discretion of the government. In the absence of any more reliable criteria, the position adopted by the Committee on Freedom of Association would seem to be, if not the best, at least by far the most prudent. As regards specifically the requisitioning of workers in the event of a strike, the Committee considers that, although a stoppage in services or undertakings such as transport companies, railways, telecommunications or electricity might disturb the normal life of the community, it can hardly be admitted that the

---

[1] In 1966 the Supreme Court established a distinction between essential and non-essential services, whereby strike action that was not likely to endanger the public to a serious extent should be exempted from criminal prosecution. However, this criterion, which was adopted by several local courts, was abandoned in a subsequent decision of the Supreme Court on 25 April 1973 which reverted to the former principle that because they were the servants of society as a whole no public employees should be allowed to strike or to instigate strike action since existing compensation for denial of the right to strike was satisfactory and reasonable (K. Koshiro: *Wage determination in the national public service in Japan: Changes in prospects*, International Industrial Relations Association, Third World Congress, 3-7 September 1973, London, doc. 3C-73/Sect. V/1, summary).

[2] During the preparatory discussion of the Convention and in the light of the reservations that certain governments expressed with regard to the recognition of trade union rights for public service employees, the following observation was made: "It has been considered that it would be inequitable to draw any distinction, as regards freedom of association, between wage earners in private industry and officials in the public services, since persons in either category should be permitted to defend their interests by becoming organised, even if those interests are not always of the same kind. However, the recognition of the right of association of public servants in no way prejudges the question of the right of such officials to strike, which is something quite apart from the question under consideration." (ILO: *Freedom of association and industrial relations*, Report VII, International Labour Conference, 30th Session, Geneva, 1947, p. 109.)

[3] A German usage distinguishes between officials *(Beamten)* whose terms of service are governed by special regulations, and workers covered by collective agreements. However, the former sharp distinction between *Beamten* and workers is disappearing (T. Ramm: *Labour relations in the public sector in the Federal Republic of Germany*, International Industrial Relations Association, Third World Congress, 3-7 September, 1973, London, doc. 3C-73/Sect. V/6/R).

stoppage of such services is by definition such as to engender a state of acute national emergency. It therefore considers that the measures taken to mobilise workers at the time of disputes in services of this kind are such as to restrict the workers' right to strike as a means of defending their occupational and economic interests. [1] Nevertheless, a government may have to assume the responsibility of ensuring the maintenance of such services and, to this end, may consider it expedient to call in either persons from the armed forces to perform the duties which have been suspended as a result of the labour dispute,[2] or the requisitioned workers themselves, provided it is an essentially temporary measure and all other methods of settlement of the dispute provided by law have been exhausted. [3]

More generally, the Committee on Freedom of Association has stressed the importance which it attaches, whenever strikes in essential services (which should not be taken in too wide a sense) or in the civil service are forbidden, to ensuring adequate guarantees to safeguard to the full the interests of the workers thus deprived of an essential means of defending their occupational interests. It has also pointed out that the restrictions should be accompanied by adequate, impartial and speedy conciliation and arbitration procedures, in which the parties can take part in every stage and in which the awards are binding in all cases on both parties. These awards, once they have been made, should be fully and promptly implemented. [4]

The introduction of delaying procedures may also help to put off the outbreak of strikes. Requirements of advance notice of the intent to strike may be found in the national legislation of several countries; [5] elsewhere, strikes may be prohibited during a certain period, particularly during proceedings for the settlement of a dispute. In other countries the legislation contains requirements concerning a strike ballot or prior approval by the unions [6] or

---

[1] Committee on Freedom of Association, 93rd Report, Cases Nos. 470 and 481, paras. 274 and 275.

[2] Committee on Freedom of Association, 13th Report, Case No. 82, para. 112; 30th Report, Case No. 177, para. 83; 71st Report, Case No. 273, para. 73.

[3] Committee on Freedom of Association, 2nd Report, Case No. 31, para. 113.

[4] Committee on Freedom of Association, 110th Report, Case No. 519, para. 79; 112th Report, Case No. 385, para. 75; 108th Report, Cases Nos. 589 and 594, para. 60, and Case No. 573, para 194; 120th Report, Case No. 604, para. 150.

[5] In Malaysia, for example, regulations provide that no person shall go on strike in breach of contract *(a)* without giving to the employer notice of strike within six weeks before striking, or *(b)* within 14 days of giving such notice, or *(c)* before the expiry of the date of strike specified in any such notice (ILO: *Freedom of association and procedures for staff participation in determining conditions of employment in the public service*, op. cit., p. 90).

[6] In Mexico, in order to be lawful a strike must be decided by a two-thirds majority of the employees of the government agency concerned, and the unions must produce before a tribunal a statement of their demands together with a record of the meeting which decided on the strike (ibid., p. 91).

includes provisions regarding strike behaviour. [1] Similarly, to avoid strikes, several developing countries in Asia [2] and Africa [3] have adopted the principle of compulsory arbitration. In theory at least, arbitration should not be incompatible with the principle of the right to collective bargaining. [4] It remains to be seen, however, whether this procedure, like the others, is as effective as some people seem to hope in achieving the desired objective, that is, ensuring that trade union action does not reduce the total supply.

[1] In Madagascar and Malaysia any behaviour entailing violence, intimidation or molestation used with a view to compelling other persons to abstain from doing or to do any act may mar the legality of a strike and give rise to the imposition of criminal penalties (ILO: *Freedom of association and procedures for staff participation in determining conditions of employment in the public service*, op. cit., p. 91).

[2] Several countries have legislation whereby the authorities, on their own motion, may refer any dispute to adjudication by arbitration court or tribunal if the parties fail to reach an agreement during the negotiation and conciliation proceedings. This is the case, in particular, in India, Malaysia, Singapore and Sri Lanka. In Pakistan the authorities may refer a dispute to compulsory arbitration if the strike has lasted more than 30 days. Legislation in some countries also provides for compulsory arbitration and strike prohibition in certain special circumstances. This is the case in Indonesia when a dispute may endanger public or state interests, and in the Philippines if the dispute takes place in an industry considered by the President of the Republic as being indispensable to the national interest (ILO: *Freedom of association for workers' and employers' organisations and their role in social and economic development*, op. cit., p. 32).

[3] Ghana in 1958 and Tanzania in 1962 extended to all sectors of employment the system formerly applicable only to the designated essential services. Strikes and lockouts may now take place only after the competent authorities have been notified that a dispute exists and a certain interval has elapsed without their taking steps to refer the dispute to arbitration. In Sudan and Ethiopia, where strikes unrelated to disputes about the terms and conditions of employment are illegal, any dispute may be referred to an arbitration tribunal by the Minister concerned without the consent of the parties. The right of the parties to refuse to accept an arbitrated award has been maintained in the Central African Republic, Guinea, Niger and Madagascar, whereas Gabon, the Ivory Coast, Mali, Mauritania, Senegal and Upper Volta have adopted measures allowing the Minister to have disputes settled by arbitration when he feels that a strike or lockout would prejudice public order and be contrary to the general interest (Roberts and Greyfié de Bellecombe, op. cit., pp. 65-67, 75).

[4] At a conference on industrial relations which was held in Tokyo in 1967, the Chief of the Labour Law and Labour Relations Branch of the ILO, J. de Givry, stated: "There has perhaps been too great a tendency in the past to distinguish systematically between collective bargaining based on free discussion by the parties with possible recourse to the strike weapon and the system of compulsory arbitration, under which an arbitrator or arbitration court makes the decision, and to consider these two methods to be incompatible. It seems that in many developing countries there has been a willingness to promote the development of collective bargaining while at the same time provision is made as a last resort for a procedure of orderly and impartial arbitration aimed at avoiding disputes which might jeopardise economic development." (Japan Institute of Labour: *Labor relations in the Asian countries*, Proceedings of the Second International Conference on Industrial Relations, Tokyo, Japan, 1967, pp. 41-42.) Similarly, Roberts and Greyfié de Bellecombe consider that "it is fair to say that while the trend in the English-speaking and non-English-speaking countries is in the direction of greater regulation and more government interference in connection with the exercise of the right to strike there is still a good deal of room for voluntary discussion and the autonomous negotiation of agreements" (op. cit., p. xvi).

Effectiveness of restrictions

The effectiveness of government efforts to restrict the right to strike is perhaps not very great, as the following examples will show.

To take first of all the most radical measure, namely the pure and simple prohibition of any strike, it is quite obvious that the legislation in Spain, to which reference has already been made, did not prevent strikes from occurring. Before 1967 the number of workers involved in disputes was not published. In 1967, however, 192,135 workers took part in total work stoppages, and 148,379 in partial stoppages. More significant, since strikes are only one of innumerable ways of expressing worker discontent, is the fact that over the years there had been a sharp increase in manifestations of extreme discontent in the form of total or partial stoppages (see table 13).

Moving on to less radical measures, such as the prohibition of the right to strike for certain categories of workers, it stands out that the least respected regulations are probably those that are widest in scope. An unduly extensive definition of the category of "public service employees" seems to be incompatible with the provisions of Convention No. 98; [1] the list of so-called "essential" services loses all credibility once it becomes too long, [2] and its

[1] In 1973 the ILO's Committee of Experts on the Application of Conventions and Recommendations stated: "With regard to public servants, who are covered without any distiction by Convention No. 87, Article 6 of Convention No. 98 establishes that the Convention does not deal with the position of public servants engaged in the administration of the State, nor shall it be construed as prejudicing their rights or status in any way. The Committee has expressed the view that, while the concept of public servant may vary to some degree under the various national legal systems, the exclusion from the scope of the Convention of persons employed by the State or in the public sector, but who do not act as agents of the public authority (even though they may be given a status identical with that of public officials engaged in the administration of the State) is contrary to the meaning of the Convention. The Committee considered that this is made even clearer in the English text of Article 6 of the Convention, which permits the exclusion solely of public servants 'engaged in the administration of the State'. In the opinion of the Committee one could not admit the exclusion from the terms of the Convention of important categories of workers employed by the State merely on the grounds that they are formally assimilated to public officials engaged in the administration of the State. If this were the case, the Convention might be deprived of much of its scope. The distinction to be drawn, therefore, according to the Committee, would appear to be, basically, between civil servants employed in various capacities in government ministries or comparable bodies, that is, public servants who by their functions are directly engaged in the administration of the State as well as lower-ranking officials who act as supporting elements in these activities, and other persons employed by the government, by public undertakings or by autonomous public institutions." (ILO: *Freedom of association and collective bargaining*, op. cit., p. 61.)

[2] In Indonesia, for example, the denial of the right to strike applies to plantations, the petroleum industry and airlines. Similarly, in its examination of a complaint relating to India, the Committee on Freedom of Association noted the fact that the legislation established a list of government services in which strikes were prohibited and which included such activities as dock work, aircraft repairs and all transport services, and that the Government was also authorised to extend the list (118th Report, Cases Nos. 589 and 593, para. 91). In Pakistan the trade unions protested that, although the authorities had ratified Conventions Nos. 87 and 98, the Industrial Disputes Ordinance, 1959, gave public utilities such a wide definition that it was tantamount to denying the unions the right to strike altogether.

Table 13. Spain: Most frequent manifestations of worker discontent, 1963-67

Year	Form of action	Number of disputes	Percentage of the total number of disputes
1963	Tension	354	32
	Total stoppage	241	21.9
	Go-slow	141	12.8
	Claims to the Trade Union Organisation	111	10
1964	Total stoppage	126	23.8
	Go-slow	73	13.8
	Dialogue	61	11.5
	Tension	57	10.8
1965	Partial stoppage	82	34.1
	Total stoppage	68	28.3
	Go-slow	46	19
	Tension	20	8.3
1966	Total stoppage	69	36.1
	Go-slow	39	20.4
	Partial stoppage	39	20.4
	Tension	18	9.4
1967	Partial stoppage	273	48.2
	Total stoppage	240	42.4
	Tension	19	3.3
	Go-slow	16	2.8

Source: ILO: *The labour and trade union situation in Spain*, op. cit., p. 227.

extension is apt to give rise to international difficulties. [1] Moreover the fact is that walk-outs of public servants have been frequent in countries where strikes are prohibited and comparatively rare in countries which have explicitly granted the right to strike. [2] It therefore seems advisable to limit strictly the use of such measures, restricting them to certain clearly defined categories, [3] perhaps even to certain specific jobs. [4]

As regards delaying methods, their purpose is presumably less to prevent strike action than to regulate the form such action takes; their economic effectiveness, however, is open to discussion. On the one hand, it is undeniable

[1] Protest from the British Trades Union Congress and the International Confederation of Free Trade Unions against the tendency in Tanganyika and Kenya to extend the concept of essential services led to a reversal of that policy (Roberts and Greyfié de Bellecombe, op. cit., p. 61, footnote).

[2] ILO: *Freedom of association and procedures for staff participation in determining conditions of employment in the public service*, op. cit., p. 82.

[3] The legislation of Chad, Mauritius, Mexico and Nigeria prohibits strike action by members of the armed forces and police. In Madagascar, Malaysia and Uganda firemen are prevented from striking; in Mexico certain categories of prison and security officers as well as magistrates and the personnel in charge of communication in the Ministry of the Interior are also prohibited from striking (ibid., pp. 89-90).

[4] In Mexico the law of 28 December 1963 denies the right to strike to certain responsible officials *(trabajadores de confianza)* while in Madagascar the same exclusion applies to all officials vested with authority or discretionary power (ibid., pp. 88-90).

that such measures are not all as contrary to the interests of the worker as they might at first appear. In Africa, for example:

> It is true that the limitations on the right to strike have not aroused the hostility of the unions that might be expected. This in part is because not all awards have been favourable to the employers, and arbitrators have sometimes fixed wages at levels that it would have been hard for the unions to obtain, given the relative strength of the parties, by free bargaining and even strike action. Moreover, many union leaders are thankful to be relieved of the responsibility of calling for strike action which might well end in disaster. [1]

Similarly in India, where trade unions are weak, they are easily persuaded that they stand a better chance of gaining some of their demands from a tribunal than through bargaining. [2] By and large, whenever trade unions are weak they tend to prefer arbitration, as a way of substituting political power for the economic power that they lack. [3] In certain cases—in Pakistan for example—compulsory arbitration may even represent a second line of defence when strike action has failed to produce results. [4] On the other hand, compulsory arbitration may have a negative effect on the promotion of a system of industrial relations, since it accentuates tensions and animosities and, because of the cumbersome legal process and heavy financial burden it imposes, aggravates the climate of social antagonism. [5] Not only does the use of arbitration as a substitute for bargaining hinder the development of industrial relations,[6] it also runs the risk of provoking offshoots of worker discontent which may ultimately be more costly than a strike[7] and of hardening opposition to the government.[8]

---

[1] Roberts and Greyfié de Bellecombe, op. cit., p. 67.

[2] Kennedy, op. cit., pp. 110.

[3] Millen, op. cit., pp. 75.

[4] M. A. Raza: "Aspects of public labour policy in Pakistan", *British Journal of Industrial Relations*, July 1967, p. 207.

[5] S. D. Punekar: "Aspects of State intervention in industrial relations in India: An evaluation", in Ross (ed.): *Industrial relations and economic development*, op. cit., p. 37.

[6] Kennedy, op. cit., p. 110.

[7] The experience of the Tata Iron and Steel Company in India is illuminating: "It is widely felt that, given the present state of labor-management relations, free collective bargaining will necessarily be characterized by widespread strikes and conflict before mature bargaining relationships can evolve. It has been argued that an underdeveloped economy cannot pay the price of such industrial idleness. The inference has therefore been drawn that compulsory adjudication is preferable. However, we must consider the other side of the picture. The Tata story, by illustrating the willingness and the capacity of the workers to strike, even against the clear opposition of the formal authority of law and government, has demonstrated once again that there can be bitter industrial disputes even under a system of compulsory adjudication. But this is by no means a full measure of the 'cost' of compulsory adjudication, even as the man-days lost are not a full measure of the 'loss' incurred in the Tata strike. We should know further what 'loss' to the economy results from the frustration and suppressed discontent of the workers. We should consider the cathartic value of protest." (S. Kannappan: "The Tata steel strike: Some dilemmas of industrial relations in a developing economy", in *Journal of Political Economy*, Oct. 1959, p. 505.)

[8] State intervention in the labour dispute may draw upon the government all the hostility that may develop in an industrial environment. Moreover, in the context of a divided labour

To sum up, it may be easy enough to understand why governments, in the interests of economic development, try to limit the potential impact of trade union action on total supply,[1] but one cannot help wondering just how appropriate the various approaches to the problem of labour and unionism are in developing countries, especially that which implicitly underlies the analyses and regulatory procedures referred to above. Three different hypotheses have been suggested: the first (that of Kerr, Dunlop, Harbison and Myers), sees labour only as one of the components of a vaster system of industrialisation in which the nature of the governing élite plays the fundamental role; the second (Millen, Sufrin) looks at trade unionism essentially through its relationship with political parties, which usually take the form of participation in nationalist movements before independence and disputes with nationalist leaders after independence; the third (de Schweinitz, Mehta) judges trade unions in the light of the strikes they call, the wage claims they submit, and the contribution they make to industrial discipline. Another possible approach[2] sees the trade unions as regulating disputes,[3] by giving them an explicit form and by taking account of the long-term interests of their members, and therefore as holding in check the tensions that inevitably arise in a process of industrialisation; if they do not do so, it is because of the other parties' failure to recognise the legitimacy of their position or because there are no facilities for dialogue.

If, for present purposes, this last approach is regarded as correct, some important conclusions can be drawn:

A more complete range of legal repressive weaponry seems unlikely to bring about a restriction of the exercise of the right to strike. The latter is so fundamental that there can be no question of repressing it or denying it; instead it must be reassessed

movement, compulsory adjudication may accentuate the feeling that the public authorities favour one group as against another (ibid.).

[1] "In developing countries where major collective disputes such as strikes may present particularly serious thereats to the economy, there tends to be a desire from governments to intervene in the event of failure of negotiation and conciliation. Fears that such disputes may be used for political ends also play a strong part. Government intervention in dispute settlement is further explained by the need to protect the public interest and by the increasing economic role of the State as the main employer. The requirements of development planning which may be jeopardised by large-scale disputes is often given as another reason. Collective disputes, because of their implications for the economy and because of the number of workers involved, are likely to attract a good deal of public attention." (ILO: *Report of the Seminar on the Role of Workers' and Employers' Organisations in Economic and Social Development in Africa*, op. cit., p. 56.)

[2] R. H. Bates: "Approaches to the study of unions and development", in *Industrial Relations* (Berkeley), Oct. 1970, p. 371.

[3] R. Dahrendorf, who defends this concept, states that effective conflict regulation presupposes the presence of at least three factors: both parties to a conflict have to recognise the necessity and the reality of the conflict situation and, in this sense, the fundamental justice of the cause of the opponent; the interest groups must be organised; and, finally, the opposing parties in social conflict have to agree on certain formal rules of the game that provide the framework of their relations (*Class and class conflict in industrial society* (London, Routledge and Kegan Paul; Stanford, California, Stanford University Press; 1959), pp. 225-226).

and given greater meaning. Far from penalising the exercise of the constitutional right to strike, this right must be re-examined so that it can be given its proper place in modern industrial relations, bearing in mind that these relations require that this right, more than any other, should be exercised—inasmuch as it is a means of expression and such means are becoming increasingly rare. The problem does not stem from the right to strike; what is perhaps more serious, more disturbing, is that the problem has to do with the whole framework of labour-management relations and requires each one of us to forget such considerations as immediate feasibility so as to devise a model of industrial relations for the future, even though this may mean looking beyond existing or currently possible systems; accordingly no descriptive approach can suffice. [1]

DEMAND

As has been pointed out—

In emerging lands government is the political substitute for the economic market, providing mechanisms of wage and hour determination, and making decisions based on criteria different from those which guide the operation of the economic markets of the Western world. . . . Thus, collective bargaining plays a lesser role in the new societies than in the old, but politics play a greater role, even though the effectiveness of new governments may be limited. [2]

Objectives of wage policy in the developing countries

Numerous observers have noted [3] that wages are regulated by the government in a great many developing countries. Such government intervention in wage determination is of course attributable to the weakness of the trade unions, and to that extent it is a substitute for faulty labour market machinery. However, it seems to a far greater extent to be the outcome of a determination not to be the slave of market mechanisms but rather, in the interests of economic growth, to act in their stead.

The wage system has been said to have three basic functions: [4]

(a) to guarantee the best possible distribution of income among wages, profits and government resources;

(b) to help to increase the productivity of labour; and

(c) to encourage the redeployment of labour to sectors of the economy—usually high productivity sectors—in which demand for labour is on the increase.

---

[1] Translation of a passage from J. C. Jardillier: "La partie 'obligatoire' de la convention collective", in *Droit social* (Paris), Apr. 1971, p. 264.

[2] Sufrin, op. cit., pp. 29-30.

[3] Millen, op. cit., p. 76; Turner, op. cit., p. 47; N. N. Franklin: "Minimum wage fixing and economic development", in A. D. Smith (ed.): *Wage policy issues in economic development* (London, Macmillan, 1969).

[4] A. C. Reynolds: "Objectives of wage policy in developing countries", in A. D. Smith (ed.), op. cit.

Obviously, therefore, wages play a vital role in any development policy. However, as only one of the forms of income, wages cannot be considered in isolation from the remuneration of other factors of production; and the requirements of social justice create a link between the generation of income and its distribution. The conclusions reached by a meeting of experts convened by the ILO Governing Body in September and October 1967 to study the determination of minimum wages and related problems, with special reference to developing countries, are as relevant today as they were then:

> Because of the extent of poverty the overriding need in these countries is economic development. The mass of the labour force has no hope of getting well paid jobs unless and until much more advanced stages of development have been reached. On the other hand, moves towards a more equal distribution of income normally accompany economic development, and there is good reason to believe that without such moves development will prove of little significance to the worker and will sooner or later be held up. It follows from the above that in developing countries minimum wage fixing has to be seen as one of a battery of measures in the strategy of an attack on poverty, its major objective. These can be considered under two headings, both of which are designed to achieve this fundamental objective: measures to accelerate development and measures to change the distribution of income. [1]

The fact is that, although the first objective is always incorporated in the wage policies of developing countries, the second usually appears only in a very special form.

One of the objectives of the income policies of developing countries is to determine the role of wages in economic development. This point has already been raised in connection with de Schweinitz's thesis. It can be summed up as follows:

> Unions and their leaders have to choose or compromise between the short-term interests of the workers—e.g. a wage raise which will permit an increase in consumption—and their long-term ones—e.g. the accumulation of capital which will permit, for instance, the development of vocational training schemes. . . . Unions have to consider that a wage policy has an effect on consumption, on prices, on investments and also on the attitude of the workers towards economic growth and nation-building.[2]

—or again as follows:

> On the one hand, the demand for consumer goods which workers badly lack and for better living conditions are difficult for trade unions to ward off over long periods of time without risking alienation of their members. On the other hand, the precariousness of the economic situation in most developing countries seems to require curtailing of trade union demands focused on immediate wage gains. What are trade unions to do in these circumstances? [3]

---

[1] ILO: *Minimum wage-fixing and economic development*, Studies and Reports, New Series, No. 72 (Geneva, 1968), pp. 148-149.

[2] ILO, Asian Seminar on the Role of Trade Unions in Development Planning, Delhi, 30 September-11 October 1968: *Working paper*, doc. WED/S.9/D.2, pp. 3-4.

[3] ILO: *Report of the Seminar on the Role of Workers' and Employers' Organisations in Economic and Social Development in Africa*, op. cit., p. 58.

In a desire, somehow or other, to strike a balance which satisfies both the requirements of the economic planner and the minimum demands of the industrial worker, [1] several arguments have been advanced to justify wage controls. It is said, for instance, that high wages have four negative effects on economic development: [2]

(a) they cause government services and government capital expenditures to contract as a result of the pressure that they exert on the public treasury in countries where a high proportion of the labour force is employed by the government, which, in Africa for example, pays between 25 and 60 per cent of the total wage bill;

(b) they reduce the volume of employment or slow its growth in four ways: (i) unskilled labour becomes more expensive and employers seek to economise in its use; (ii) the change in relative prices makes it worth while to substitute machines for men; (iii) some firms find it impossible to pay the higher wage rates and are forced out of business; (iv) some potential enterprises, particularly in agriculture, never get started;

(c) they increase pressure on the balance of payments by increasing the demand for imports or, because of the consequent rise of national prices, by reducing exports; and

(d) they prevent the expansion of the agricultural sector by introducing a redistribution of income in favour of wage earners and at the expense of the rural population, owing both to the increase in taxes that they lead to and the change in relative prices that they bring about.

The conclusions to be drawn from this kind of analysis are obvious: in developing countries the steady advance of wages must be curtailed in order to promote economic development.

The additional argument is sometimes heard that, where real wages in developed countries have risen roughly in proportion with average national productivity, in the developing countries they have increased faster than the product per head, which suggests, for example, that almost the whole benefit of economic development during the 1950s was transferred to African wage earners [3] and that, by widening the gap between town and country, these wage increases accelerate rural-urban migration. [4]

It is generally, and sometimes wrongly, believed that the wage increases obtained by union members in the modern sector, which in developing countries

---

[1] Galenson (ed.): *Labor and economic development*, op. cit., p. 14.

[2] Berg: "Major issues of wage policy in Africa", op. cit., pp. 200-205.

[3] Turner, op. cit., pp. 13-14.

[4] Kilby, op. cit., p. 500.

is also very often the urban sector, are indirectly responsible for economic distortions as a result of the pull that they exercise on the economic system; hence the rural-urban migration which widens the gap between town and country and leads to substantial urban unemployment. Although this line of reasoning may seem eminently logical and although it was used, for example, by Arthur Lewis [1] to develop his well known model that was subsequently taken up by Fei and Ranis, [2] its basis in fact is perhaps less sound, because rural migration tends to be much more the result of a push from the countryside.

> . . . In the developing world, . . . the urban explosion is much less attributable to the attraction of jobs and high living standards in the cities. Most cities in the developing world do not have the industrial base with which to provide a sufficient number of new jobs to absorb the rural immigrants. Nor do they have the resources needed for urban housing, services, infrastructure, administration and social security. People seek the towns, despite the little that they offer, because they are fleeing the countryside. The crux of the problem is the generally primitive state of the rural economy: an archaic social structure; highly inequitable systems of land tenure; and, in many countries, the pressure of a rapidly growing population on the land. [3]

An initial justification for a wage policy in the developing countries can thus be found in the requirements of economic development; a second justification is to be found in the requirements of social justice. The view is frequently shared by political leaders in developing countries, particularly in Africa, that "urban wage earners, and particularly unionised groups, must not be allowed to extend their already advantageous position relative to the rural population".[4]

---

[1] Lewis: "Economic development with unlimited supplies of labour", op. cit.

[2] Fei and Ranis: *Development of the labour surplus economy: Theory and policy*, op. cit.

[3] ILO: *Freedom by dialogue: Economic development by social progress*, op. cit., p. 16.

[4] Kassalow: "Trade unionism and the development process in the new nations: A comparative view", op. cit., p. 72. It is true that the author goes on to say: "Whether this policy of holding stable or reducing the income gap between favored urban or modern sector workers and those in the rural, traditional areas is consonant with effective development policy is at least debatable; but it is prevalent, and it heightens social tensions in Africa." This point was also raised in the working document prepared by the ILO for a seminar held in Addis Ababa in December 1968: "The urban African wage earners' position as a 'privileged minority' in relation to the lower income and lack of facilities and amenities on the part of the majority of the rural wage earners and smallholders is also frequently raised, often without due consideration of the extra cost of living in towns and the easy access of the rural population to basic foodstuffs. African trade unions are therefore under great pressure to curtail their rights to wage demands—even when considered justified—in return for obtaining other rights such as a guaranteed participation in tripartite policy-making in economic and social matters. Yet experience shows that mere acceptance of wage restraint and even support of government policies by trade unions cannot by themselves allay tensions and crises arising out of the rank-and-file's discontent with wage levels. Members' understanding and acceptance of union policies of restraint may require long educational efforts and some visible improvement of living standards by gaining their members certain material advantages such as provision of social services and fringe benefits such as paid holidays, housing, food and health services of various kinds." (*Report of the Seminar on the Role of Workers' and Employers' Organisations in Economic and Social Development in Africa*, op. cit., p. 59.)

Sometimes referring to certain statistical data,[1] but more often than not using purely qualitative criteria, it is argued that the main objective of a wage policy in developing countries should be to bring about a more equitable distribution of the benefits of growth. This argument is sometimes amplified as follows:

Several of these problems are difficult to handle because those who are the "haves" are articulate, relatively powerful and often well enough organised to present their case forcefully. Too often they get more and the "have-nots" get less. The worker who is employed in the monetary economy in Kenya is a fortunate person. He has a wage; he has the provident fund; there is a health centre in his area; his union may organise and present his views. On the other hand the "have-nots" in society normally are not well organised and must rely on the Government or the political parties to represent their interests. For example, high wages in urban areas are fine for the employed union members, but the Government must bear in mind that the person who is unemployed has to pay the same prices as are paid by those fortunate enough to be employed. Indeed, at times, increases in wages in marginal industries may force business firms to lay off workers or induce them to mechanise to the detriment of those still seeking employment.[2]

Whether the argument put forward is that of economic development or that of social justice, the fact remains that numerous plans in developing countries contain provisions relating to a price and wage policy. In Asia, for instance, this is the case in Afghanistan where "it is stipulated that continuous review will be made of the level of wages and of prices to maintain an appropriate balance", in India where "the main emphasis in price policy should be to ensure that a spiralling of costs, prices and money incomes through mutual interaction is avoided", in the Republic of Korea where "price stability will help to ensure that real wages reflect rising labour productivity", in Pakistan where "in the name of economic justice the Government will have to intervene with a policy of industrial wages" by establishing minimum wages and by implementing an incomes policy based above all on increasing productivity.[3]

Of course, if one's view of the link between trade union action and economic development is based on the assumption that the higher wages slow down the accumulation of capital, this gives undue importance to a causal relationship

[1] Kilby, op. cit., p. 500, gives the following figures for Nigeria:

Year	Urban real wages				Per capita gross domestic product
	Lagos	Ibadan	Enugu	Kaduna	
1953	100	100	100	100	100
1965	146	185	164	159	117

[2] T. J. M'boya: "Incomes policies for developing countries?", in *Bulletin* (Geneva, International Institute for Labour Studies), Nov. 1967, pp. 5-6.

[3] ILO, Asian Seminar on the Role of Trade Unions in Development Planning, Delhi, 30 September-11 October 1968: *The contents of a plan*, doc. WED/S.9/D3, pp. 29-35.

which has in any case been found to be highly debatable. On the other hand, if trade union action leads to a more equitable distribution of income, far from being an evil, this may be a positive advantage—a point which has not passed unnoticed:

> The more equal enjoyment of the good things of life is first and foremost a question of social justice and, indeed, of common morality, but it also has an important economic aspect. To the extent that raising the income levels of the disadvantaged masses of the population can lead to improvements in human productive capacity and thus to increased productivity, to an enlargement of national markets and to a positive change in the structure of demand, it is a valid contribution to the process of economic modernisation. Distortions in income distribution hinder development. Economic growth makes possible higher incomes, and to sacrifice growth to other considerations would be self-defeating; but a policy geared exclusively to economic growth which did not ensure a more equitable distribution of its fruits and the protection of vulnerable and disadvantaged social groups would also fail to make its full contribution to the development process. [1]

Means of implementing a wage policy

There are several ways of bringing about a more equitable distribution of income. First of all, a minimum can be fixed below which remuneration for work cannot drop, irrespective of market anomalies. This is the idea behind minimum wage legislation, which has been influenced by the Minimum Wage-Fixing Machinery Convention of 1928 (No. 26), the Minimum Wage Fixing Machinery (Agriculture) Convention (No. 99) and Recommendation (No. 89) of 1951, and the Minimum Wage Fixing Convention (No. 131) and Recommendation (No. 135) of 1970. Minimum wage policies usually have four objectives: [2]

(a) to eliminate the "sweating of labour" through very low wages and bad conditions of employment generally that take advantage of the relatively weak bargaining position of unorganised labour; comparison with the wages paid to workers carrying out similar tasks could serve as an approximate criterion;

(b) to exert upward pressure on the general wage level itself; [3]

(c) to eliminate unfair competition by establishing a set of minimum standards for entrepreneurs; and

---

[1] ILO: *Freedom by dialogue: Economic development by social progress*, op. cit., p. 10. The same points are made forcefully in the International Development Strategy which was unanimously approved by the United Nations General Assembly on 24 October 1970 and is quoted on pp. 4, 21-22 and 25-26 above.

[2] ILO: *Minimum wage-fixing and economic development*, op. cit., pp. 5-9.

[3] This was no doubt the underlying purpose of minimum wage legislation in Argentina in 1964. See A. R. Campañó: "The Minimum Wage Act in Argentina", in *International Labour Review*, Sep. 1966.

(d) to ensure rapid growth and equitable distribution of national income, while bearing in mind the other objectives of the economic development policy, some of which may be in conflict with such an objective.

The implications of this kind of policy are complex. Any attempt to bring lower wage rates up to the average tends to raise not only the average level itself but also the median, in view of the resistance against any attempt to reduce wage differentials. [1] The result is that total remuneration will tend to follow fairly closely the trend of minimum wages. This is particularly true if the number of workers earning the minimum rate is very high, as seems to be the case in many developing countries, particularly in Africa. On the other hand, although minimum wage fixing may push up prices by increasing the cost of production, it may also bring about improvements in productivity

---

[1] This process is not peculiar to the developing countries. The way in which it operates has been very clearly explained by Y. Gaillard and G. Thuillier in a text which, for all its length, is well worth translating here in full: "The ritual of union claims is always the same. It begins with loud protestations of inferiority, backed up by reference to conditions in similar occupations. From then on it is a question of tactics. If the discussion is about financial aspects, nothing is said of the bonuses and perquisites that go with them (coal for the miners, cut-price electricity for employees of the state electricity corporation, free annual trips for employees of Air France). If it is a question of [other aspects], then all the talk is about career development and promotion problems, while security of employment, for instance, is entirely glossed over. Experience of such confrontations has given rise to a whole routine in which the initiated are well versed: at whatever level, the emphasis is on the least privileged, even when their existence is only theoretical (the civil servant at base 100); a specific bonus negotiated on a confidential basis is subsequently extended step by step to other workers as a result of contamination and 'leaks'; and above all, intermediate scales and 'special grades' are created, or else whole grades are merged. Over a long period a kind of sinusoidal progression can be discerned: at one moment, the bargaining is all about the lower echelons—which are granted special benefits—and then, as a result of the closing of differentials and the disappearance of relative advantages, these benefits are taken to be part and parcel of the basic wage or salary. At another moment, the wage or salary spread is opened at the top by the creation—for the 'best' employees—of new grades which subsequently give rise to a general upward movement. It is significant that priority in this pendular motion is given sometimes to financial factors and sometimes to non-financial factors (professional qualifications, career prospects, even the possibility of reorganising a government department or carrying out administrative reforms). In the private sector methods are by and large much the same as in the public sector, but because of the complexity of the occupational structure they are particularly varied: the levelling process as regards benefits often takes place from one workshop to another in the same factory, or from one branch to another in the same company. As often as not, collective agreements merely make official and generalise more or less under-the-counter practices that a shortage of manpower, for example, or widespread membership of a trade union, had brought into being. Sometimes the unions bring pressure to bear on rapidly expanding enterprises which are best able to meet the demand of the moment; at others, they tackle a firm that is the weakest in a particular trade and would be incapable of withstanding a strike. The fact is that the collective agreements and plant agreements that evolve from these two forms of bargaining contain clauses relating not only to wages but also to related factors such as promotion, training and career development facilities, even scholarships for children. The most important component, however—and one which is closely bound up with the wage—is grading. It is through the latter that hidden increases in income are introduced—special brackets for the exceptionally highly qualified, shifts in grading, intermediate scales and so on." ("Pour une approche psychologique de la politique des revenus", in *Droit social*, Apr. 1965, p. 219).

which can more or less offset the higher production costs—improvements deriving from a corresponding improvement in the physical capacity of the workers [1] or from the fact that they may work harder. [2] Against these positive effects, however, there may be negative repercussions on the capacity and motivation of other groups of the population—workers who lose their jobs, rural communities that have to pay higher taxes, and so on. As to the effects on employment, one would have to take account of so many variables and possible variations in particular cases that the combinations and permutations of adjustment may seem almost limitless. [3]

However, there is no getting away from the fact that a great many countries use minimum wage fixing as an instrument of policy. [4] The Asian and African countries that follow the British pattern use industry or regional wage boards whose recommendations, although not binding, are very widely observed by management and labour. In countries following the French pattern, particularly in equatorial Africa, a joint commission may be consulted

[1] According to Berg, the underlying hypotheses are "(1) that the wage earner's poor physical condition is due mainly to improper diet and living conditions in wage employment; (2) that increases in wage income will be spent on more nutritious food and other items which directly affect the physical capacity to produce; (3) that better health will increase individual effort and effectiveness which will mean significantly greater output per worker" ("Major issues of wage policy in Africa", op. cit., p. 190). However, he considers that there is little chance that all these conditions will be met in underdeveloped countries and that there are in any case other ways of improving the state of health than through wage policies. See also ILO: *Minimum wage-fixing and economic development*, op. cit., p. 30.

[2] Very substantial improvements in productivity would seem to have resulted from the fixing of minimum wages in Puerto Rico, Mauritius and Tanzania (ILO: *Minimum wage-fixing and economic development*, op. cit., p. 32).

[3] R. A. Lester: "Economic adjustments to changes in wage differentials", in G. W. Taylor and F. C. Pierson: *New concepts in wage determination* (New York, McGraw-Hill, 1957), p. 220. The most that can be said is that "possible management responses to higher wages are many and diverse, and in some situations adverse effects on employment may be weak or absent, but normally some adverse effect on employment is to be expected except in three sets of conditions: *(a)* if higher wages increase the marginal productivity of a group of workers of a given size by an amount equal to or exceeding the wage increase; *(b)* if there is no effective competition among employers for the services of workers and wages are below the levels that competition would establish; *(c)* if there is general surplus capacity that could be brought into employment by action to raise aggregate demand, coupled with a situation in which the payment of higher wages will increase aggregate demand and not merely transfer purchasing power among different groups. On the whole these conditions appear to be rather exceptional in developing countries." (ILO: *Minimum wage-fixing and economic development*, op. cit., pp. 137-138.)

[4] The effect of this on wage levels is far from negligible, and people responsible for formulating general policies are not altogether wrong in their belief that, under prevailing conditions in the developing countries, the raising of minimum wages has a marked influence on the wages paid (see Franklin, op. cit., p. 341). For example, "in Africa, unlike most advanced regions, minimum wage policy directly affects the majority of wage earners. It is an 'effective' rate in most cases, above prevailing rates. It determines the wage paid to that 50 per cent or thereabouts of the wage-earning labour force which is unskilled and paid at the established minimums. It is also the key rate in the wage structure; when minimum wages change, the entire wage structure tends to move with it." (Berg: "Major issues of wage policy in Africa", op. cit., p. 186.)

first under a legal procedure that is sometimes coupled with compulsory mediation and arbitration. [1]

A second way of influencing wage trends in many developing countries is through the indirect pressure that governments can exert on the general wage level because of the preponderance of public sector employment. Since a large number of undertakings model their own wage policy on that of the government, decisions taken by the latter have a substantial effect on the level of remuneration in the private sector also. [2]

A third form that wage policies can take in developing countries involves influencing collective bargaining. In this particular respect, industrial relations systems in underdeveloped countries tend to be submitted to stricter government control than in the industrialised countries. [3] There can be few questions that have been more widely discussed than collective bargaining in the developing countries. The forms it can take are unquestionably extremely varied, ranging from bargaining on ad hoc issues between groups of non-unionised workers and their employers to formal systems of bargaining with the participation of the unions. [4] The situation varies from country to country. In Pakistan, for instance, there is very little collective bargaining, [5] whereas in the Philippines the former law on industrial relations encouraged, for economic, political and ideological reasons and sometimes even against the wishes of the weakest unions, the switch from a system of compulsory arbitra-

---

[1] Turner, op. cit., pp. 46-47.

[2] Millen, op. cit., p. 76; A. D. Smith: "A conspectus of wage trends in developing countries", in *Wage policy issues in economic development*, op. cit.

[3] As the Director-General of the ILO pointed out: "Governments, in pursuing policies of faster growth, will no longer be able to content themselves with their position as impartial observers in the collective bargaining process, but have of necessity to take a direct interest in some of the questions which have hitherto been tackled exclusively by collective bargaining between employers and workers. In so doing, the government is introducing into the bargaining process the concept of the national, common or public interest, which it considers its responsibility to define and assert in addition to the sectional interest represented by employers' and workers' organisations." (*The role of management and trade unions in the years ahead*, speech by David A. Morse to the Industrial Welfare Society, London, 21 April 1964.)

[4] ILO: *Institutional aspects of labour-management relations inside undertakings in Asia*, Labour-Management Relations Series, No. 26 (Geneva, 1966), p. 104. Similarly, according to Roberts and Greyfié de Bellecombe: "A collective agreement regulating the terms and conditions of employment may be adopted in a number of different ways. At one end of the scale it may be reached at the end of negotiations between a trade union and an employers' association within a legal framework which gives to both parties the maximum degree of freedom to settle their differences on mutually acceptable terms. At the other end of the scale collective agreements may be drafted by a department of government, as part of the process of the administration of economic and social policy; the agreements are legally binding upon unions and employers, who are obliged to carry out their terms. The extreme cases are easily recognised, but the difficult question to decide is exactly at what point collective bargaining ceases to exist and is superseded by the process of administration" (op. cit., p. 46).

[5] ILO: *Report on the visit of a joint team of experts on labour-management relations to Pakistan and Ceylon*, op. cit., p. 12.

tion to one of collective bargaining patterned on the United States system. [1] Consequently, opinions as to the evolution of collective bargaining during recent years vary from author to author. Whereas, on the one hand, at a 1965 Asian regional seminar it was asserted that since the Second World War "collective bargaining has been on the increase in almost all Asian countries", [2] H. A. Turner on the other hand considers that in most of the undeveloped countries there is little development of collective bargaining, at least in a sense that would be recognisable by trade unions in the United Kingdom or the United States. [3]

The usefulness and effectiveness of the collective bargaining system in developing countries are often publicly questioned. The feeling is that as regards economic structure there is not much of a free market in these countries, which tend instead to have a large public sector, and that industrial peace and harmonious industrial relations are ideologically essential for economic development. It would follow that in India, for example, rather than making futile attempts to introduce the type of collective bargaining system used in the United States or the United Kingdom it would be more fruitful to establish, first, a coherent wage policy which would give guidance to the wage-fixing tribunals or the courts arbitrating in industrial disputes and fix wage levels; secondly, standing wage-fixing and arbitration tribunals, instead of ad hoc groups, in order to develop a body of consistent principles and procedures; and thirdly, special machinery for legally enforcing the decisions of the tribunals, whether in the public or the private sector. [4] It would therefore be more appropriate to pattern the Indian system on the Australian model. Nigeria is in a similar situation. [5] This has been expressed in more general terms as follows:

> It is frequently suggested that the promotion of collective bargaining as a method of determining the terms and conditions of employment of workers in Africa was a foolish error on the part of the former British and French Governments. The ILO

[1] D. Wurfel: "Trade union development and labor relations policy in the Philippines", in *Industrial and Labor Relations Review*, July 1959.

[2] ILO: *Institutional aspects of labour-management relations inside undertakings in Asia*, op. cit., p. 104.

[3] op. cit., p. 10. The author feels that effective collective bargaining depends on certain prerequisites that are generally lacking in developing countries: a "stabilised" and "structured" labour force; a trade union movement that produces competent leaders who are identified with the workers they represent; trade unions which are concerned with achieving limited, gradual and detailed economic advances rather than general social or political transformations and which are not so deeply divided on non-economic lines (political, racial, religious and so on) that they find it difficult to co-operate on a continuing basis for limited economic purposes; a situation in which workers' and employers' organisations have not become used to other methods of regulating labour conditions; a State that is not the dominant employer; and the absence of a massive surplus of labour (op. cit., pp. 34-35).

[4] Dufty, op. cit., pp. 160-161.

[5] See Kilby, op. cit.

and such trade union organisations as the International Confederation of Free Trade Unions and the trade union centres of Britain, Scandinavia and the USA are severely criticised for perpetuating the error. The fact that many of the countries, since gaining their independence, have introduced a greater degree of administrative regulation of collective bargaining may be cited as evidence of the inadequacy of the classical model of industrial relations for the countries of Africa. The first argument against the suitability of the collective bargaining model rests upon the contention that unions in Africa are too weak to bargain effectively and therefore it is socially undesirable to leave the standards of employment to be established by all-powerful and, by implication, ruthless employers. The second argument that is advanced, often at the same time as the first though they are mutually contradictory, is that collective bargaining will lead to an unfair advantage being gained by organised workers and that the gains will create inflation, undermine economic stability and reduce the rate of economic growth. [1]

This kind of attitude, which is very widespread, explains why more and more countries place legal restrictions on the right to bargain collectively. This they may do by specifying the problems that are excluded from collective bargaining. In Singapore (Industrial Relations Act, 1968), for instance, no trade union may include in a notice setting out proposals for a collective agreement a proposal in relation to such matters as promotion, transfers within an enterprise, employment, termination of the services of an employee by reason of a reduction in the staff, dismissals and reinstatements, or assignments to specific duties. Japan excludes from collective bargaining in public enterprises matters relating to their administration and operation. In Tunisia no collective agreements can be negotiated on wages (article 51 of the Labour Code). In Cuba matters relating to wages, hours of work, annual holidays and working conditions in general are excluded from collective bargaining by the administration. [2]

Another restriction on the freedom to bargain collectively consists of prohibiting collective agreements from containing clauses more favourable than those of the legislation in force. As far as conditions of employment are concerned, this is the case with pilot enterprises in Malaysia and Singapore, where a provision of this kind was adopted within the framework of the national policy designed to encourage the investment of new capital. It is also the case in Brazil, where wages obtained through collective bargaining cannot

[1] Roberts and Greyfié de Bellecombe, op. cit., pp. xvii-xviii.

[2] Provisions of this kind have been condemned repeatedly by the ILO Committee on Freedom of Association, which considers that the right to bargain freely with employers with respect to conditions of work constitutes an essential element in freedom of association, that trade unions should have the right to seek to improve the living and working conditions of those whom they represent and that the public authorities should refrain from any interference which would restrict this right or impede the lawful exercise thereof (44th Report, Case No. 202, para. 137; 65th Report, Case No. 266, para. 65; 67th Report, Case No. 303, para. 291; 75th Report, Case No. 341, para. 78; 85th Report, Cases Nos. 300, 311, 321, para. 152; 116th Report, Case No. 551, para. 106; 118th report, Case No. 559, para. 120).

exceed the official scale. [1] Similarly, it may be made compulsory for collective agreements to be approved before they enter into force, approval being withheld if the competent authority considers that the agreements are harmful to the economy or do not conform to official guidelines in respect of wages and conditions of employment: provisions along these lines exist in several countries (Chad, Kenya, Libyan Arab Republic, Singapore, Spain, Syrian Arab Republic, Tanzania). [2] Finally, the application of an agreement or of some of its provisions can be suspended or declared null and void.

Effectiveness of wage policies

Now that the objectives of the public authorities in endeavouring to regulate global demand have been pinpointed and the principal means at their disposal have been examined, it is time to consider the effectiveness of such policies.

The disruptive effect of a wage increase is of course not necessarily related to the share of wages in the national income. And yet in a whole series of developing countries the smallness of the wage-earning sector raises a certain number of questions. A glance at the structure of wage-earning employment in Africa, for example, shows that around 1960, out of a total labour force amounting to about 40 per cent of the population, an average of 20 per cent were wage earners, the figure varying from about 6 per cent in West Africa to 15 per cent in East and Central Africa and as much as 33 per cent in North Africa. [3] It is therefore fair to ask to what extent reasonable wage increases, which are in any case conducive to higher productivity, are capable of having a really significant effect on total consumption, especially since as often as not such increases are intended more to restore a purchasing power that has been undermined by inflation than to raise real wages. Turning from the consideration of the size of the wage-earning sector to the calculation of the incomes, one comes up against conceptual and statistical difficulties: there is not one concept of income but several; available information is unreliable and inadequate on certain countries in Asia (India, Malaysia, Philippines, Sri Lanka), the Middle East (Lebanon) and Latin America (Colombia, Mexico,

[1] The Committee on Freedom of Association considers that legislation establishing that the Ministry of Labour has powers to regulate wages, working hours, leave and conditions of work and that these regulations must be observed in collective agreements is not in harmony with Article 4 of Convention No. 98 (116th Report, Case No. 551, para. 109).

[2] The Committee on Freedom of Association considers that a legal provision which could be applied so as to supersede the conditions laid down in collective agreements or to prevent the workers from negotiating such conditions as they wish in future collective agreements would infringe the rights of the persons concerned to bargain collectively through their trade unions (15th Report, Case No. 102, para. 185).

[2] K. C. Doctor and H. Gallis: "Size and characteristics of wage employment in Africa: Some statistical estimates", in *International Labour Review*, Feb. 1966.

Puerto Rico, El Salvador); what is available is less the product of systematic and co-ordinated surveys than a series of assessments or opinions.

With these reservations, a few broad trends can nevertheless be discerned.[1] In the underdeveloped countries there is *(a)* a marked inequality in the distribution of available income and a marked absence or numerical weakness of intermediate groups; and *(b)* a much higher percentage of income accruing to the richest families than in the developed countries.[2] The more underdeveloped the country, the more acute these features will be found to be. A study by Kuznets of 41 countries, for instance, shows a close link between the size of the labour force in the agricultural sector and the income concentration ratio, which is 0.10 in the industrialised countries (where the agricultural labour force ranges from 10 to 25 per cent) and 0.35 in the underdeveloped countries (where the agricultural labour force constitutes between 60 and 75 per cent of the total).[3] The largest share of income is derived from real estate. Bearing in mind, moreover, that entrepreneurs themselves make up a sizeable fraction of the labour force and that the part of their income which falls in the category of labour is not included in income from property, the conclusion is quickly reached that an increase in the share of wages and salaries will tend to promote a certain levelling of income.[4]

The utmost prudence must be used when introducing a wage policy:

Many things have been confidently, not to say dogmatically, asserted about the effects of wage increase; these are for the most part "theoretical" propositions based on the construction of simplified models of what goes on in the real world. The

[1] E. Gannage: "La répartition des revenus dans les pays sous-développés", in *Le partage du revenu national*, Rapports et débats du colloque organisé par l'Association internationale des sciences économiques (Paris, Cujas, 1971), pp. 325-347.

[2] The shares of the national income accruing to the richest families is as follows (Gannage, op. cit., p. 341):

Underdeveloped countries	Top 10% of the income scale	Top 5% of the income scale	Developed countries	Top 10% of the income scale	Top 5% of the income scale
India (1950)	43.0	33.4	United States (1950)	30.3	20.4
Ceylon (1952/53)	40.6	31	Great Britain		
Lebanon (1950)		31.5	(1951-52)	30.2	20.9
Mexico (1957)	46.7	37	Federal Republic of		
El Salvador (1946)	43.6	35.5	Germany (1950)	34.6	23.6
Puerto Rico (1953)	32.9	23.4	Denmark (1950)	30.7	20.1
			Netherlands (1950)	35.0	24.6

[3] S. Kuznets: "Quantitative aspects of the economic growth of nations: VIII. Distribution of income by size", in *Economic Development and Cultural Change*, Jan. 1963, Part II.

[4] E. Gannage, op. cit., p. 339.

dangers of applying to the real world conclusions based on simplified theoretical models, and particularly of using such conclusions as a basis for advice to policy-makers, are familiar. Firstly, the model may be so unlike the real world that what happens in it may throw little light on what happens in the real world. For example, a model incorporating a competitive labour market may throw little light on reasons for the "stickiness" of wages in many real-world situations; or a model may exclude some relationships that may be important in the real world, such as the effects of higher wages on the efficiency of managements and workers. Secondly, even if the model is close enough to reality to throw light on real situations it may tell us only the direction and nothing about the magnitude of the effects to be expected. . . . What is important for policy purposes is not to be able to describe the effects of higher wages in general terms; the objective of inquiry should be to identify—and this in "operational" terms—the circumstances in which particular effects can be expected to manifest themselves, and to know how important these effects will be. Many governments are anxious that wages should rise as rapidly as the economic circumstances of their countries permit, but are apprehensive about the effects of "excessive" wage increases. Countries seeking rapid economic development and fair sharing of the proceeds need to be able to determine as accurately as possible the "room" for wage increases—to know how far and how fast wages should rise, given the objectives of economic and social policy, and the means and resources available for achieving these objectives. [1]

In the light of these comments, which are both a statement of fact and a recommendation, three remarks are in order.

To begin with, the structural peculiarities of the developing countries must be borne in mind. Reference has often been made to their dualistic nature, in the sense that in a developing country there co-exist a traditional and a modern economy, a subsistence and a market economy, and so on. These distinctions obviously have their usefulness, but the distinction that is likely to be particularly useful here is that between national enterprises and multinational enterprises. The latter are autonomous decision-making centres. To use C. Kerr's term, there is therefore a "balkanisation" of labour markets with "internal markets" [2] having different standards and patterns of behaviour. The wages paid by multinationals (petroleum enterprises in the Middle East and Latin America, mining enterprises in Zambia, bauxite enterprises in Jamaica, and so on), whose productivity as a rule is substantially above the average, are usually much higher than those paid by other firms. The same applies to fringe benefits [3] and, by and large, to working conditions. The

[1] Franklin, op. cit., pp. 342-343.

[2] The concept, which is Doerlinger's, describes the complex equilibrium which evolves between occupational structures, administrative regulations instituting models and networks of internal movements, procedures for the recruitment, hiring, training and remuneration of the labour force, special working conditions, etc.

[3] In Mexico these supplements or *prestaciones* (bonuses, allowances, social insurance and a wide variety of payments in kind) tend to be below 15 per cent of wages in the case of Mexican-owned firms and above 25 per cent in the case of foreign subsidiaries (W. P. Strassman: *Technological change and economic development: The manufacturing experience of Mexico and Puerto Rico* (Ithaca, New York, Cornell University Press, 1968), p. 134).

difficulty of implementing a national wage policy in these circumstances is tremendous:

> Such disparities between those who have employment in high-paying industries and other workers, coupled with the common disparity between an urban wage-earning minority and a rural majority consisting of small cultivators, accentuates a fundamental dilemma extending beyond multinational companies but often exemplified in them: how to reconcile the principle of allowing workers to share in the productivity of the industry in which they are employed with the broader social objectives of reducing gross inequalities of incomes and living standards, expanding employment opportunities and generally enabling the entire population to benefit from the development of the productive resources of the country. [1]

The existence of multinational enterprises is one of the structural factors that have to be taken into account; the domestic peculiarities of the labour market are another. This is reflected in two related characteristics: a less balanced occupational structure compared with that of industrialised countries, and bigger income differentials between categories of employees. Although the figures in it date from about 1960, table 14 illustrates these two points quite well. [2] It also shows that a wage policy can hardly be a satisfactory substitute for a vocational training policy as a means of reducing such considerable gaps.

Secondly, and in the light of the foregoing observations on structural factors, a close look should also be given to the problem of the means that are available. Here two further points should perhaps be made. On the one hand, the compartmentalisation of the economy means that the kind of action that the government can take will have only a limited effect. In particular, the process whereby changes in the public sector are followed automatically by corresponding changes in the private sector will be restricted; the findings of an ILO study on Sri Lanka are particularly revealing in this connection, in so far as they cover a fairly long space of 20 years (1948-68).

The main conclusions of this study are as follows [3]:

(1) Government pay policies exert influence only on those industries or firms that are characterised by the presence of "institutional factors"—a minimum wage fixing apparatus, collective bargaining or union pressure, managerial policies which can be pursued with some degree of independence from the market forces of supply and demand. Although the government is by far the largest employer, its pay policies have not influenced to any noticeable degree the reservation price (or wage) of hundreds and thousands of persons employed in a variety of small establishments; the wage movements of

---

[1] ILO: *Multinational enterprises and social policy* (Geneva, 1973), p. 73.

[2] C. Morrisson: *La répartition des revenus dans les pays du tiers monde* (Paris, Cujas, 1968), pp. 68, 71.

[3] ILO: *Government pay policies in Ceylon* (Geneva, 1971), pp. 65-67.

Table 14. France and certain African countries: Occupational distribution and comparative remuneration of employed persons

Country	Occupational distribution of employed persons (percentages)					Remuneration indexes (remuneration of labourers = 100)					
	Year	Unskilled labourers	Other manual workers	Salaried employees	Executive and supervisory staff	Year	Manual workers		Salaried employees	Executive and supervisory staff	
							Semi-skilled	Skilled		Middle management	Senior management
France (private sector)	1953	18	45	25	12	1952	140		160	280	510
Mauritania (private sector)	1962	58.8	25.7	4.5	11	1962	.		550	700	1 600
Senegal:											
Africans	1957	46.1	23.9	28.4	1.6	1957	.		260	1 500	
Europeans	1957	1.6	9.8	39.1	49.5						
Niger	1959	66.2	20.8	9.9	3.1	1959	300		.	4 400	
Ivory Coast:											
Africans	1958	66.2	19.3	11.3	3.2	1956	.	215	230	.	.
Europeans	1958	—	3.4	27.5	69.1						
Upper Volta	1960	51.8	17.0	25.7	5.5	1961	.	290	330	1 000	1 640
Congo	1958	49.9	18.5	26.6	5.0	1951	140	220	.	1 150	2 300
Gabon:											
Africans:	1959	51.6	25.5	21.7	1.2	1960	180	280	320	1 400	2 200
Europeans	1959	—	—	15.7	84.3						
Madagascar	1960	59.4	18.6	17.0	5.0	1953	280		560	.	.

Source: Morrisson, op. cit., pp. 68 and 71.

these establishments have reflected rather the influence of supply and demand.

(2) The "institutional factors", although necessary for the transmittal of government influence to the private establishments, have not constituted a sufficient condition: in the tea-growing, rubber-growing and coconut-growing trades, the economic factors have imposed rather narrow limits on the process of wage decisions.

(3) Government influence has been most pronounced in the trades where institutional forces are at their strongest and where the economic environment does not provide very narrow limits on wage determination (in the engineering trade specialising in equipment for the domestic market, and the tea export and rubber export trades, in which, because their activities account for a small proportion of the total cost of the exported commodity, the economic environment provides room for a relatively large degree of discretion in wage determination).

(4) The influence of government policies has been less pronounced during periods of stability of government pay. During this phase (1958-67), the mercantile and banking trades did not hesitate to negotiate increases in wages.

(5) Even when the government pay policies were at their most active, they never influenced more than 20 per cent of paid employment in the private sector outside of agriculture and estates.

On the other hand, even assuming that such a pay policy could really be effective, a satisfactory combination still has to be devised of the four criteria on which pay policies have usually been based: [1]

(1) The criterion of the workers' needs, used by several countries (Mexico in 1941, Uruguay in 1953, India in 1957), raises tremendous problems, since it is necessary to define what is meant by a living wage, to decide for how many people the minimum wage should serve as a living wage and, finally, to determine how far governments should try to solve problems of poverty by means of minimum wage systems alone and how far by means of other instruments.

(2) The criterion of the capacity to pay, which several countries take into account (Argentina, Chile, Colombia, Costa Rica, Dominican Republic, Mexico), is an extremely elusive and difficult concept to define. If a choice can be made between its evaluation at the level of a particular industry or

[1] ILO: *Minimum wage-fixing and economic development*, op. cit., pp. 59-76.

at that of the economy as a whole, the second solution would seem preferable in so far as it can be defended on grounds both of equity and of economic efficiency.

(3) The criterion of relative living standards is referred to, for example, in the Minimum Wage-Fixing Machinery Convention, 1928 (No. 30), and the Minimum Wage Fixing Machinery (Agriculture) Recommendation, 1951 (No. 89). In this case, a decision has to be taken as to what gaps can be usefully maintained in a context of industrialisation between industrial wages and agricultural incomes. [1]

(4) The criterion of economic development means that "minimum wages cannot be set without taking account of the total social and economic context, including the amount of unemployment, the size of the peasant population and the existing relationship between peasant incomes and wages, both rural and urban. Because of the importance of a country's economic development to its wage earners no less than to other classes, the process of wage determination must take into account the proper role of wages in creating markets for mass production of consumer goods, as well as the likely impact of wage changes on the volume of employment. All this has, moreover, to be seen against the background of the government strategy." [2]

Thirdly, wage policies must make allowance for the behaviour of the economic agents whom they affect. Here, two factors deserve mention. The first is that industrialising élites have certain preferences where remuneration is concerned, for example as regards the portion to be paid in kind, the share of the various components of remuneration (basic wage, fixed and variable portions of the direct income, various indirect income components), differentials according to professional skills or social and professional status, even methods of wage payment (time rates or piece rates). [3] The second is that the imple-

[1] Without attempting to suggest any particular percentage, H. A. Turner believes that a certain margin in favour of the wage earner would be required "to compensate for the reduced leisure involved in full-time employment and as an incentive to the cultivator to leave his traditional way of life" (Turner, op. cit., p. 57). Arthur Lewis for his part considers that "urban wages will always exceed farm incomes, partly because the cost of living in towns is higher, partly because a more rapidly growing sector has to offer higher real earnings in order to attract labour, partly because working eight hours a day for five or six days a week throughout the year requires a greater input of food than working the farmer's year, and partly because working eight hours every day for wages in towns is less pleasant than working on one's farm, and therefore demands higher compensations. The equilibrium wage for unskilled workers is therefore normally about 50 per cent higher than the average agricultural income." (*Development planning: The essentials of economic policy* (London, George Allen and Unwin, 1966), p. 92.)

[2] ILO: *Minimum wage-fixing and economic development*, op. cit., p. 159.

[3] In this connection see the extremely useful table drawn up by Kerr, Dunlop, Harbison and Myers, op. cit., pp. 216-219.

mentation of a wage policy may spark off certain reactions in the trade unions:

If a trade union policy of wage restraint is difficult to implement in developed countries, due to pressure from members, and requires very skilful handling on the part of trade union leadership, is that not even more true in developing regions where trade union organisation is less securely anchored and where the paucity of reliable statistics, the weakness of administrative machinery and the dearth of effective means of influencing prices and incomes render the preparation and implementation of national policies in this field difficult and uncertain in results? [1]

However, if employers' and workers' organisations are to play a positive role in the making of economic policy decisions and actually contribute to the success of the policy, support of the trade unions rather than control or suppression would appear to be the wiser policy. [2]

THE DEVELOPMENT PROCESS

The influence of trade union action on the development process must accordingly be examined irrespective of the considerations of supply and demand referred to above. It can be assumed that trade unions reflect the interests of their members, but those interests are multiple and have to be harmonised; moreover, the unions have their own preferences as regards both the type of society they wish to promote and the best means of bringing it about. In other words, the development process will differ according to whether it takes place in keeping with or in spite of the views of the unions regarding ends and means.

Ends

Quite apart from the differences between the various employers' and workers' organisations, the explicit objectives of trade unions sometimes seem to be quite contrary to those advanced by the authorities, as can be seen from the burst of "counter-plans" that greets any official development plan. In such circumstances freedom of association is not so much a hindrance or constraint as the vehicle for a necessary confrontation of ideas and a reflection of the need for compromise between aims that are not always compatible. This raises the more general problem of the compatibility of the values traditionally associated with freedom of association and the manner in which most governments of developing countries envisage the place and role of the

[1] ILO: *Report of the Seminar on the Role of Workers' and Employers' Organisations in Economic and Social Development in Africa*, op. cit., p. 58.

[2] Fisher, op. cit., p. 113.

trade union movement in the development process. This aspect can be looked at from several angles.

The Western conception of human rights that gave birth to freedom of association implies curtailing the powers of the State so as to ensure maximum individual freedom and the recognition of collective rights in a pluralist society that reconciles industrialism, capitalism and democracy. Perhaps that conception may be superseded by another, which frequently prevails in countries that are late developers and under which the emphasis is on collective rights that strengthen the State's power to facilitate modernisation. This possibility was hinted at earlier on in this book when the positions of the various industrialising élites were briefly discussed; it is now time to look at it more closely. It will be seen that whereas the international scene has since 1950 witnessed a decline of traditional oligarchies and a slight retreat of reconciliation régimes, there has by contrast been an upsurge in mobilisation or authoritarian régimes. This is shown in table 15, on the basis of a classification whose appropriateness can be questioned, but which does at least have the advantage of illustrating the trends. [1]

A rapid calculation from the classification tables drawn up by Haas [2] on the basis of empirical material (monographs, reference works, consultation of experts, etc.) reveals that most of the modernising, mobilisation and authoritarian régimes are in developing countries (see table 16). Of course, the assignment of a country to any particular category is always open to argument—

[1] See Haas, op. cit. The author defines his categories on pp. 38-40. A *reconciliation* régime has values that are preponderantly instrumental; its authority structure is pyramidal; the government uses little coercion; norms are sanctioned by the constitution and by custom; the participation and integration of the individual are more or less assured; resource allocation is based on market forces or on wide consultation with private enterprise; and consent groups are co-opted into the government structure. A *mobilisation* régime is the exact opposite: the authority structure is hierarchical; a single "party" serves as the source of norms and the integrative mechanism; a "political religion" provides the symbolic reverent and a national identity; recruitment into the élite rests on loyalty to the party; resources are allocated according to a plan; and consent groups are manipulated to achieve rapid modernisation. *Authoritarian* régimes are milder and more relaxed forms of mobilisation régimes: a "presidential monarch" attempts to be the source of new, modernising and progressive norms, using a single party and a bureaucracy as the integrative device; instrumental values dominate and moderate amounts of coercion are used; allocation of resources is to a large extent reserved to private enterprises and mixed corporations; here too consent groups are manipulated. A *modernising oligarchy* is a régime led by a junta of civilian or military rulers; the authority structure is hierarchical in principle but far less efficient and rigorous in practice than in an authoritarian system; values tend to be instrumental in practice; the enforcement of norms is rigid in principle but haphazard in practice; modernising oligarchies have little staying power and readily develop into authoritarian or mobilisation régimes. A *traditional oligarchy*, in which the people live in tribal or village units, is controlled by a small group linked by family-tie status. A *modernising autocracy* is a régime whose traditional ruler attempts to adapt traditional norms and integrating mechanisms to the demands of social and economic modernisation.

[2] The tabulations referred to will be found in the methodological appendix to the Haas study, p. 137 ff.

Table 15. Poiltical régimes in member States of the United Nations, 1946-67

Year	Total number of UN member States	Percentage distribution by kind of régime					
		Reconciliation régime	Mobilisation régime	Traditional oligarchy	Modernising oligarchy	Modernising autocracy	Authoritarian régime
1946	53	*43*	*11*	*34*	*4*	*6*	*2*
1950	60	*50*	*13*	*25*	*5*	*5*	*2*
1953	61	*46*	*13*	*19*	*8*	*7*	*7*
1958	82	*43*	*19*	*10*	*6*	*15*	*7*
1967	120	*37*	*18*	*5*	*5*	*10*	*25*

Source: Haas, op. cit., p. 13.

Table 16. Political régimes in underdeveloped countries, 1945-68
(Figures in Roman type from Haas; in italics from Cox and Jacobson)

Kind of régime	1945-47	1948-51		1952-55	1956-60		1961-68	
Reconciliation	11	19	*4*	16	21	*3*	21	*3*
Mobilisation	2	2	*1*	2	4	*6*	8	*4*
Authoritarian	3	3	*25*	6	20	*19*	27	*35*
Modernising autocracy	2	6	—	7	10	—	12	—
Traditional oligarchy	21	17	—	13	8	—	9	—
Modernising oligarchy	—	2	—	6	6	—	5	—
Not classifiable	—	—	—	—	—	—	1	—
Not independent	67	51	*42*	49	26	*31*	—	*1*

Note: The figures do not include the countries whose economic institutions, in the Haas coding, have been placed in the socialist category nor the countries which, in the Haas and Cox-Jacobson coding, are considered from the point of view of economic development as growing, developed or highly developed (irrespective of any other objections that may be raised against the classification used).

Sources: Haas, op. cit., pp. 141-155; R. W. Cox and H. K. Jacobson: "Decision-making in international organizations: An interim report", paper delivered at the 65th annual meeting of the American Political Science Association, New York, 1969.

as a comparison of the Haas and Cox-Jacobson [1] codings shows—but only the general tendency is important here.

Although the nature of a régime denotes its attitude towards individual and collective rights, its approach will in practice vary according to the type of problem involved. An analysis of human rights votes in the United Nations General Assembly, whether in committee or in plenary session, casts some light on this problem by illustrating the differences between Western and developing countries. [2]

[1] R. W. Cox and H. K. Jacobson: "Decision-making in international organizations: An interim report", paper delivered at the 65th annual meeting of the American Political Science Association, New York, 1969.

[2] Haas, op. cit., p. 18. Here again, the general tendency is of more concern than the details. As Arthur Lewis pointed out, it is better to rely on statistics than on guesswork, even though the statistics may themselves have been based on guesswork.

The same problem of the compatibility of the traditional values associated with freedom of association with the officially appointed role of the trade union movement in the development process can be tackled from another angle, as was done by Kerr, Dunlop, Harbison and Myers, [1] who consider that—

Any general interpretation of the industrialization process and its relation to workers and managers must provide answers to the following groups of questions:

(1) Does industrialization have an inner logic? What are the inherent tendencies of the industrialization process, and what impact do they necessarily have upon workers, managers, and governments?

(2) Who are the leaders who plan the strategy and direct the industrialization process? What are the implications of each strategy for the relation among workers, managers and governments? What are the origins and evolutionary trends of these groups?

(3) What are the pre-existing cultural factors and the economic constraints that uniquely shape the industrialization process in every nation? What are the major questions which confront a country seeking to industrialize and how do the ways in which these questions are decided influence the relations among workers, managers and governments?

(4) What is the role of enterprise management in the industrializing society? What are the consequences of alternative policies and philosophies of managements upon economic development and the pattern of industrial relations? How are enterprise managers generated and developed?

(5) How is an industrial labor-force recruited, developed and motivated in the course of industrialization?

(6) What are some of the universal impacts of the industrialization process upon workers? What are the responses of workers? Who organises them? Are there any general patterns of worker response that emerge over industrial time?

(7) Into what types of institutions are workers organized, and what are the major patterns of interrelations that are established among workers, managers, and governments in the industrialization process?

(8) Do industrializing societies, regardless of their origins and leadership, tend to become more similar to each other, or do they retain the variations of their pre-industrial background or develop new diversities? [2]

This approach [3] to the subject has the merit of setting out the problems and issues clearly, by highlighting the basic economic options (summarised in table 17) that are implicit in the various policies pursued and in the resulting attitudes of the workers and employers. It is precisely those attitudes that are

[1] Whereas E. B. Haas engaged in quantitative historical analysis, their approach hangs on the socio-economic logic of typological constructions.

[2] Kerr, Dunlop, Harbison and Myers: *Industrialism and industrial man*, op. cit., pp. 11-12.

[3] Which is a mixture of structuro-functionalism and social change theory, admittedly has a strong bias in favour of the technological variable, plays down the class issue inherent in Marxist ideology and is ultimately founded on a debatable theory of the convergence of systems. The class issue, by showing society in terms not only of decision-making but also of power structures, leads, for example, to the adoption of industrialisation as a major political goal—a point made by T. Burns: *Industrial man* (Harmondsworth, Middlesex, Penguin Books, 1969), p. 7.

Table 17. Summary of policies of industrializing élites

Basic issues	Kind of élite				
	Middle class	Dynastic	Revolutionary intellectuals	Colonial administrators	Nationalist leaders
Pace of industrialization	Pace set by prospects of private gain, individual choices and limited actions of government. Moderate pace.	No faster than necessary to preserve the traditional élite and its values. Military needs may dictate a more rapid pace.	The fastest possible pace under an extensive set of controls.	Dependent solely upon the advantage of the mother country.	High aspiration and promises but uncertain rate.
Sources of funds	Market decisions by voluntary household and business savings, bank credit and international capital market. Continuity depends an uncertainty and variations of the market. International sources sometimes significant.	Paternalistic grants and protection. Agricultural rents may be significant. Continuity of funds depends upon government favors which vary. International sources rarely significant.	Forced restriction of consumption by taxation and other means to secure very large proportion of net national income for capital formation. Continuity stable. Largely domestic supply.	Funds from budget of mother country; continuity depends on budget pressures.	Tends to seek large sums from abroad to supplement domestic savings but difficulties great, supply variable and short-term.
Priorities in development	Agriculture compressed by international competition. Sequence depends on market, and traditional pattern is from consumers to basic industry. Housing depends on market.	Preserve and protect agriculture; public works, monuments and paternalistic projects including housing.	Agriculture compressed by draining manpower and preventing individual agricultural enterprises. Priority to basic industry with a vengeance. Housing compressed.	Industries developed which furnish materials or consumption goods to mother country or supply foreign exchange.	Aspires to a broad industrial base, expands on the range of the previous colonial administrator. Prestige items.
Pressures on enterprise managers	Strong pressure: competitive product	Weak pressure: Cartelized product	Strong pressure: bureaucratically	Weak pressure: domestic and interna-	Complex and difficult problem of

	markets domestically and internationally. Labor organizations oriented toward the plant level generate pressure on managers.	markets and tariffs restrict international competition. Labor organizations have little interest in the plant level.	determined production plan targets are supported by party, labor organizations and career interests.	tional product markets have little impact, and labor organizations are oriented to nationalist interests. Labor shortages may generate some pressure in some cases, but other methods of recruiting cheap labor are likely to be emphasized.	organizing the environment of the enterprise manager. Little pressure on the whole.
The educational system	Liberal education; mass education; educational system a major instrument in vertical mobility for workers and their families.	Preserves traditional values; higher education limited to élitists; universities have little role in industrialization; workers have only elementary education.	Education bound to revolutionary ideology; high priority to science and specialized fields: workers receive specialised training	Education adapted from mother country; higher education limited to few natives and training often only in mother country.	Educational system designed to be independent and to seek prestige. Dilemma of general education versus training of high level manpower.
Self-sufficiency or economic integration	The financial and commodity markets tend to create a high degree of international interdependence.	A relatively high degree of self-sufficiency particularly where military considerations important.	A high degree of self-sufficiency.	Integrate with the mother country.	Conflict between the aspirations for self-sufficiency and the need for integration for development.
Population	Population a response to few public policies; largely depends upon market forces, incomes and public expenditures on health which may be indirectly encouraging. Permits immigration.	A variety of policies tend indirectly to stimulate growth. No encouragement to immigration.	A variety of policies are designed to constrict the tendency of population to increase in response to industrialization. No immigration.	No concern with population if labor supply adequate. Otherwise recruit labor in the colony or abroad.	Conflict between means to decrease death rate and the impediment of population increases in "crowded" countries.

Source: Kerr, Dunlop, Harbison and Myers: *Industrialism and industrial man*, op. cit., chart 5A, pp. 106-109.

Table 18. Implications of policies of industrializing élites for workers and managers

Basic issues	Kind of élite				
	Middle class	Dynastic	Revolutionary intellectuals	Colonial administrators	Nationalist leaders
Pressure to constrict consumption	Savings arise from voluntary savings and taxes of democratic government.	Relatively little pressure since slow pace.	Stringent constriction of consumption for rapid pace.	Depends on needs of mother country.	High aspirations but pressure dfficult to apply.
Methods of restricting consumption	Private savings.	Inflation.	Direct controls on a broad front.	Direct controls on a few items, particularly imports.	Inflation.
Policies toward agriculture	Contraction by market forces alone.	Minor structural dislocation except to increase efficiency for export surplus to cities.	Sweeping reorganization to release sources and increase output.	Develop in specialized directions for mother country.	Tendency to neglect in program for industrial development.
Methods of allocation of labor	Reliance upon the labor market and public training.	Family and community ties limit mobility of labor and make for greater need for mobility of capital.	Direct allocation and training with emphasis upon monetary incentives.	Direct allocation of native labor and importation of high-level skills.	Training of nationals to replace foreigners.
Methods of motivating labor force	The personal ethic of hard work and money rewards.	Layalty to tradition, family and church.	An ideological compulsion and money rewards.	Limited compulsion, limited acceptance into ruling group in a few cases.	Nationalism as an ideal.

Source: Kerr, Dunlop, Harbison and Myers: *Industrialism and industrial man*, op. cit., table 5B, pp. 110-111.

the potential source of social conflicts. Such conflicts may derive from too fast a rate of industrialisation (a frequent cause of social tensions), from reduced incomes and forced savings in order to finance investment (when the policy proves to be too demanding), from development priorities entailing too sudden or too prolonged a sacrifice of consumption, or simply from the methods chosen to apply economic policy (table 18). Conflicts are in fact as likely to arise in connection with the objectives as with the means of a development policy: they can arise in connection with the objectives because, to use the catch phrase, a choice always has to be made between guns or butter (or, more accurately, regarding the share to be allocated to each); and they can arise in connection with the means, since capital formation can be financed in a variety of ways. [1]

The matter at hand can also be viewed as the compatibility of two value systems, freedom of association and economic development, that are subscribed to when defining economic policy objectives. It is in fact not enough to consider, as was done by Haas, whether, as they evolve, political régimes in developing countries find it more or less easy to accept freedom of association and the civic and political rights that go with it; nor is it enough to make an abstract comparison between the development policies associated with the various types of industrialising élites and the development policies that entail the exercise of freedom of association, so as to identify the possible sources of social conflict arising in an industrial context during the development process: it is also necessary to examine the specific ideologies of the trade unions and the extent to which they are compatible with the chosen development model.

Of course, "ideology" is difficult to define exactly; Gurvitch lists at least 14 possible interpretations. At the risk of over-simplifying, however, three conceptions will suffice here. To start with, an ideology is a set of representations, a view of the world which is reflected in every manifestation of individual and community life, [2] the total framework of society's reflections on itself. Secondly, it is a force for mobilising energy and, as such, a possible substitute for coercion; it accordingly finds its goal in the action to which it gives rise. Thirdly, it can mask reality entirely, act as a more or less deliberate attempt to camouflage the real nature of a situation; [3] in this sense, it is self-justificatory

[1] Domestic savings on a fixed or growing income, by means of *(a)* a voluntary reduction of consumption, *(b)* a change in the distribution of income in favour of the social classes that have a natural propensity to save, *(c)* taxation, *(d)* inflation that may curtail the consumption of certain social groups, *(e)* a cut in imports, or *(f)* international transfers of capital.

[2] A. Gramsci: *Œuvres choisies* (Paris, Les éditions sociales, 1959), p. 47.

[3] K. Mannheim: *Ideology and utopia: An introduction to the sociology of knowledge* (London, Routledge and Kegan Paul, 1954), p. 49.

and a source of mystification for its own sake, often employed to perpetuate and vindicate existing institutions, and serves as a kind of pseudo-conscience. These three interpretations, which all seem to have something to offer, can be combined and condensed into a single definition which sees ideology as a system of representations (images, myths, ideas or concepts, as the case may be), with its own logic and its own set of rules, and which has its existence and plays a historic role within a given society. [1] A social system is made up of sub-units—exerting political forces, economic forces, social forces—each sub-unit having its own ideology which is at one and the same time distinct from and complementary to that of the other sub-units. As far as the protagonists in the industrial-relations sub-system are concerned, the ideology can be described as a set of ideas and beliefs commonly held by the actors that helps to bind or to integrate the system together as an entity. "The ideology of the industrial-relations system is a body of common ideas that defines the role and place of each actor and that defines the ideas which each actor holds towards the place and function of the others in the system. The ideology or philosophy of a stable system involves a congruence or compatibility among these views and the rest of the system." [2]

Now that a definition of ideology has been put forward, some of its possible manifestations can be discerned in the dominant political philosophy of the developing countries. Nationalism for the purpose of modernisation is one ingredient of this ideology, which can assume a great many different forms—the consciencism of Nkrumah, the basic democracy of Ayub Khan, the guided democracy of Soekarno, the middle way of Frei, the *ujamaa* of Nyerere, the *aprismo* of Haya de la Torre, the co-operative democracy of Nasser, and the democratic centralism of Touré, to mention but a few of the examples which history provides, [3] not to mention the countless "models" which are nowadays vaunted as original concepts in Brazil, Peru, the Philippines or Singapore. For all their diversity, these ideologies have a number of common features. In some way or other they all advocate a kind of fusion of consciences, which is a feature of a community as distinct from a society. The ideology picks out likenesses while throwing a cloak over differences, sometimes—in a number of African countries, for instance—to the extent of denying class differentiation. It is easy, then, to find ready-made labels—one people, one nation, one party, one leader. In this way, the ideology favours certain references and advocates and organises loyalty—loyalty towards the nation automatically excluding loyalty to any other sub-groups (profession, class or ethnic group) and the education system being designed in such a way as to foster such loyalty by

[1] L. Althusser: *Pour Marx* (Paris, Maspero, 1966), p. 238.
[2] Dunlop: *Industrial relations systems*, op. cit., pp. 16-17.
[3] See Sigmund, op. cit.

means of the priority it accords to national history and national culture. At the top of the ideological pyramid is the leader, in whom the spirit of the people is personified and in whom the three aspects of the ideology described earlier merge and intermingle: the structural organisation of the representations, the channelling of behaviour towards an ultimate objective, but also the masking and reversal of reality. As they evolve, then, ideologies disguise differences and place a premium on likenesses; these likenesses are translated into a very limited number of dominant themes, according to the continent.

In Africa ideology has three major undercurrents. The first, which is *négritude* or the defence of Negro achievements, is essentially cultural in inspiration. *Négritude*, which can be defined objectively as the body of constituent values of a civilisation and subjectively as a determination to cultivate, perpetuate, use and adopt these values, has many facets; it is at one and the same time a philosophy based on the life force, a certain view of mankind according to which creation is never-ending, and a certain concept of art; these various elements are ultimately distilled into a kind of humanism. [1] The second undercurrent, panafricanism, [2] is more political; although the aspect most frequently cited is the tendency to harp on the theme of independence and African unity, the very title of George Padmore's book *Panafricanism or communism?*, [3] which was in a sense its manifesto, reveals another aspect which over the years has come increasingly to the fore. Its rejection of communism is first and foremost a refusal to believe in White superiority, however much it may subsequently be backed up by socio-economic arguments repudiating the division of Africa south of the Sahara along class lines. The third undercurrent, that of African socialism, has economic overtones and represents an attempt to offer intellectuals an alternative to Marxist theory: faced with the impossibility of subscribing to archaic collectivist structures that are on the way out any more than to Western capitalism, this form of socialism, which owes more to Atatürk than to Marx—and which, were it not for the pejorative implications of that expression, could be described as "nationalist socialism" [4]—purports to turn communalism into a specifically African solution.

The implications for trade unionism are nowhere better described than in a paper prepared by a former trade unionist for the Kenyan Cabinet: [5]

> The first responsibility of the unions must be to develop a disciplined, skilled and responsible labor force. The nation's welfare and that of the workers depend much

---

[1] L. Senghor: "Deux textes sur la négritude", in *Cahiers ivoiriens de recherche économique et sociale*, No. 3.

[2] Ph. Decraene: *Le panafricanisme* (Paris, Presses universitaires de France, 1959); Y. Bénot, op. cit.

[3] G. Padmore: *Panafricanism or communism?* (New York, Doubleday, 1971).

[4] Sigmund, op. cit., p. 17.

[5] Quoted in Sigmund, op. cit., pp. 277-278; see also M'boya, op. cit.

more on hard, productive work than on strikes and walkouts. Unions must concern themselves with training programs, apprentice programs, and workers' discipline and productivity. In addition, trade unions assisted by government should take an active role in organizing consumer co-operatives, generating savings for development, promoting co-operative housing development, initiating producer co-operatives, and making workers aware of their contribution to the development of the nation. Strikes cost the nation output, the workers wages, the companies profits, and the government taxes. Wages in excess of those warranted by productivity increase the unemployment, encourage the substitution of capital for labor, and lead to bankruptcies. In order to avoid these drags on development, legislation will be needed providing for the compulsory arbitration of major issues not resolved through the regular bargaining process. Special legislation may be needed in sensitive industries and the government to avoid the economic paralysis that could result from work stoppages in these areas.

In Latin America, where ideological conflicts often mirror those of Europe, the dominant ideology has two underlying themes—anti-imperialism, which is its outward aspect, and populism, which is its inward aspect. Anti-imperialism can easily be explained by the integration of Latin America into the Western economic system as a consequence, first, of the export of primary products and, subsequently, of a process of industrialisation based on import substitution. Economic dependence has therefore always been keenly felt and is the framework on which Raul Prebisch, who has had a profound influence on economic thought in Latin America, based his explanation of the deterioration in the region's terms of trade. When as a result of the depression of 1929 and the Second World War the dependency relationship was modified, it heralded the rise of populism, of which Vargas in Brazil and Perón in Argentina were the leading exponents. As in the case of Bonapartism, the industrial bourgeoisie mobilised the masses to shore up its power and defend it against the great landowners through a ubiquitous state apparatus. Briefly, the fundamental ideological themes of populism are as follows: the nation is above classes, industrialisation is identified with development, and the people necessarily benefit from growth and from the limited redistribution of income that goes with it. Given this ideological context, the trade union movement may well be used for manoeuvring purposes in the occasional struggle against multinational enterprises but, on the other hand, it is limited in its ambitions and restricted in its means of action the moment it threatens to jeopardise industrialisation.

Consideration of these three factors—the positions adopted at the United Nations when voting on the fundamental human rights on which freedom of association is based, the various ways in which the industrialising élites envisage the process of development, and the ideological preferences that find expression in the developing countries—has brought to light a conception of freedom of association that is more restrictive than that formulated by the International Labour Organisation. Government objectives are not necessarily incompatible with the formal recognition of freedom of association but, in the event of conflict, the objectives of freedom of association tend to be regarded as less important than those of the State, to which they are accordingly liable to be somewhat sacrificed.

Means

A study of the relationship between freedom of association and economic development cannot stop short at the principles and objectives that determine policy: it must also consider means and methods. Once again, clarification can be sought in several quarters. Economic development, which necessarily entails accumulation of capital, also involves mobilising the labour force. During the Industrial Revolution, the promotion of the Lombard Street goldsmiths from mere treasurers to bankers on whom the prosperity of the City of London depended was inextricably bound up with the mass migration towards the factories of smallholders driven from the countryside by the Enclosure Acts; today similar events are taking place in countries on the road to industrialisation. The first step, therefore, is to consider the various ways in which this mobilisation of manpower can take place according to the development model adopted. However, because trade unions exist and have to be taken into account, the rules of the game in any system of industrial relations may in turn be partly determined by the particular method of industrialisation selected; in an analysis which is ultimately a matter of discovering the right combination of ends and means in the industrialisation process, this raises a further series of problems.

In any industrialisation process, workers have to be recruited, made to feel committed, and guaranteed a certain amount of job mobility and security of employment and social security. Even as regards these standard requirements, however, practice may differ widely from one country to another, whether in respect of recruitment (through family or tribal ties, through labour market institutions or through direct assignment), motivation (financial or ideological, individual or social), advancement (on-the-job or formal training, promotion according to skills or seniority), social security institutions (company schemes on a joint basis or not, formal social security systems administered by the State and supervised by the trade unions or not), or attitudes towards unemployment and any state machinery responsible for dealing with the problem. [1]

It will be appreciated from table 19 that, ultimately, labour legislation is the outcome of social forces stemming from the specific institutions of the society concerned. [2] Depending on the importance attached to the trade union

[1] For more details see Kerr, Dunlop, Harbison and Myers: *Industrialism and industrial man*, op. cit., pp. 140-166.

[2] Baldwin, op. cit., p. 9.

Table 19. Characteristics of workers' organizations as determined by the nature of the industrializing élite

Aspect of workers' organizations and the setting in which they operate	Nature of industrializing élite				
	Middle class	Dynastic	Revolutionary intellectuals	Colonial administrators	Nationalist leaders
Ideology	Reformist.	Class-conscious and revolutionary except for a minority.	Preserve the true revolution.	Independence.	Nationalism.
Functions of workers' organizations	Regulates management at the local and industry level. Independent political activity accepted. Does not challenge the élite.	Social functions at plant level; little constraint upon management. Provides minimum industry conditions by legislation. Political activity challenges the élite.	Instrument of party to educate, lead workers and to stimulate production. No political activity except through the party.	Largely a part of the independence and nationalist movement	Confronts the conflicting objectives of economic development and protection of workers.
Role of labor organizations at workplace	Active role under established procedures. Regulate management.	Little role, competitive with works councils. Co-operate with management.	Little direct role; influence through party. Increase productivity.	Little role, force for nationalism and independence.	Little direct role; influence through government tribunals. Increase productivity.
Division of authority on rule making	Pluralistic with workers, management and State having an active role.	State and management dominant.	Party and State, with management and labor organizations as instruments.	Manager dominant with support of mother country.	Nationalist state and enterprise managers.
Broad or detailed systems of rules	Detailed regulation at the workplace primarily through collective agreement.	General rules at the industry level with management free at the workplace.	Detailed regulation at industry and work levels prescribed by the State.	General rules prescribed by State with management free at the workplace.	General rules prescribed by State with management often free at the workplace.

Competition among workers' organizations	Exclusive representation and keen competition. Some rivalry between plant and industry levels over allocation of functions.	Limited rivalry at the plant level and the distribution of functions between the local and industry levels. No exclusive representation.	No rivalry or competition allowed.	Divided by ideological, tactical, regional and personal leadership factions.	Tendency for consolidation among organizations recognized as loyal by nationalistic élite. Advantage over those not so recognized.
Structure of workers' organizations	A variety of structural forms. Confederations not centralized. Organizations perform a wide range of functions.	Relatively large number of industrial unions. Centralized confederation often limited by rival confederations. Unions perform narrow range of functions.	A few industrial unions. Centralized confederation. Organizations perform a narrow range of functions.	A wide variety of structures. Organizations not well developed, often personal.	Tendency toward industrial unions with one confederation acceptable to élite.
Sources of funds	Substantial resources secured by regular dues; regulatory functions require administrative organizations and large budgets.	Meagre resources from irregular dues payments and indirect government allowances. Financial success not highly regarded by workers' organizations.	Substantial resources secured by assessment of all workers; financial resources present no problem with support of régime.	Meager funds often raised outside workers' organizations.	Funds often secured indirectly from government in addition to meager dues. Officers receive other salaries.
Sources of leadership	The ranks through lower levels of workers' organizations. They have an established career.	Intellectuals and those ideologically oriented toward political activity. The leaders' income position is often insecure.	Reliable party leaders with experience in workers' organizations. They have an established career.	Nationalist and independence leaders. Intellectuals with a personal following.	National leaders and intellectuals except where confined to manual workers.

Source: Kerr, Dunlop, Harbison and Myers: *Industrialism and industrial man*, op. cit., pp. 204-207.

movement as a social institution and on the role it is expected to play in what is in fact an active manpower policy, the degree of conflict or, on the contrary, of co-operation will be more or less great. It may be wondered whether the dynamic élites that have used worker organisations as a breeding ground for nationalism and as an instrument of national independence will be inclined to keep the union movement within narrow bounds so as to secure at least its compliance if not its actual co-operation or whether, realising that growth has to be brought about not in spite of people but on their behalf, they will give unionism a leading role in the society they are building. This is no idle question from the strictly economic point of view, since the answer will condition the rapidity of capital formation and hence of economic take-off.

Of particular interest to the economist, an active manpower policy such as has been sketched above is one of the means to be used to apply the decisions of the industrialising élites. There are two others of fundamental importance: the first has to do with the structure of the trade union movement and, consequently, the concept of freedom of association that is embodied in Convention No. 87, and the second with the rules governing labour-management relations and so with the question of collective bargaining as it is defined in Convention No. 98.

As regards the structure of the trade union movement, it may be possible to identify the problems through the ideologies of the labour organisations, their functions, the extent of inter-union rivalry, their institutions and the source of their funds and of their leadership—all of which are covered in table 19 in the light of the different types of industrialisation associated with the different governing élites. This immediately suggests a number of consequences as far as freedom of association is concerned. In cases in which a dynastic élite is faced with class-conscious revolutionary trade unions, the conflict in values may be particularly serious, in which case it is highly probable that certain restrictions will be placed on the exercise of trade union rights—strict controls over the constitution of employers' and workers' organisations, restrictions on international affiliation, supervision of union administration and funds, condemnation of "political" activities and so on, the counterpart of restrictions of this kind being possibly a broadly paternalistic policy.

In more general terms, the desire to reconcile potentially antagonistic aims is apt to induce governments to interfere in union affairs and thereby curtail freedom of association. The most radical measure is of course to restrict the right to establish organisations. While countries where trade union rights are not recognised (Afghanistan, for example) are few and far between, there are quite a number where the right to establish organisations is still denied to certain categories of workers such as public servants (Bolivia, Brazil, Dominican Republic, El Salvador, Jordan, Liberia, Nicaragua, Turkey) or at any rate to certain sections of the public service. Although the right of agricultural workers to organise is normally recognised by law certain statutory provisions may add to the economic or social obstacles they encounter (lack of education, instability of employment, distance from built-up areas, opposition of landowners). This is the case of countries which specify requirements concerning the size of the farm (more than 10 full-time workers in the Dominican Republic and Honduras, for instance), when industrial unions are prohibited by law from engaging in any activity on behalf of rural workers, or when the legislation is enforced differently according to the category of workers (as used to be the case in Angola and Mozambique). Restrictions can also take the form of distinctions based on race (apartheid in South Africa) nationality (Colombia, Honduras, Jordan, Libyan Arab Republic) and political affiliation (Philippines, Turkey).

Another means of curtailing freedom of association is to make the establishment of a trade union dependent on certain formalities. These may be compulsory and make registration a condition for the organisation to operate (Argentina, Brazil, United Republic of Cameroon, Costa Rica, Cyprus, Ecuador, Ethiopia, Ghana, Greece, Guatemala, Jamaica, Kenya, Libyan Arab Republic, Malawi, Malaysia, Mexico, Nigeria, Sierra Leone, Singapore, Spain, Tanzania, Venezuela, Zaire). Though this is more often than not a mere formality, legislation may also grant the competent authorities greater discretionary powers which may be incompatible with the principle of freedom of association. [1] Elsewhere this formality may be optional but secures unions major advantages, such as special immunity, tax exemption, the right to initiate action for the settlement of disputes or the right to be recognised as the sole bargaining agent for a particular category of workers (India, Pakistan, Philippines, for instance).

Such provisions as these have to do with the establishment of trade unions; others relate to their actual operation. Although Article 3 of Convention No. 87 recognises the right of workers' and employers' organisations to draw up their constitutions and rules and to organise their administration, some governments may disregard this right and themselves draw up the constitution of the country's central workers' organisation (Kenya, Tanzania), or demand that the by-laws should include a statement to the effect that the organisation will co-operate with the public authorities and other bodies in a spirit of social solidarity and with a view to the subordination of economic and occupational interests to the interests of the State (Brazil). Again, in developing countries union leaders often come from outside the occupation they represent, and this does much to politicise the organisation. To prevent this from happening,

[1] See Committee on Freedom of Association, Fourth Report, Case No. 20, para. 110.

many governments have introduced provisions requiring union officials to be engaged in the occupation which they represent (Cuba, Ecuador, Peru) or to have been engaged in it at some time or other for a certain period (Argentina, Brazil, Colombia, Libyan Arab Republic, Malaysia, Syrian Arab Republic, Zambia). Government interference in elections may be even more direct, because the result of the poll has to be approved by the Ministry of Labour (Brazil), or because the authorities refuse to recognise an executive that has been elected at a trade union congress, or again because the President of the country designates the secretary-general of the workers' confederation (Kenya).[1] To prevent the union movement from serving as a springboard for political opponents to the governing élites, persons who are active members of certain parties or political movements or in parties whose ideology is considered to be incompatible with the interests of the nation (Brazil) or persons convicted of counter-revolutionary activities (Cuba) may be declared ineligible; conversely, there may be cases in which trade union officers have to be members of a political party (Egypt). In certain countries trade unions are prohibited from making any financial contribution to a political party or to persons standing for election to a political post (Liberia) or from taking part in party politics (Brazil, Colombia, Costa Rica, El Salvador, Ecuador, Guatemala) or engaging in any political activity whatsoever (Chad, Madagascar, Paraguay, Somalia).

All these special clauses reveal a certain suspicion of trade unions, as indicated in the following passage concerning Latin America:

> As far as the regulation of workers' organisations is concerned, originally the legislation clearly seems to have considered these organisations as weapons of protest which needed to be controlled right from the moment of their foundation. Generally speaking, more pains were taken with superintending the existence of trade unions than with stimulating the development of sound, stable and independent organisations. In some countries the forming of trade unions was prohibited in certain sectors (such as agriculture and the civil service, for example), or recognition was refused to national confederations, or attempts were made to promote the development of a specified type of trade union, such as the works union. This kind of restrictions on freedom of association prevented the trade union movement from expanding to the full or weakened certain organisations. Even though the trade union movement is relatively powerful in some countries, in most of them the trade union membership figures still fall below 15 per cent of the organisable labour force. Moreover, the harshness of the statutory provisions was partly to blame for the foundation of *de facto* organisations which in some cases have acquired such standing that they have come to form a trade union world apart.

What kind of effects can the above-mentioned features of the legislation on trade unions be seen to have had on development? In principle, it might be stated that these features have mainly affected social development, or rather the striking of a

[1] Examples of these many and varied kinds of government interference in the internal affairs of trade unions can be found in G. Weiss: *Doctrine et action syndicales en Algérie* (Paris, Cujas, 1970).

satisfactory balance between economic and social development. The lack of an organised trade union movement in some sectors or its non-representativeness in others may indeed have hampered the spread of aspirations and claims and the adequate defence of occupational interests. Nevertheless, it might also be argued that to a certain extent the trade union position has affected economic development, in that freedom of association is one of the prerequisites for active participation of the population in the development process and that this participation is deemed today to be essential to the speeding up of this process. Furthermore, the non-recognition of certain organisations or the underdevelopment of the trade union movement may have encouraged a tendency to anomy which could not be prevented by legal means, with inevitable disruptive effects on the production process. It might further be claimed that the little progress made by the trade union movement has reduced the supporting functions of the social institutions in development, including that of adapting workers to industrial life. [1]

Of course legislation has not always been so restrictive, and has sometimes been designed, on the contrary, to encourage the establishment of unions capable of contributing to economic development. To avoid their proliferation, the law has sometimes prohibited the existence of more than one organisation for all the workers of a given enterprise or institution (Colombia, Honduras, Panama) or, without including such an explicit prohibition, has given the official responsible for registering trade unions the power to refuse to register a union if another already exists (Malaysia, Singapore, the British Solomon Islands and the Seychelles). More and more countries (Congo, Cuba, Egypt, Kuwait, the Libyan Arab Republic, the Sudan, the Syrian Arab Republic, Tanzania and Zambia) impose a single trade union system at every level, along with a compulsory check-off system. [2] This raises a major problem since Convention No. 87, while not excluding the possibility of a trade union monopoly, accepts it only if it is on a voluntary basis.

To turn now from the role of employers and workers in economic development to the rules of the game, a number of comments can be made. This is a vast topic that covers the nature of the organisations concerned (workers' and employers' organisations, state institutions), the greater or lesser degree of flexibility at various levels (enterprise, industry or the entire economy) of the system set up by law or by collective agreement and the procedure for settling disputes (conciliation, arbitration or decision of the public authorities). As regards disputes—

The right to strike is subject to restrictions in many countries, but the scope and severity of these restrictions may vary to a considerable extent, ranging from temporary prohibition and prohibition for only certain categories of workers, to prohibition of a general character applicable to all workers. A general prohibition of strikes may result from specific provisions in the law, and it may also result, for all practical purposes, from the cumulative effect of the provisions relating to

[1] Córdova, op. cit., pp. 469-470.

[2] E. Córdova: "The check-off system: A comparative study", in *International Labour Review*, May 1969.

the established dispute settlement machinery, according to which labour disputes are channelled through compulsory conciliation and arbitration procedures leading to a final award or decision which is binding on the parties concerned. A similar situation may arise in cases where in the absence of an agreement reached by the parties, disputes can be settled by compulsory arbitration or decision at the discretion of the public authorities. Severe restrictions may also occur where the procedure to be followed before a strike can be called is so cumbersome that in practice lawful strike action becomes almost impossible; the effect of restrictions of this kind is accentuated where the workers have not yet been able to develop strong and experienced organisations. [1]

As to collective bargaining, this can be promoted in several ways:

(a) the use of a procedure for recognising or registering trade unions as organisations representing economic interests, for example by determining the most representative organisation (Costa Rica, Honduras, Mexico, Pakistan, Philippines, Singapore, Trinidad and Tobago, Turkey);

(b) the application of sanctions in the event of the employers' refusal to negotiate, for example by means of special enforcement procedures (Argentina, Japan, Philippines);

(c) the establishment of conciliation bodies to induce the parties to negotiate (Benin, United Republic of Cameroon, Central African Republic, Chad, Colombia, Guinea, Ivory Coast, Madagascar, Niger, Nigeria, Peru, Senegal, Tunisia, Venezuela, Zaire); and

(d) the creation of joint collective bargaining commissions or boards whose agreements may subsequently be extended to an entire economic sector (Benin, Central African Republic, Chad, Ivory Coast, Gabon, Guinea, Mali, Morocco, Senegal, Togo, Tunisia).

At the same time, more and more countries have legislation that restricts collective bargaining by listing certain matters as not being open to bargaining (Malaysia, Singapore), by making the enforcement of a collective agreement or certain of its clauses subject to the prior approval of the administration or of labour courts (Kenya, Singapore, Tanzania), or by granting the authorities the right to declare an agreement or certain parts of it null and void (Cuba).

There is, then, a whole shifting pattern of mutual adjustments between the industrial relations system and economic and social development. Development influences social practice:

It appears that in the case of limitations on collective bargaining and the right to strike, often the real concern of governments is that trade unions should play a more constructive role in labour relations—that they should display a more co-operative attitude in regard to the government's development programme and its policy of encouraging investment and that there should be less strikes and more industrial

[1] ILO: *Freedom of association and collective bargaining*, op. cit., p. 44.

peace. There are, however, other ways—which need not involve any restrictions on trade union rights—of encouraging trade unions as well as employers' organisations to play a more constructive role as participants in the system of labour relations.
While such measures would include education and training programmes, what may be of essential importance is the development of a positive national labour relations policy specifically geared to the objectives and requirements of national development and aiming specially at the development of constructive relations and co-operation between employers and workers and their organisations. [1]

This means that, conversely, genuine economic and social development depends on changes in social practice.

To sum up, then, only participation can reconcile the requirements of development with the unqualified acceptance of the principles of freedom of association:

Genuine participation by workers' and employers' organisations in planning will depend on clear political thinking on the part of the public authorities, a certain consensus of opinion among the social partners as to the aims to be pursued, or at least the absence of any major source of conflict, and a strong determination on the part of government to associate these organisations in the formulation and implementation of its economic and social development policy. [2]

---

[1] ILO: *Freedom of association for employers' and workers' organisations and their role in social and economic development*, op. cit., p. 61.

[2] ILO: *Employers' and workers' participation in planning*, (Geneva, 1973), p. 222.

CONCLUSIONS

"What is our contribution to personal freedom? What is our contribution to economic growth? What is our contribution to social justice? And what is our contribution to the synthesis without which none of these is complete and all are precarious?" [1] These are, in a nutshell, the fundamental questions that this book has attempted to answer. It will be useful now to sum up the main points dealt with and to see where they might lead.

SUMMING UP

Concepts

The first chapter of this book was devoted to the far-reaching, positive and dynamic significance of freedom of association. The various elements of freedom of association as a fundamental right were outlined by reference to Conventions Nos. 87 and 98, which deal with the subject specifically and which represent a commitment for the ratifying States; to certain international labour Recommendations, which have a definite bearing on its practical application even though they may not be binding; and to the resolutions, conclusions or reports of the International Labour Conference, committees of experts, regional or special conferences and various other bodies in which the spokesmen of certain economic sectors or categories of workers can be heard—and which in many ways supplement the other international standards. The general survey that has been made of the subject by the McNair Committee and the surveys dealing specifically with individual countries, [2] as well as the reports of the

[1] ILO: *Freedom by dialogue: Economic development by social progress*, op. cit. p. 2.

[2] For example, Japan (*Official Bulletin* (Geneva, ILO), 1966, No. 1, Special supplement; ibid., 1969, No. 4, Second special supplement), and Greece (ibid., 1971, No. 2, Special supplement).

Committee of Experts on the Application of Conventions and Recommendations, show how this right is sometimes curtailed, particularly in developing countries. The practical difficulties involved in enforcing this right and the numerous ways in which it can be infringed, in spite of its being recognised and even proclaimed in a country's constitution, are revealed by various complaints taken up by the Governing Body Committee on Freedom of Association. The conclusion reached in the first chapter was that two widely accepted interpretations of freedom of association were particularly relevant to the proposed investigation of the relationship between that concept and economic development: freedom of association can be regarded both as an individual freedom and as a collective right.

Chapter 1 also sought to pinpoint the nature of economic development. Accordingly, a number of distinctions were considered useful. Growth is of course necessary for development but the two terms are not synonymous: growth can at best serve as a highly unreliable indicator since, in extreme cases, it may actually be incompatible with genuine development. Quite apart from its economic objectives that can be defined in quantitative terms, development is also a matter of social objectives for which there is no such accurate yardstick—if indeed their attainment can be measured at all. This distinction has a number of consequences. In recent years economic theorists have endeavoured to make allowance for them, while thanks in no small measure to the efforts of the ILO they have also been included in economic plans. The relationship between freedom of association and development has to be considered in the light of those social objectives. Although freedom of association has been discussed essentially as a collective right affecting the pursuit of mere economic growth, the problem has many other aspects which, while secondary, should not be altogether overlooked.

Issues

Chapter 2 contained a long and painstaking discussion of a thesis that has been advanced by numerous experts, and that sees freedom of association in present-day developing countries as an obstacle to capital formation, and a source of social injustice to boot. Since the fundamental argument of the thesis involves reasoning by analogy (which is often employed in the social sciences in spite of its pitfalls) [1] it was felt necessary to make a trip into the

[1] This point was made by Gaston Berger, who remarked that there was far too great a tendency to look to the past and use three easy, but dangerous, methods of reasoning: precedent, analogy and extrapolation. In his view, analogy was a form of intellectual laziness which endeavoured to do away with analysis, by taking a bird's eye view of things and then directly transposing past solutions to the present. Though valuable as a means of suggesting hypotheses, analogies were a bad source of solutions (quoted by P. Massé in *Le choix des investissements* (Paris, Dunod, 1964), pp. 50-51).

past to look at the institutional and statistical history of the societies that were first affected by the Industrial Revolution. In those societies both the legislation prohibiting any form of coalition among workers and the spirit underlying the principles of nascent political science and economics were unquestionably hostile to trade union rights as they are understood today, that is to say in the sense of freedom of association and freedom to bargain collectively; but the same cannot by any means be said of countries in which economic take-off came later, towards the end of the nineteenth century and the beginning of the twentieth. This is a clear indication that freedom of association and economic development are not as totally antagonistic as has sometimes been claimed. Using available statistical data, two tests were carried out: the first revealed that far from declining as a result of the recognition of freedom of association, as was implied by the thesis under discussion, growth rates as a rule actually picked up; while the second showed that although no absolute parallel could be drawn between trade union membership and growth indicators, the correlation between the two curves was positive rather than negative, which again contradicts the thesis under consideration.

Leaving aside such historical analogies as manifestly inconclusive—inevitably so, since the underdevelopment of today is not the same as the lack of development of the past—the thesis was next examined in itself. First the supporting arguments (a stronger demonstration effect, a widening gap, higher cost of investment) and then the main argument (breakdown of capital formation machinery as a result of trade union pressure) were found to be insufficiently relevant to be entirely convincing. The same can be said of the arguments for restricting freedom of association not in order to facilitate capital formation but on grounds of social justice and of the primacy of full employment; and it can also be said of the more subtle theses of people who, while not wanting to do away with free trade unions, would like to see their activities restricted to purely economic affairs and geared more towards increased productivity, industrial discipline and productive effort than towards the defence of the workers' interests. The conclusion reached at the end of the chapter was that, instead of branding trade unionism as a hindrance to development, it would seem wiser to regard the absence of development as a barrier to the exercise of freedom of association. It also appeared necessary to reassess the role of the trade union movement in the developing countries and to think of it not just as a burden but also—at least in certain well defined circumstances—as a potential agent of growth. [1] The issues must therefore be looked at

[1] "There are some governments which tend more and more to restrict trade union activities because they believe, or claim to believe, that the free exercise of trade union rights is an obstacle to economic progress. This is, of course, a fallacy. It is self-evident that trade unions, provided they are given a full part in development efforts on a voluntary basis,

(footnote concluded overleaf)

differently: instead of discussing the relationship between freedom of association and economic development in absolute terms, a pragmatic approach is needed to the problems that arise in the specific context of industrial relations policies, since, in the long run, "it is not enough that the transition from an agricultural to an industrial order be successful in strictly economic terms; it must also be acceptable in socio-political terms." [1]

Industrial relations policies

The third chapter, which was concerned with policy decisions, dealt with the specific implications of freedom of association for over-all supply and demand and for the development process itself.

The influence of trade unions on the volume of supply is, as a rule, considered only in terms of the disruptive effect of a strike. However, strike action is just one point on a scale of social tension. Worker protest may take any number of forms, and this book has attempted to describe their fundamental aspects—although the latter, as Kerr, Dunlop, Harbison and Myers suggest, tend to change in the course of industrialisation. [2] The role of trade unionism is to serve as a channel for worker discontent by highlighting its social significance, that is to say by encouraging its collective, open and rational expression. In this, however, the trade union movement in developing countries comes up against all kinds of obstacles—the small size of the working class, its sectoral distribution, its lack of occupational skills, the absence of a sense of industrial commitment among the workers, the paternalism of employers, and the fact that many of the union leaders come from outside the trade concerned. In the interests of the economic development of their country, certain political leaders have felt tempted to restrict the exercise of the right to strike by various methods (total prohibition, limited ban covering a certain period and, some-

---

can be the most important social institution for promoting mass participation, whereas unorganised, illiterate and ill-informed workers contribute very little to the development of their societies" (International Confederation of Free Trade Unions: *Economic development and the free trade unions*, op. cit., p. 38). See also G. C. Lodge: "Labor's role in newly developing countries", in *Foreign Affairs*, July 1959.

[1] Kerr, Dunlop, Harbison and Myers: "The labour problem in economic development: A framework for a reappraisal", op. cit., p. 234.

[2] Of course other sequences are possible. S. Perlman, in his theory of the labour movement, suggests two stages. During the first stage, which corresponds to an immature labour movement, the emphasis is on long-term objectives (revolutionary action or at least the pursuit of social reforms), political action is common and collective bargaining is subordinated to other means of improving work conditions, such as legislation or revolutionary change. During the second stage, which corresponds to a fully mature labour movement, long-term objectives are pushed into the background, political action is regarded as suspect, the emphasis is on collective bargaining and the existing social order is accepted. In historical terms, the transition should logically be from the first to the second form of worker protest. As can be seen, there is an argument for convergence but based on other tenets than those of Kerr, Dunlop, Harbison and Myers.

times, affecting only certain categories of workers, or else the simple introduction of delaying procedures intended to put off the actual moment of the outbreak of the strike). It is questionable, however, whether these various methods are really effective in achieving the desired objective and whether strike action does not in fact serve as a means of regulating conflict.[1]

When they realise the influence that trade union action can have on over-all demand, governments are sorely tempted to use wage policies to control this vital element in production costs. Their aim in so doing may be to keep the process of economic growth under control and, possibly, to achieve greater social justice. For this purpose they have a wide choice of means at their disposal, three of which have received particular attention in this study in view of their importance. There are in fact three fundamental factors that enable governments to influence wages considerably: (*a*) governments are themselves major employers; (*b*) in some countries state arbitration procedures have a substantial effect on wages; and (*c*) governments very often assume a certain degree of responsibility by virtue of the fact that they institute minimum wage systems. The effectiveness of wage policies in developing countries is debatable, however. This is so partly because, by definition, they concern only one component of the national income, and that component is proportionately much smaller in developing countries than in the industrialised countries owing to the differences in the structure of incomes. The outcome of wage policies is also very uncertain because of the lack of economic integration, the presence of multinational enterprises, the difficulty of reconciling the four criteria on which a pay policy may be based (needs of workers, capacity to pay, relative living standards, requirements of economic development), and the preferences of the industrialising élites and the reactions of employers' and workers' organisations.

The development process was then examined once more in all its complexity, in an attempt to find out where the ideas and aims of the public authorities responsible for economic development and those of trade unions defending freedom of association differ. The focus was first on ends and then on means. Objectives were examined from three angles successively. First the attitudes that governments have adopted on the international scene were examined through their voting record on matters of trade union rights and civil and

[1] "By [regulation] we mean such forms of conflict control as address themselves to the expressions of conflicts rather than their causes, and as imply the continued existence of antagonisms of interest and interest groups" (R. Dahrendorf: op. cit., p. 225). It has been observed, for example, that whereas the argument in favour of banning all strikes is not based on any convincing theoretical or empirical demonstration that economic strikes have an adverse effect on economic growth, the prohibition of strike action may well have the effect of slowing down the process of adaptation to necessary changes by bottling up the workers' legitimate grievances. See Roberts: *Labour in the tropical territories of the Commonwealth*, op. cit., p. 323.

political liberties in the General Assembly of the United Nations or in the ILO. A classification of industrialising élites was then used to draw up a list of the main economic options that flow from different development policies, with an eye to their possible consequences for employers' and workers' organisations. Thirdly, the major ideologies prevailing in the developing countries were rapidly surveyed in order to illustrate their implications for trade unions as regards both their role and their place in evolving societies. As to the means employed under a development policy, the first point of interest was the various ways in which labour can be mobilised for development and the greater or lesser number of restrictions that they entail for employers' and workers' organisations and freedom of association. Moving on to the wider field of industrial relations policies, Chapter 3 drew attention, first, to the attitude of public authorities towards trade unions and therefore towards their freedom or control, and secondly to the kind of rules that are accepted or imposed in industrial relations.

For all the subtle differences between actual situations, a desire to participate in economic and social development is felt everywhere. However, if trade unions are to play their rightful role to the full, the legal restrictions on union rights have to be eliminated. Such restrictions are a barrier to mutual trust and understanding between trade unions and governments, and they also hinder the mobilisation of the energies that lie dormant within employers' and workers' organisations, however small their membership, however meagre their financial resources and however numerous their institutional shortcomings.

ROLE OF INTERNATIONAL STANDARDS

In so far as the establishment of genuine representative organisations is a desirable goal that public authorities and the International Labour Organisation can set themselves, there is a need to define the principles to be respected and the means to be employed. At this point it may be useful to try to identify the possible role of international standards relating to freedom of association and perhaps, subsequently, to make a few constructive suggestions. The first step will be to gauge the influence of the standards in the legal field, the second to assess their educational role in the creation of an international code of conduct in social and economic matters, and the third to examine how the cause of freedom of association can be advanced through the technical assistance activities of the ILO in developing countries. [1]

[1] This brings us back to the three traditional spheres of activity of the ILO: "When the ILO was founded in 1919 it was thought that it would have to rely mainly if not wholly on the setting of international standards in order to achieve its objectives. Since then, and

Influence in the legal field

As a legal standard, an international Convention must fulfil certain conditions if it is to ensure the promotion of a universal set of values: [1] the right to be protected must reflect a widely shared set of expectations among significant actors, governmental and non-governmental, although these expectations need not be identical; it must be general in nature so as to be capable of triggering activity and demands in social and economic fields close to, but not identical with, the original area of concern; the right to be protected must nevertheless be specific enough to permit the investigation and rational evaluation of charges of violations; it must be important enough to be valued by its constituency apart from and beyond the particular political context of the time and place; and it must be protected by a minimum international machinery. Freedom of association fulfils all these conditions. It is a right which broadly reflects the expectations of the social actors since the two relevant Conventions were adopted by very large majorities (127 votes to 0, with 11 abstentions, in the case of Convention No. 87; 115 votes to 10, with 25 abstentions, in the case of Convention No. 98) and are currently those that have been most widely ratified. The right is sufficiently general to apply to all kinds of economic and social contexts, as is apparent from the ratification of the relevant Conventions by countries at such diverse stages of economic development as France and Upper Volta, with such diverse political régimes as the USSR and Belgium, and with such different legal traditions as Nigeria and Senegal. The right is nevertheless specific enough to have given rise to a whole body of case law. [2] It is important enough to have been embodied in the constitution of a number of countries. In addition, as has been seen, it is protected by special legal machinery which is both original and effective. Obviously then, its effectiveness as a legal instrument has been considerable; [3] but this does not make its influence any easier to assess. [4] As for unratified standards, their influence may be felt when they come up for examination by the competent national authorities, since that process gives national parliaments an initial opportunity of taking international standards into account in connection with the framing of policy and legislation on labour matters; it may also be felt as

---

especially over the past 20 years, its methods have in fact been diversified considerably, with strong emphasis on technical co-operation and education." (N. Valticos: "Fifty years of standard-setting activities by the International Labour Organisation", in *International Labour Review*, Sep. 1969, p. 201.)

[1] Haas, op. cit., pp. 20-23.

[2] ILO: *Freedom of association: Digest of decisions of the Freedom of Association Committee of the Governing Body of the ILO*, op. cit.

[3] A number of *International Labour Review* articles dealing with the influence of international labour Conventions on national legislation have been listed at the end of the book.

[4] See E. A. Landy: "The influence of international labour standards: Possibilities and performance", in *International Labour Review*, June 1970.

a result of a country's obligation to submit progress reports, since that will suggest new ways of bringing national legislation into line with the standards in question. The Recommendations serve much the same purpose since, like unratified Conventions, they do not constitute obligations but serve essentially as guidelines for national action. Because of their legal status and because of the special machinery that exists to supervise their application, however, a more direct influence is exerted by ratified standards in that they oblige countries to modify their national law or practice. [1] Given the particularly strict supervision of freedom of association that is made possible by the special machinery set up for the purpose, it may be tempting to try to measure the effect of this supervision statistically. [2] Unfortunately, as long as there is no system for following up the action taken pursuant to the recommendations of the Committee on Freedom of Association, the figures, and therefore the conclusions reached, could not be claimed to have a reliable scientific basis.

In any case, any assessment of the effectiveness of legal procedures must be based on a fairly broad view of the subject:

> This continuous progress in supervisory procedures has led to an enlargement in two respects. In the first place, the scope of the supervision has been extended, since it does not confine itself to checking observance of the obligations arising out of ratification of the Conventions but promotes application of the standards more

---

[1] The ratification of Conventions Nos. 87 and 98 by Costa Rica in 1960, for example, entailed an amendment of the Labour Code which had the effect of making it impossible to dissolve trade unions by administrative decision and of authorising trade union federations and confederations to affiliate with international workers' and employers' organisations. In another instance, "the effect of ratifying ILO Convention No. 87 in Japan has been unquestionably to bring about considerable change both inside the unions in government employment and in their relations with the government, as employer". (A. H. Cook: "The ILO and Japanese politics; II. Gain or loss for labor?", in *Industrial and Labor Relations Review*, Apr. 1969, p. 398). Similarly, in 1967, the Committee of Experts on the Application of Conventions and Recommendations noted that a recent Act in Niger expressly excluded trade unions from the scope of an earlier ordinance which allowed them to be dissolved by decree, contrary to the provisions of the Freedom of Association and Protection of the Right to Organise Convention, 1948 (No. 87). (See ILO: *Report of the Committee of Experts on the Application of Conventions and Recommendations*, Report III (Part IV), International Labour Conference, 51st Session, Geneva, 1967, p. 90.) The matter had been raised for the first time in 1962. To take some more recent cases, the Committee of Experts noted the following developments in 1975: in Barbados, adoption of provisions designed to protect workers against acts of anti-union discrimination in employment; in Ecuador, adoption of provisions prohibiting an employer from interfering in activities that are strictly union matters and from violating the right to carry on such activities freely and requiring the administrative authorities to be careful to prevent such acts of interference; in Greece, repeal of various restrictive provisions relating, inter alia, to the freedom of trade unions to elect their representatives, the constitution of federations and confederations, and the right to bargain collectively without interference; in Upper Volta, modification of provisions according to which the declaration of a strike was deemed to be unlawful (ILO: *Report of the Committee of Experts on the Application of Conventions and Recommendations*, Report III (Part IVa), International Labour Conference, 60th Session, Geneva, 1975, pp. 106, 118, 129 and 130).

[2] Cf. Haas, op. cit., pp. 77, 83.

generally, irrespective of the formal obligations assumed. Secondly, the methods have been diversified to meet the variety of situations and needs encountered. This diversification has not, however, entailed a dispersal of effort, for all the procedures are complementary, in that one takes over where the other leaves off or else they are mutually supporting. Furthermore, despite their own special features, the procedures have certain common characteristics that give the system as a whole an underlying unity. For one thing, the fact that the procedures are accompanied by such safeguards as recourse to independent figures and quasi-judicial methods results in objective, impartial assessments and ensures the general confidence which is essential if any form of international supervision is to be effective. For another, the fact that the employers' and workers' organisations take part in the supervision procedure at appropriate stages not only produces additional information but enhances the effectiveness of the supervision. Thirdly, all the procedures are based on careful, detailed research designed to ensure that supervision is based on accurate knowledge of the facts. And fourthly, there is the combination of the discretion required by the investigation and conciliation stages with the publicity required for action by the Conference and, more generally, for keeping public opinion informed. [1]

The last observation shows how necessary it is to consider freedom of association not just in its strictly legal context but also in the light of the broader, educational role that its promotion can play on the international scene.

Educational role

Quite apart from its purely legal aspect, the international supervision of the application of standards has a definite didactic function in that, by publicising widely the ideals set forth in all the international instruments, it can have a positive influence on public opinion and government practice. The constitutions, declarations, charters, conventions, recommendations and resolutions adopted over the years by international organisations, whose highest expression is to be found in the Universal Declaration of Human Rights and in the two international Covenants adopted by the United Nations on economic, social and cultural rights and on civil and political rights, give a very special meaning to the ILO's activities. Because of the number and importance of the rights recognised in the International Covenant on Economic, Social and Cultural Rights, the International Labour Organisation is one of the agencies mainly responsible for implementation of the provisions of the instrument. This is particularly fitting in view of its experience, its standards, its structure, the powers conferred on it in its Constitution, and its procedures, which guarantee these rights better protection than can be provided by other international organisations, [2] which are rarely equipped to do more than furnish information on follow-up action.

---

[1] Valticos, op. cit., pp. 235-236.

[2] "Broadly speaking, the methods of implementation prescribed by the Covenants and the procedure for supervising the application of international labour Conventions differ considerably. In particular, the Covenants do not provide for such detailed and varied

(footnote concluded overleaf)

Just as the reports on ratified Conventions are a means of verifying the application of international standards, the reports on non-ratified Conventions and those of the Committee on Freedom of Association are an excellent means of bringing pressure to bear on countries to observe the rules of an international code of conduct. The practical effect of the Committee's recommendations is in fact much greater than that of a formal condemnation: in these recommendations, several countries have been invited to bring their legislation into line with the international commitments they have undertaken or, more generally, with principles relating to freedom of association. However, it is a fact that the willingness of countries to accept international criticism depends very much on general political considerations.

The influence of international standards can be roughly gauged by applying a criterion of legitimacy and a criterion of authority. [1] Legitimacy refers to the extent to which countries demand international standards, refer to them and apply them willingly; authority refers to the extent to which the international organisation can bring pressure to bear on a country to fulfil its obligations. The "conformity score" [2] measures the frequency (or fidelity) with

---

supervisory procedures as those applicable to international labour Conventions and Recommendations. Even the complaints procedure provided for in the Covenant on Civil and Political Rights, which goes further in this respect than the Covenant on Economic, Social and Cultural Rights, differs from that of the ILO, mainly in that complaints may only be presented by States Parties which have recognised the competence of the Human Rights Committee to deal with such matters, whereas under the Constitution of the ILO the complaints procedure may be invoked by one Member against another when both have ratified the Convention to which the complaint relates, by a delegate to the Conference or by the Governing Body acting on its own initiative; furthermore, under the Covenants, a complaint may not be referred to an ad hoc conciliation commission without the prior consent of the States Parties concerned, whereas under the ILO procedure the decision to refer a complaint to a commission of inquiry is taken by the Governing Body alone, and such referral implies an obligation to co-operate with the commission" (ILO: *The ILO and human rights*, op. cit., p. 23). An interesting view of the problem discussed here is provided by Haas, op. cit., which contains a table (pp. 6-7) summarising and comparing the supervisory and enforcement provisions for human rights—prevention of genocide, International Labour Code, freedom of association, discrimination in education, civil and political rights, racial discrimination, religious intolerance.

[1] Haas, op. cit. The hypotheses that the author endeavours to test (p. 31) are the following: (1) international Conventions dealing with human rights enjoy more authority and legitimacy than do other kinds of international labour Conventions; (2) international labour Conventions are most legitimate and authoritative in reconciliation régimes with mixed economic institutions and developed economies; they are least legitimate and authoritative in totalitarian and authoritarian régimes with socialist or capitalist institutions and underdeveloped economies; such Conventions enjoy increasing authority and legitimacy in incipient reconciliation régimes with growing economies; (3) international Conventions dealing with human rights show an exaggerated tendency towards high or low legitimacy and authority, as compared with other Conventions, in all types of nations; (4) over time, complaining trade unions will concentrate less and less on issues with world political implications and will focus instead on immediate issues of human rights at the national level. Haas's subsequent calculations are an attempt to confirm or invalidate these theses.

[2] E. A. Landy: *The effectiveness of international supervision: Thirty years of ILO experience* (London, Stevens and Sons, 1966), p. 68.

Table 20. Legitimacy and authority of ILO Conventions, 1927-64

Item	Acceptance	Conformity	Implementation
All Conventions (100)	0.26	0.70	0.42
Human rights Conventions (7)	0.61	0.73	0.22

Source: Haas, op. cit., p. 48.

which countries include international standards they have ratified in their legislation, according to the formula

$$1 - \frac{\text{critical observations}}{\text{actual ratifications}}.$$

The "implementation score" measures the frequency with which countries improve their legislation in the light of observations by the international organisation, according to the formula

$$\frac{\text{action in full} + 0.5\ (\text{action in part})}{\text{critical observations}}.$$

These two tests have to do with the principle of authority. The principle of legitimacy is measured by an "acceptance score", according to the formula

$$\frac{\text{actual ratifications}}{\text{possible ratifications}}.$$

Haas's analysis of all ILO Conventions adopted between 1927 and 1964 is summarised in table 20.

By and large, human rights standards have a better legitimacy score than technical labour Conventions, but they do not have a higher authority score. If, instead of looking at the over-all picture, the classification described in Chapter 3 is used, the figures are as shown in table 21.

Haas reaches the following conclusions:

> A closer examination of the attitudes of various types of régimes and economies has disclosed that human rights texts do not enjoy unusual legitimacy among reconciliation and authoritarian régimes, but are generously ratified by mobilisation polities. Economic development does not show a striking correlation with the acceptance of human rights norms; socialist countries find them more attractive than countries with capitalist or mixed institutions. With respect to authority, however, the picture is different. As predicted, human rights texts are most authoritative for reconciliation polities with developed or growing economies and mixed economic institutions, least authoritative for mobilisation régimes with socialist economies, and of indifferent interest to authoritarian régimes, capitalist institutions, and underdeveloped economies.[1]

[1] Haas, op. cit., pp. 54-55.

Table 21. Legitimacy and authority of ILO Conventions for selected types of member States

Kind of member State	All Conventions, 1927-64				Human rights Conventions, 1948-64			
	Number of countries	Accept	Con-form	Imple-ment	Number of countries	Accept	Con-form	Imple-ment
Reconciliation	28	0.32	0.75	0.53	36	0.63	0.82	0.32
Mobilisation	8	0.21	0.84	0.20 [1]	16	0.76	0.72	0.18
Authoritarian	14	0.19	0.84	0.40	15	0.61	0.66	0.07
Modernising autocracy	0	—	—	—	5	0.54	0.92	0.50 [2]
Capitalist	42	0.16	0.75	0.31	42	0.55	0.72	0.25
Mixed	5	0.43	0.61	0.45 [3]	32	0.67	0.84	0.27
Socialist	5	0.25	0.90	0.25 [1]	12	0.80	0.64	0.14 [4]
Underdeveloped	69	0.19	0.70	0.34	69	0.59	0.75	0.21
Growing	6	0.35	0.77	0.59 [3]	8	0.57	0.92	0.50 [2]
Developed	0	—	—	—	5	0.69	0.90	0.17 [1]

[1] For three countries only. [2] For two countries only. [3] For five countries only. [4] For eight countries only.
Source: Haas, op. cit., table 5, p. 50.

These conclusions would seem to have a direct relevance to the problem dealt with here. Underdevelopment is not incompatible with freedom of association as far as principles are concerned, since the standards are usually accepted and ratified (legitimacy principle). On the other hand, there can be no doubt that their practical implementation often poses difficulties, as was seen in Chapter 3, thereby weakening the authority principle (especially as regards the implementation score). What these countries need to do, therefore, is to reconcile the legitimacy principle with the authority principle by fostering freedom of association through persuasion rather than coercion, and by influencing national practices from within rather than endeavouring to impose reputedly more satisfactory practices from elsewhere.

Promotion of international standards through technical assistance

It has been seen that legal supervision in the field of freedom of association has played a major role, and that the education of employers and workers and the promotion of a code of industrial relations is making steady progress thanks to the pressure exerted by reports on Conventions, whether ratified or not, and by various international surveys. The cause of freedom of association is also advanced by means of technical assistance.

Technical assistance and promotional activities seem destined to play an increasingly important part in the future development of international action for the promotion and protection of freedom of association. Some of the other procedures which we have examined, and notably the review of credentials and the formal procedures of representation and complaint and in large measure the examination of the allegations of infringements of trade union rights, represent the pathology rather than the normal healthy operation of international action for the protection of freedom of association. The basic problem is one of strengthening the forces which are working towards a fuller measure of freedom of association, mutual recognition by industrial organisations, collective bargaining and collaboration by such organisations with each other and with the State in pursuit of the common weal. Machiavelli, for all his shrewdness, took a short-term view when he declared that it is better to be feared than to be loved. The occasional use of litigation and coercive methods is inseparable from the government of large masses of men and procedures savouring of litigation and of at least moral coercion therefore have an essential part to play in the international promotion and protection of freedom of association; but the only basis on which the International Labour Organisation can build up its strength as an effective influence in favour of freedom of association is the value of the contribution which it makes to the lives of the citizens of its Members and the loyalty towards it which that contribution to their lives inspires. It is for this reason that the technical assistance and promotional activities of the International Labour Organisation in relation to freedom of association and industrial relations have an importance altogether disproportionate to their immediate impact on the body of law and precedent. [1]

A number of economic and social development experiments have been carried out along essentially technocratic lines, no allowance being made for the potential contribution of employers' and workers' organisations to the process. The failure of those experiments is a matter of record. Freedom of association, then, is much more than just a value worth preserving; it is an instrument whose use should be promoted. Quite logically, therefore, technical co-operation for that purpose should expand. [2] Freedom of association will not come about unaided; it is not an automatic offshoot of economic growth or development; on the contrary, it must be part of a deliberate and carefully planned policy. Thanks to its experience in this field, the ILO can do a great deal to help. Of course, "the Office does not decide on the content of projects and governments have the final say in this connection. In the last resort it is up to the employers and workers themselves, in consultation with the authorities, to devise ways and means of participating more actively in official decisions". [3] Its technical assistance can, however, be extremely useful, and several

[1] Jenks: *The international protection of trade union freedom*, op. cit., pp. 499-500.

[2] "These programmes, which are not normally regarded as falling directly within the sphere of action in favour of human rights, are nevertheless essential elements in such action, and this for two reasons. In the first place, the material fulfilment of economic, social and cultural rights with which these programmes are mainly concerned also helps—sometimes decisively—to realise fundamental aspirations to freedom and equality. . . . Again, economic and social rights, while an end in themselves, cannot be achieved without promoting fundamental rights and freedoms. The essential justification for freedom of association is thus the defence of the economic and social rights of those concerned" (ILO: *The ILO and human rights*, op. cit., p. 6).

[3] ILO: *The ILO and technical co-operation*, Report VIII (Part I), International Labour Conference, 51st Session, Geneva, 1967, p. 42; see also pp. 55-56.

examples can be given of fields in which such activities may be particularly valuable as a means of promoting freedom of association.

In the first place, it often appears necessary in developing countries to strengthen departments of labour so as to improve their ability to carry out their responsibilities in respect of economic and social development and in respect of the defence of trade union rights. It will therefore probably be necessary to step up the ILO's technical assistance in this area inasmuch as it helps departments of labour to identify the social factors that must find a place in the country's economic policy, to compile and analyse information on social and labour matters and to devote more attention to the establishment of constructive relations between employers' and workers' organisations. [1] Labour administration will then be in a position to play a simultaneously preventive, executive and in some cases quasi-judicial role in the promotion, protection and defence of economic and social rights, a field in which it can hope to be particularly active when other machinery with the same social aim, such as a collective bargaining system, proves inadequate.

Secondly, the trade union movement in developing countries has often been described as weak, and some of the signs and origins of this weakness have already been discussed. However, the fact that strong employers' and workers' organisations are one of the instruments of economic and social development means that any technical assistance that they receive will be all the more useful. The colonial authorities in the past, [2] the workers' or employers' organisations in the countries administering the colonies during the same period, [3] and the international trade union movements today [4] have all provided

[1] ILO: *Report on the Asian Round Table on Labour Administration and Development Planning, Manila, September 1959*, document ILO/OTA/AFE/R.17 (Geneva, 1970), p. 92.

[2] For example, the Colonial Development Act of 1929, which legalised trade unionism in British colonial territories, also encouraged its development (J. I. Roper: *Labour problems in West Africa* (Harmondsworth, Middlesex, Penguin Books, 1958), p. 57), and in 1938 labour officers were specially appointed to encourage trade union organisation, the granting of financial aid being made dependent on the facilities granted to the development of unionism. Similarly, in France, unions in the colonial territories received legal sanction through a decree issued by the Popular Front Government in 1937, and the reformist policy followed after the Second World War, and culminating in 1952 in the enactment of a special labour code for the overseas territories, further encouraged the development of the union movement (Neufeld, op. cit., pp. 115-116). In the Belgian colonial territories, the legalisation of the union movement and establishment of a complex system of works councils, unions, and local and regional workers' committees dates from 1946 (C. A. Orr: "Trade unionism in colonial Africa", in *Journal of Modern African Studies* (London), May 1966, p. 76).

[3] The participation of French or British workers' organisations in the development of the African trade union movement has been described in many works (Berg: "French West Africa", op. cit.; J. Meynaud: *Le syndicalisme africain: Evolution et perspectives* (Paris, Payot, 1963); A. November: *L'évolution du mouvement syndical en Afrique occidentale* (Paris, Mouton, 1965)).

[4] The World Federation of Trade Unions and the International Confederation of Free Trade Unions are both well known for the assistance they provide (A. Zack: *Labor training in developing countries: A challenge in responsible democracy* (New York, Praeger, 1964)).

the trade unions in developing countries with assistance. The ILO's contribution in this field could also be substantial, especially perhaps in one of the most neglected fields, namely the formation of agricultural associations to represent independent rural workers and farmers. Consideration should therefore be given to the suggestion made at the Seventh Session of the ILO Permanent Agricultural Committee that short missions should be sent to interested countries to encourage the creation of agricultural organisations or to increase the effectiveness of those that exist already.

> In many countries something could be done in this respect if peasants' associations were created at the bottom of the ladder (as counterweights to the co-operatives) with, at the top, well organised federations maintaining close, intimate links with the public authorities. Otherwise, we shall create inward-looking pockets of development which, lacking the tonic of contacts with the outside world, will be quickly absorbed by the traditional way of life. [1]

It is interesting to note that the ILO has recently made significant progress in the development of rural workers' organisations with the adoption in 1975 of Convention No. 141 and Recommendation No. 149, which deal with such organisations and with their role in economic and social development. The Recommendation in particular contains specific reference to action that governments should take within the framework of a policy of active encouragement to these organisations, in the form of legislative and administrative measures, public information, education and training, and financial and material assistance.

Thirdly, if the ideal is a trade union movement that is "responsible" in the sense that it responds to development aims rather than to restrictive measures which, as has been seen, are very likely to be ineffectual, workers' education is of paramount importance. Because workers' organisations are short of funds, it is often government policy to encourage and assist trade unions in their training and education work: workers' education programmes in India and at the Asian Labor Education Centre of the University of the Philippines are just two examples of the efforts made in that direction in

---

Such activities may sometimes have compromised the independence of nascent trade unions, but they have also unquestionably had a valuable contribution to make: "Leaving aside issues relating to the transfusion of ideology, there can be no question that one broad result of external assistance will be the strengthening of labor movements in developing countries. Of course examples could be cited where competitive assistance from East and West have contributed to fractionalism, to the creation of rival unions, to internecine struggles, and to the corruption of promising individual leaders, and these will doubtless be repeated. But on balance the infusion of new skills can only contribute to stronger trade unions. In this way the assistance programs may well contribute to the maintenance and growth of pluralism in the developing countries." (H. K. Jacobson: *Ventures in polity shaping: External assistance to labor movements in developing countries*, International Political Science Association, Working paper submitted to the Grenoble round table meetings, 14-18 September 1965, p. 13.)

[1] X. Flores: *Agricultural organisations and development*, Studies and Reports, New Series, No. 77 (Geneva, ILO, 1970), p. 559.

developing countries. [1] In some cases, as certain observers have pointed out, "there may be a need for a re-orientation of training programmes to the objectives and requirements of development and for giving increased emphasis in the programmes on the promotion of better understanding of labour and social problems of industrial development and economic growth, and of the ways for building up constructive relations and co-operation between employers and workers and their organisations". [2]

The ILO's technical co-operation programme has taken and can take many different forms, including aid, advice and assistance in connection with workers' education programmes (whether private or partly government-run), help in the establishment of trade union research services, help with training programmes for personnel management staff, study grants for the officials of employers' or workers' organisations, and regional seminars. [3] However, it must not be forgotten that workers' education rarely reaches the vast mass of unorganised workers; it reaches rural workers even less, if at all, and this is a major shortcoming to be remedied.

These suggestions are not in any way exhaustive. Another major way of promoting the development of trade unions and their activities, for instance, is the system of direct contacts, under which a representative of the Director-General of the ILO, along with a representative of the government that requests or accepts the contacts, can study the best way of tackling problems arising from the application of Conventions, including those concerning freedom of association. Under this system, contact is also made with workers' and employers' organisations so that they are kept in touch with the subject being discussed and have an opportunity to state their views. As concerns free collective bargaining and economic development specifically, direct contacts of this kind recently took place with the Government of Singapore in connection with the observations of the Committee of Experts on the Application of Conventions and Recommendations regarding national legislation restricting collective bargaining in the case of newly established enterprises.

---

[1] ILO: *Directory of labour relations institutes* (Geneva, 1973); idem: *Labour relations institutes: Structure and functions* (Geneva, 1973).

[2] ILO: *Freedom of association for workers' and employers' organisations and their role in social and economic development*, op. cit., p. 57.

[3] An Asian seminar on the role of trade unions in development planning was held in New Delhi in September-October 1968: an Asian round table on labour administration and development planning was organised by the ILO in Manila in September 1969; another round table on the role of employers' organisations in Asian countries took place in Tokyo in December 1970; an African seminar on the role of trade unions in development planning was held in Dakar in November-December 1966; a seminar on the role of workers' and employers' organisations in economic and social development in Africa was held in Addis Ababa in December 1968; seminars on the role of trade unions in development planning have also been held in Latin America (in Santiago, Tegucigalpa, Managua and San José).

The ILO has also felt it desirable to step up its information activities directed towards certain groups of people who, by reason of the position they occupy, can contribute a great deal to a greater awareness of the principles of freedom of association or are called upon to participate in the implementation of relevant national legislation. These include university lecturers on labour affairs, judges, and public servants in the field of labour administration. A first symposium on freedom of association in Latin America was recently held in Mexico City with the participation of members of these professions and employers' and workers' representatives. Its purpose was to familiarise them with the ILO's principles and standards in this field and to discuss the problems connected with their application in the region.

The reason for laying so much emphasis, in these few examples, on the role of technical assistance as a means of supplementing the drafting of international standards and educating nations and workers' organisations, is that there is a definite interplay among these various aspects.

> Operational programmes . . . cannot be dissociated from the standard-setting activities of the ILO. On the one hand, operational programmes must be inspired by the principles enunciated in Conventions and Recommendations, while facilitating their effective implementation, and, on the other, in framing standards inspiration and guidance should be sought in the operational programmes, with due allowance being made for the circumstances peculiar to each country resulting from its degree of economic and social advancement and its general political system. While there are cases where it seems possible to combine successfully these two major forms of ILO action, it cannot be said that integration has always been fully achieved. One way of helping to bring this about would be for regional conferences and technical meetings to discuss the difficulties encountered in the practical application of standards and to indicate how technical co-operation activities may best contribute to overcoming them. [1]

This last remark shows that an important question still remains to be asked about the relationship between freedom of association and development. The Director-General of the ILO, speaking about the general objectives of the Organisation, phrased the question in the following terms:

> It may doubtless also be asked whether the ILO has succeeded in achieving a reasonable balance between the desire to advance the cause of human rights and freedoms through the adoption of provisions as close to the ideal as possible and the concern to adopt standards that are not too high to secure acceptance by the greatest possible number of States—in short, whether the ILO has succeeded in solving the fundamental problem of formulating standards that, while themselves representing a minimum, can nevertheless stimulate further progress. Has it, in particular, ensured that the ILO's concern for realism and flexibility does not jeopardise its essential objective, which is to raise labour standards in all countries? In some quarters the ILO is the subject of reproach because of the modest results obtained, and the flexibility of its standards is regarded, for example, more as a mark of ambiguity than of realism. [2]

---

[1] ILO: *The ILO and human rights*, op. cit., p. 24.

[2] ibid., pp. 15-16.

The search for new international standards

Obviously, it would be useful to look into new ways of ensuring greater respect of trade union rights in the widest sense of the term. Accordingly, in a resolution concerning trade union rights and their relation to civil liberties adopted in 1970, the International Labour Conference indicated that special attention should be given to the following questions: right of trade unions to exercise their activities in the undertaking and other workplaces; right of trade unions to negotiate wages and all other conditions of work; right of participation of trade unions in undertakings and in the general economy; right to strike; right to participate fully in national and international union activities; right to inviolability of trade union premises as well as of correspondence and telephonic conversations; right to protection of trade union funds and assets against intervention by the public authorities; right of trade unions to have access to media of mass communications; right to protection against any discrimination in matters of affiliation and trade union activities; right of access to voluntary conciliation and arbitration procedures; right to workers' education and further training. A first step in the implementation of this vast programme of new activities drawn up in 1970 was the adoption of the Workers' Representatives Convention, 1971 (No. 135) and Recommendation, 1971 (No. 143). Certain other objectives of the programme are of priority importance.

One of these is the right to strike which, for the moment, has not yet been embodied in any Convention or Recommendation. It is, of course, a fact that the resolution concerning the abolition of anti-trade-union legislation in the States Members of the ILO, adopted by the Conference in 1957, called upon governments to adopt laws "ensuring the effective and unrestricted exercise of trade union rights, including the right to strike, by the workers", and that a resolution concerning freedom of association and protection of the right to organise, adopted by the First African Regional Conference of the ILO, held in Lagos in 1960, appealed for the recognition of "the right of all workers to go on strike in defence of their economic and social interests, after having exhausted all conciliation procedures provided for to this end, by the legislation, or failing legislation, by the practice of the country concerned". If effective guarantees of freedom of association are to be adopted and to lead to practical action, it would be desirable for the right to strike, already recognised in the International Covenant on Economic, Social and Cultural Rights, to be embodied in an international instrument. The case law of the ILO's supervisory bodies responsible for trade union rights, which defines the limits and conditions within which restrictions can reasonably be imposed on the right to strike (e.g. procedure to be followed before calling for strike action, restriction of the right to strike in certain essential services, guarantees to compensate for such restrictions), contains sufficient material that could be drawn upon for this purpose.

The right of trade unions to exercise their activities in the undertaking and other workplaces is a second aspect that deserves particular attention. There are at least three reasons for advocating the recognition of trade unions at the workplace. The first is a legal one: ways must be found of applying legislation which, although it proclaims freedom of association, does not indicate what steps should be taken to make this freedom a reality (posting of notices, collection of dues, circulation of trade union news, union meetings). The second is economic: modern economic conditions make it increasingly necessary to have a trade union at the workplace, since owing to such factors as urbanisation and shift work, the enterprise is often the only place where workers can get together. The third reason is that the trade union branch within the undertaking is the only means of combining and co-ordinating the various forms of labour action. The undertaking is the place where labour-management relations and conflicts of interest are put to the test day by day; it is therefore also the place where the defence of occupational interests has to be organised.

A third fundamental aspect, which is in fact inseparable from the other two, has to do with procedures for the settlement of disputes. It is true that ordinary courts of law and conciliation and arbitration courts and boards are already playing a very useful role. However, it appears necessary, with a view to the possible adoption of international standards, to lay down principles to serve as a basis for administrative and judicial procedures, supervisory and conciliation machinery, appeals, petitions and hearings, and participation and representation guarantees.

The total or partial adoption of the programme outlined here would no doubt fulfil the aspirations of trade unions, one of whose aims is "to strengthen institutions able to contribute to the adoption of constructive industrial relations policies and appropriate labour standards". [1]

[1] ICFTU: *Economic development and the free trade unions*, op. cit., p. 37.

APPENDIX: BIBLIOGRAPHY

1. MATERIAL PUBLISHED OR ISSUED BY THE ILO

A. Books and miscellaneous documents

African labour survey (1958).

Agricultural organisations and development, by X. Flores (1970).

Directory of labour relations institutes (1973).

Eligibility for trade union office (1972).

Employers' and workers' participation in planning (1973).

Freedom by dialogue: Economic development by social progress—The ILO contribution, Report of the Director-General, Part 1, International Labour Conference, 56th Session, Geneva, 1971.

Freedom of association: An international survey (1975).

Freedom of association: Digest of decisions of the Freedom of Association Committee of the Governing Body of the ILO (second edition, revised, 1976).

Freedom of association and collective bargaining, Report III (Part 4B), International Labour Conference, 58th Session, Geneva, 1973.

Freedom of association and industrial relations, Report VII, International Labour Conference, 30th Session, Geneva, 1947.

Freedom of association and procedures for staff participation in determining conditions of employment in the civil service, Report II, Joint Committee on the Public Service, First Session, Geneva, 1970.

Freedom of association for workers' and employers' organisations and their role in social and economic development, Report III, Seventh Asian Regional Conference, Teheran, 1971.

Government pay policies in Ceylon (1971).

Human resources development: Objectives, problems and policies, Report of the Director-General, Sixth Asian Regional Conference, Tokyo, 1968.

Institutional aspects of labour-management relations inside undertakings in Asia, Labour-Management Relations Series, No. 26 (1966).

Labour relations: Existing problems and prospects for the future, Report of the Director-General, Part I, International Labour Conference, 45th Session, Geneva, 1961.

Labour relations institutes: Structure and functions (1973).

Minimum wage-fixing and economic development (1968).

Multinational enterprises and social policy (1973).

Prosperity for welfare: Social purpose in economic growth and change, Report of the Director-General (Part I), International Labour Conference, 58th Session, Geneva, 1973.

Protection and facilities afforded to workers' representatives in the undertaking, Report VIII (1), International Labour Conference, 54th Session, 1970.

Report of the Committee of Experts on the Application of Conventions and Recommendations, Report III (Parts IV and IVA), International Labour Conference, 60th Session, 1975.

Report on the Asian Round Table on Labour Administration and Development Planning, Manila, September 1959, document ILO/OTA/AFE/R.17 (1970).

Report of the Seminar on the Role of Workers' and Employers' Organisations in Economic and Social Development in Africa (1969; document ILO/OTA/AFR/R.10).

Report on the visit of a joint team of experts on labour-management relations to Pakistan and Ceylon, Labour-Management Relations Series, No. 10 (1961).

Some aspects of labour-management relations in Asia, Labour-Management Relations Series, No. 3 (1958).

The ILO and human rights, Report of the Director-General (Part 1), International Labour Conference, 52nd Session, Geneva, 1968.

The labour and trade union situation in Spain (1969).

The public authorities and the right to protection of trade union funds and property (1974).

The trade union situation in Chile: Report of the Fact-Finding and Conciliation Commission on Freedom of Association (provisional edition, 1975).

The impact of international labour Conventions and Recommendations (1976).

The ILO and technical co-operation, Report VIII (Part I), International Labour Conference, 51st Session, Geneva, 1967.

B. Articles in the *International Labour Review*

Abdeljaouad, A. "The influence of international labour Conventions on Tunisian legislation", Mar. 1965.

Anon. "The influence of international labour Conventions on Nigerian legislation", July 1960.

Ayissi Mvodo, V., and Le Faou, R. "Influence of international labour standards on the legislation of Cameroon", Aug.-Sep. 1973.

Badaoui, A. Z. "The influence of international labour Conventions on the Arab Labour Standards Convention", Nov. 1970.

Berenstein, A. "The influence of international labour Conventions on Swiss legislation", June 1958.

Campaño, A. R. "The Minimum Wage Act in Argentina", Sep. 1966.

Cashell, M. "Influence on Irish law and practice of international labour standards", July 1972.

Córdova, F. "Labour legislation and Latin American development: A preliminary review", Nov. 1972.

Dahl, K. N. "The influence of ILO standards on Norwegian legislation", Sep. 1964.

Daya, E. "Freedom of association and industrial relations in Asian countries", Apr.-May 1955.

Doctor, K. C., and Gallis, H. "Size and characteristics of wage employment in Africa: Some statistical estimates", Feb. 1966.

Hallsworth, J. A. "Freedom of association and industrial relations in the countries of the Near and Middle East", Nov.-Dec. 1954.

Johnston, G. A. "The influence of international labour standards on legislation and practice in the United Kingdom", May 1968.

Kerr, C., Dunlop, J. T., Harbison, F. H., and Myers, C. A. "The labour problem in economic development: A framework for a reappraisal", Mar. 1955.

Landy, E. A. "The influence of international labour standards: Possibilities and performance", June 1970.

Menon, V. K. R. "The influence of international labour Conventions on Indian labour legislation", June 1956.

Morellet, J. "The influence of international labour Conventions on French legislation", Apr. 1970.

Pešić, R. "International labour standards and Yugoslav legislation", Nov. 1967.

Plata-Castilla, A. "International labour standards and Colombian legislation", Feb. 1969.

von Potobsky, G. "Protection of trade union rights: Twenty years' work by the Committee on Freedom of Association", Jan. 1972.

Riva Sanseverino, L. "The influence of international labour Conventions on Italian labour legislation", June 1961.

Rosner, J. "Influence of international labour Conventions on Polish legislation", Nov. 1965.

Schnorr, G. "The influence of ILO standards on law and practice in the Federal Republic of Germany", Dec. 1974.

Troclet, L. E., and Vogel-Polsky, E. "The influence of international labour Conventions on Belgian labour legislation", Nov. 1968.

Valticos, N. "The influence of international labour Conventions on Greek legislation", June 1955.

— "Fifty years of standard-setting activities by the International Labour Organisation", Sep. 1969.

Vernengo, R. "Freedom of association and industrial relations in Latin America", May-June 1956.

C. Reports of the Governing Body Committee on Freedom of Association

No. of report	Reference
1-3	*Sixth report of the International Labour Organisation to the United Nations* (1952), Appendix V.
4-6	*Seventh report of the International Labour Organisation to the United Nations* (1953), Appendix V.
7-12	*Eighth report of the International Labour Organisation to the United Nations* (1954), Appendix II.

The following reports have been published in the *Official Bulletin* of the International Labour Office:

No. of report	Issue of the *Bulletin*
13-14	Vol. XXXVII (1954), No. 4.
15-16	Vol. XXXVIII (1955), No. 1.

No. of report	Issue of the *Bulletin*
17-18	Vol. XXXIX (1956), No. 1.
19-24	Vol. XXXIX (1956), No. 4.
25-26	Vol. XL (1957), No. 2.
27-28	Vol. XLI (1958), No. 3.
29-45	Vol. XLIII (1960), No. 3.
46-57	Vol. XLIV (1961), No. 3.
58	Vol. XLV (1962), No. 15.
59-60	Vol. XLV (1962), No. 2, supplement I.
61-65	Vol. XLV (1962), No. 3, supplement II.
66	Vol. XLVI (1963), No. 1, supplement.
67-68	Vol. XLVI (1963), No. 2, supplement I.
69-71	Vol. XLVI (1963), No. 3, supplement II.
72	Vol. XLVII (1964), No. 1, supplement.
73-77	Vol. XLVII (1964), No. 3, supplement II.
78	Vol. XLVIII (1965), No. 1, supplement.
79-81	Vol. XLVIII (1965), No. 2, supplement.
82-84	Vol. XLVIII (1965), No. 3, supplement II.
85	Vol. XLIX (1966), No. 1, supplement.
86-88	Vol. XLIX (1966), No. 2, supplement.
89-92	Vol. XLIX (1966), No. 3, supplement II.
93	Vol. L (1967), No. 1, supplement.
94-95	Vol. L (1967), No. 2, supplement.
96-100	Vol. L (1967), No. 3, supplement II.
101	Vol. LI (1968), No. 1, supplement.
102-103	Vol. LI (1968), No. 2, supplement.
104-106	Vol. LI (1968), No. 4, supplement.
107-108	Vol. LII (1969), No. 1, supplement.
109-110	Vol. LII (1969), No. 2, supplement.
111-112	Vol. LII (1969), No. 4, supplement.
113-116	Vol. LIII (1970), No. 2, supplement.
117-119	Vol. LIII (1970), No. 4, supplement.
120-122	Vol. LIV (1971), No. 2, supplement,
123-125	Vol. LIV (1971), No. 4.
126-133	Vol. LV (1972), supplement.
134-138	Vol. LVI (1973), supplement.

Subsequent reports are at present available only in the form of Governing Body documents.

2. OTHER PUBLICATIONS

Adler, J. H. "World economic growth: Retrospect and prospects", in *Review of Economics and Statistics*, Aug. 1956.

Agarwala, A. N., and Singh, S. P. *The economics of underdevelopment* (Oxford University Press, 1958).

Althusser, L. *Pour Marx* (Paris, Maspero, 1966).

American labor's role in less developed countries, report on a conference held at Cornell University, October 12-17, 1958.

Ashton, T. S. *The Industrial Revolution*, 1760-1830 (London, Oxford University Press, 1958).

Bairoch, P. *Révolution industrielle et sous-développement* (Paris, Société d'édition d'enseignement supérieur, 1963).

Baldwin, G. B. "Labor problems in a developing economy", in *Current History* (Philadelphia), Aug. 1959.

Barkin, S., and others (ed.). *International labor* (New York, Harper and Row, 1967).

Bastianetto, R. *Essai sur le démarrage des pays sous-développés* (Paris, Cujas, 1968).

Bates, R. H. "Approaches to the study of unions and development", in *Industrial Relations* (Berkeley), Oct. 1970.

Bénot, Y. *Idéologies des indépendances africaines* (Paris, Maspéro, 1972).

Berg, E. J. "French West Africa", in W. Galenson (ed.): *Labor and economic development* (New York, Wiley, 1959).

— "Major issues of wage policy in Africa", in A. M. Ross (ed.): *Industrial relations and economic development* (London, Macmillan, 1966).

Bernstein, H. *Underdevelopment and development: The Third World to-day* (Harmondsworth, Middlesex, Penguin Books, 1973).

Blanpain, R. *Public employee unionism in Belgium* (University of Michigan, Institute of Labor and Industrial Relations, 1971).

Bloom, G. F., and Northrup, H. R. *Economics of labor relations* (Homewood, Illinois, R. D. Irwin, 1969).

Bolino, A. C. *The development of the American economy* (Columbus, Ohio, 1968).

Burns, T. *Industrial man* (Harmondsworth, Middlesex, Penguin Books, 1969).

Camerlynck, G. H., and Lyon-Caen, G. *Droit du travail* (Paris, Dalloz, sixth edition, 1973).

Carré, J.-J., Dubois, P., and Malinvaud, E. *La croissance française* (Paris, Editions du Seuil, 1972).

Chalmers, W. E. *Crucial issues in industrial relations in Singapore* (Donald Moore Press, 1967).

Coates, K., and Silburn, R. *Poverty: The forgotten Englishmen* (Harmondsworth, Middlesex, Penguin Books, 1970).

Cook, A. H. "The ILO and Japanese politics; II: Gain or loss for labor?", in *Industrial and Labor Relations Review*, Apr. 1969.

Cox, R. W. "Approaches to a futurology of industrial relations", in *Bulletin of the International Institute for Labour Studies* (Geneva), 1971, No. 8.

Cox, R. W., Harrod, J., and others. *Future industrial relations—An interim report* (Geneva, International Institute for Labour Studies, 1972).

Cox, R. W., and Jacobson, H. K. "Decision-making in international organizations: An interim report", paper delivered at the 65th Annual Meeting of the American Political Science Association, New York, 1969.

Cuisenier, J. "Sous-développement, industrie, décolonisation: Perspectives et questions", in *Esprit* (Paris), Oct. 1961.

Dahrendorf, R. *Class and class conflict in industrial society* (London, Routledge and Kegan Paul; Stanford, California, Stanford University Press; 1959).

David, P. A. "New light on a statistical dark age: US real product growth before 1840", in *American Economic Review*, May 1967.

Davis, H. B. "The theory of union growth", in *Quarterly Journal of Economics*, Aug. 1941.

Deane, P. "The implications of early national income estimates for the measurement of long-term economic growth in the United Kingdom", in *Economic Development and Cultural Change*, Nov. 1955.

— "Contemporary estimates of national income in the first half of the nineteenth century", and "Contemporary estimates of national income in the second half of the nineteenth century", in *Economic History Review*, Apr. 1956 and Apr. 1957.

Decraene, P. *Le panafricanisme* (Paris, Presses universitaires de France, 1959).

Deyrup, F. J. "Organized labor and government in underdeveloped countries: Sources of conflict", in *Industrial and Labor Relations Review*, Oct. 1958.

Dieterlen, P. "La monnaie, auxiliaire du développement. Contribution à l'étude de l'inflation séculaire", in *Revue économique* (Paris), July 1958.

Dollot, L. *Les migrations humaines* (Paris, Presses universitaires de France, 1958).

Dowd, D. F. "Some issues of economic development and of development economics", in *Journal of Economic Issues*, Sep. 1967.

Dufty, N. F. *Industrial relations in India* (Bombay, Allied Publishers, 1964).

Dunlop, J. T. *Industrial relations systems* (Southern Illinois University Press, 1970).

— "The role of the free trade union in a less developed nation", in *American labor's role in less developed countries*, report on a conference held at Cornell University, October 12-17, 1958.

Elkan, W. "Migrant labor in Africa: An economist's approach", in *American Economic Review*, May 1959.

Fei, J. C. H., and Ranis, G. *Development of the labor surplus economy: Theory and policy* (Homewood, Illinois, R. D. Irwin, 1964).

Fisher, P. "Unions in the less developed countries: A reappraisal of their economic role", in E. M. Kassalow (ed.): *National labor movements in the postwar world* ([Evanston, Illinois], Northwestern University Press, 1963).

Flanders, A. *Trade unions* (London, Hutchinson University Library, 1960).

Fockstedt, S. *Trade unions in developing countries*, lecture given on 20 June 1966 at the International Institute for Labour Studies, Geneva (doc. ILO/INST/L.S.17).

Fohlen, C. *Qu'est-ce que la révolution industrielle?* (Paris, Laffont, 1971).

Franklin, N. N. "Minimum wage fixing and economic development", in A. D. Smith (ed.): *Wage policy issues in economic development* (London, Macmillan, 1969).

Freedman, R. "Industrialization, labor controls and democracy: A comment", in *Economic Development and Cultural Change*, Jan. 1960.

Gaillard, Y., and Thuillier, G. "Pour une approche psychologique de la politique des revenus", in *Droit social* (Paris), Apr. 1965.

Galenson, W. *Labor in developing economies* (Berkeley, University of California Press, 1962).

— (ed.) *Labor and economic development* (New York, Wiley, 1959).

Gallman, R. E. "Gross national product in the United States, 1834-1909", in P. Temin (ed.): *New economic history* (Harmondsworth, Middlesex, Penguin Books, 1973).

Gannage, E. "La répartition des revenus dans les pays sous-développés", in *Le partage du revenu national*, Rapports et débats du colloque organisé par l'Association internationale des sciences économiques (Paris, Cujas, 1971), pp. 325-347.

Garruccio, L. *L'industrializzazione tra nazionalismo e revoluzione* (Bologna, Società editrice Il Mulino, 1969).

Gaude, J. *Emploi agricole et migrations dans une économie dualiste* (Geneva, Droz, 1972).

Goldberg, J. P. "Changing policies in public employee labor relations", in *Monthly Labor Review* (Washington), July 1970.

de la Gorce, P. M. *La France pauvre* (Paris, Grasset, 1965).

Gramsci, A. *Œuvres choisies* (Paris, Les éditions sociales, 1959).

Guillain, R. "Le Japon éclate sur lui-même", in *Le Monde* (Paris), 10-17 Nov. 1959.

Haas, E. B. *Human rights and international action: The case of freedom of association* (Stanford, California, Stanford University Press, 1970).

Harbison, F. H. "Egypt", in W. Galenson (ed.): *Labor and economic development* (New York, Wiley, 1959).

Harrington, M. *The other America: Poverty in the United States* (New York, Macmillan, 1962).

Henderson, W. O. *The industrial revolution on the Continent: Germany, France, Russia, 1880-1914* (London, Frank Cass, 1967).

— *The industrialisation of Europe, 1780-1914* (London, Thames and Hudson, 1969).

Higgins, B. *Economic development: Principles, problems and policies* (New York, Norton and Co., 1959).

International Confederation of Free Trade Unions. *Economic development and the free trade unions* (Brussels, 1971).

Jacobson, H. K. *Ventures in policy shaping: External assistance to labor movements in developing countries*, International Political Science Association, Working paper submitted to the Grenoble round table meetings, 14-18 September 1965.

Japan Institute of Labour. *Labor relations in the Asian countries*, Proceedings of the Second International Conference on Industrial Relations, Tokyo, . . . 1967.

Javillier, J. C. "La partie 'obligatoire' de la convention collective", in *Droit social*, Apr. 1971.

Jenks, C. W. *The international protection of trade union freedom* (London, Stevens & Sons, 1957).

— *The right to organise and its limits: A comparison of policies in the United States and selected European countries* (Washington, Brookings Institution, 1950).

Johan, M. "La CGT et le mouvement de mai", in *Les temps modernes* (Paris), Aug.-Sep. 1968.

Jorgenson, D. W. "Surplus agricultural labour and the development of a dual economy", in *Oxford Economic Papers*, Nov. 1967.

de Jouvenel, B. "Sur la croissance économique", in Stoléru, L. (ed.): *Economie et société humaine*, . . . exposés et . . . débats des Rencontres internationales du Ministère de l'Economie et des Finances, . . . Paris, . . . 20, 21 et 22 juin 1972 (Paris, Denoël, 1972).

Kanappan, S. "The Tata steel strike: Some dilemmas of industrial relations in a developing economy", in *Journal of Political Economy*, Oct. 1959.

Kassalow, E. M. *Trade unions and industrial relations: An international comparison* (New York, Random House, 1969).

— (ed.) *National labor movements in the postwar world* (Evanston, Illinois, Northwestern University Press, 1963).

— "Trade unionism and the development process in the new nations: A comparative view", in S. Barkin and others (ed.): *International labor* (New York, Harper and Row, 1967).

Kennedy, V. D. *Unions, employers and government: Essays on Indian labour questions* (Bombay, Manaktalas, 1966).

Kerr, C., Dunlop, J. T., Harbison, F. H., and Myers, C. A. *Industrialism and industrial man* (New York, Oxford University Press, second edition, 1966).

Kerr, C., and Siegel, A. "Industrialization and the labor force: A typological framework", in R. L. Aronson and J. Windmuller (ed.): *Labor management and economic growth*, Proceedings of a conference on human resources and labor relations in underdeveloped countries (Cornell University, 1954).

Kilby, P. "Industrial relations and wage determination: Failure of the Anglo-Saxon model", in *Journal of Developing Areas*, July 1967.

Knowles, W. H. "The British West Indies", in W. Galenson (ed.): *Labor and economic development* (New York, Wiley, 1959).

— "Industrial conflict and unions", in W. E. Moore and A. S. Feldman (ed.): *Labor commitment and social change in developing areas* (New York, Social Science Research Council, 1960).

— "Trade unionism in the British West Indies", in *Monthly Labor Review*, Dec. 1956.

Koshiro, K. *Wage determination in the national public service in Japan: Changes in prospects*, International Industrial Relations Association, Third World Congress, 3-7 September 1973, London, doc. 3C-73/Sect. V/1, summary.

Kuznets, S., assisted by Elizabeth Jenks. *Capital in the American economy: Its formation and financing*, National Bureau of Economic Research, Inc., Studies in capital formation and financing, No. 9 (Princeton University Press, 1961).

— "Quantitative aspects of the economic growth of nations", in *Economic Development and Cultural Change*: "VI. Long-term trends in capital formation proportions", July 1961, and "VIII. Distribution of income by size", Jan. 1963, Part II.

Kuznets, S., Moore, W. E., Spengler, J. J. (ed.). *Economic growth: Brazil, India, Japan* (Durham, North Carolina, Duke University Press, 1955).

Labi, M. *La grande division des travailleurs: Première scission de la CGT, 1914-1921* (Paris, Les éditions ouvrières, 1964).

Landsberger, H. "The labor elite: Is it revolutionary?", in S. M. Lipset and A. Solari (ed.): *Elites in Latin America* (London, Oxford University Press, 1967).

Landy, E. A. *The effectiveness of international supervision: Thirty years of ILO experience* (London, Stevens and Sons, 1966).

Lebret, L. J. *Dynamique concrète du développement* (Paris, Les éditions ouvrières, 1961).

Lefranc, G. *Le mouvement syndical de la libération aux événements de mai-juin 1968* (Paris, Payot, 1969).

Lesire-Ogrel, H. *Le syndicat dans l'entreprise* (Paris, Editions du Seuil, 1967).

Lester, R. A. "Economic adjustments to changes in wage differentials", in G. W. Taylor and F. C. Pierson (ed.): *New concepts in wage determination* (New York, McGraw-Hill, 1957).

Lewis, A. *Development planning: The essentials of economic policy* (London, Allen and Unwin, 1966).

— "Economic development with unlimited supplies of labour", in *Manchester School of Economic and Social Studies*, May 1954.

— *The theory of economic growth* (London, Allen and Unwin, 1955).

Lipset, S. M., and Solari, A. (ed.). *Elites in Latin America* (New York, Oxford University Press, 1967).

Lodge, G. C. "Labor's role in newly developing countries", in *Foreign Affairs*, July 1959.

Mannheim, K. *Ideology and utopia*, An introduction to the sociology of knowledge (London, Routledge and Kegan Paul, 1954).

Marczewski, J. "Some aspects of the economic growth of France, 1660-1958", in *Economic Development and Cultural Change*, Apr. 1961.

— "Y a-t-il eu un 'take-off' en France?", in *Cahiers de l'Institut de science économique appliquée*, Supplement, No. 111, Series AD, No. 1, Mar. 1961.

Margerison, C. J. "What do we mean by industrial relations: A behavioural science approach", in *British Journal of Industrial Relations*, July 1969.

Massé, P. *Le choix des investissements* (Paris, Dunod, 1964).

M'boya, T. J. "Incomes policies for developing countries?", in *Bulletin* (Geneva, International Institute for Labour Studies), Nov. 1967.

McCarthy, W. E. J. (ed.). *Trade unions* (Harmondsworth, Middlesex, Penguin Books, 1972).

Mehta, A. "The mediating role of the trade union in underdeveloped countries", in *Economic Development and Cultural Change*, Oct. 1957.

Meynaud, J. *Le syndicalisme africain: Evolution et perspectives* (Paris, Payot, 1963).

Millen, B. H. *The political role of labor in developing countries* (Washington, Brookings Institution, 1963).

Moore, W. E., and Feldman, A. S. *Labor commitment and social change in developing areas* (New York, Social Science Research Council, 1960).

Morrisson, C. *La répartition des revenus dans les pays du tiers monde* (Paris, Cujas, 1968).

Morse, D. A. *The role of management and trade unions in the years ahead,* address delivered to the Industrial Welfare Society, London, 21 April 1964.

Myers, C. A. "India", in W. Galenson (ed.): *Labor and economic development* (New York, Wiley, 1959).

— *Labor problems in the industrialization of India* (Cambridge, Massachusetts, Harvard University Press, 1958).

Myrdal, G. *The challenge of world poverty: A world anti-poverty program in outline* (New York, Pantheon Books, 1970).

— *Economic theory and underdeveloped regions* (London, Duckworth, 1957).

Nef, J. U. *Cultural foundations of industrial civilisation* (Cambridge University Press, 1958).

Neffa, J. C. *The Latin-American labour movement and its social strategy* (Geneva, International Institute for Labour Studies, 1969; doc. IEME 4071).

Neufeld, M. F. *Poor countries and authoritarian rule*, Cornell International Industrial and Labor Relations Report No. 6 (Ithaca, New York, Cornell University Press, 1965).

November, A. *L'évolution du mouvement syndical en Afrique occidentale* (Paris and The Hague, Mouton, 1965).

Orr, C. A. "Trade unionism in colonial Africa", in *Journal of Modern African Affairs*, May 1966.

Padmore, G. *Panafricanism or communism?* (New York, Doubleday, 1971).

Parker, C. H. *The casual laborer and other essays* (New York, Harcourt, Brace and Howe, 1920).

Perroux, F. *L'économie du XXe siècle* (Paris, Presses universitaires de France, 1961).

— "Prises de vues sur la croissance de l'économie française, 1780-1950", in *Income and Wealth*, Series V (London, 1955).

Pollard, S., and Rosley, D. W. C. *The wealth of Britain* (London, Batford, 1968).

Prost, A. *La CGT à l'époque du Front populaire* (Paris, Colin, 1964).

Punekar, S. D. "Aspects of State intervention in industrial relations in India: An evaluation", in Ross (ed.): *Industrial relations and economic development* (London, Macmillan, 1966).

Ramm, T. *Labour relations in the public sector in the Federal Republic of Germany*, International Industrial Relations Association, Third World Congress, 3-7 September, 1973, London, doc. 3C-73/Sect. V/6R.

Raza, M. A. "Aspects of public labour policy in Pakistan", in *British Journal of Industrial Relations*, July 1967.

Reynolds, L. G. "Objectives of wage policy in developing countries", in A. D. Smith (ed.): *Wage policy issues in economic development* (London, Macmillan, 1969).

Reynolds, L. G. and Gregory, P. *Wages, productivity and industrialization in Puerto Rico* (Homewood, Illinois, R. D. Irwin, 1965).

Rioux, J. P. *La révolution industrielle, 1780-1880* (Paris, Editions du Seuil, 1971).

Roberts, B. C. *Labor in the tropical territories of the Commonwealth* (Durham, North Carolina, Duke University Press, 1964).

Roberts, B. C., and Greyfié de Bellecombe, L. *Collective bargaining in African countries* (New York, St. Martin's Press, 1967).

Roper, J. I. *Labour problems in West Africa* (Harmondsworth, Middlesex, Penguin Books, 1958).

Ross, A. M. "Public employee unions and the right to strike", in *Monthly Labor Review*, Mar. 1969.

— (ed.) *Industrial relations and economic development* (London, Macmillan, 1966).

Rostow, W. "The take-off into self-sustained growth", in *Economic Journal*, Mar. 1956.

Sauvy, A. *Histoire économique de la France entre les deux guerres (1918-1931)* (Paris, Fayard, 1965-67).

Scalapino, R. A. "Japan", in W. Galenson (ed.): *Labor and economic development* (New York, Wiley, 1959).

de Schweinitz, K. "Industrialization, labor controls and democracy", in *Economic Development and Cultural Change*, July 1959.

Seers, D. "The meaning of development", in *International Development Review* (Washington, Society for International Development), Dec. 1969.

Senghor, L. "Deux textes sur la négritude", in *Cahiers ivoiriens de recherche économique et sociale*, No. 3.

Sigmund, P. *The ideologies of the developing nations* (London, Praeger, 1967).

Smith, A. D. (ed.): *Wage policy issues in economic development* (London, Macmillan, 1969).

Spitaels, G. *Les conflits sociaux en Europe: Grèves sauvages, contestation, rajeunissement des structures* (Bruges, Collège de l'Europe; Verviers, Editions Gérard & Cie; 1979).

Spyropoulos, G. *La liberté syndicale* (Paris, Librairie générale de droit et de jurisprudence, 1954).

Strassmann, W. P. *Technological change and economic development: The manufacturing experience of Mexico and Puerto Rico* (Ithaca, New York, Cornell University Press, 1968).

Sturmthal, A. "Unions and economic development", in *Economic Development and Cultural Change*, Jan. 1960.

Subramanian, K. N. *Labour-management relations in India* (Bombay, Asia Publishing House, 1967).

Sufrin, S. C. *Unions in emerging societies: Frustration and politics* (Syracuse, New York, Syracuse University Press, 1964).

Taylor, G. W., and Pierson, F. C. (ed.). *New concepts in wage determination* (New York, McGraw-Hill, 1957).

Turner, H. A. *Wage trends, wage policies and collective bargaining: The problems for underdeveloped countries* (Cambridge University Press, 1965).

United Nations. *Measures for the economic development of underdeveloped countries* (New York, Sales No. 1951.II.B.2).

— *Processes and problems of industrialisation in underdeveloped countries* (New York, Sales No. 1955.II.B.1).

— *Land reform: Defects in agrarian structure as obstacles to economic development* (New York, Sales No. 1951.II.B.3).

Valticos, N. "La protection internationale de la liberté syndicale vingt-cinq ans après", in *Human Rights Journal*, Vol. VII-1, 1974.

— "Les méthodes de la protection internationale de la liberté syndicale", in *Recueil des Cours*, Académie de droit international (The Hague), Vol. 144, 1975-1.

Verdier, J. M. *Syndicats* (Paris, Dalloz, 1966).

Weiss, F. *Doctrine et action syndicales en Algérie* (Paris, Cujas, 1970).

White, S. C. "Work stoppages of government employees", in *Monthly Labor Review*, Dec. 1969.

Wilber, C. K. *The Soviet model and underdeveloped countries* (University of North Carolina Press, 1969).

Williams, R., and Guest, D. "Psychological research and industrial relations: A brief review", in *Occupational Psychology* (London), Vol. 43, Nos. 3 and 4.

Wurfel, D. "Trade union development and labor relations policy in the Philippines", in *Industrial and Labor Relations Review*, July 1959.

Yesufu, T. M. *An introduction to industrial relations in Nigeria* (London, Oxford University Press, 1962).

Zachariah, K. A. *Industrial relations and personnel problems*, A study with particular reference to Bombay (Bombay, Asia Publishing House, 1954).

Zack, A. *Labor training in developing countries: A challenge in responsible democracy* (New York, Praeger, 1964).